# GENDER AND RACE MATTER: GLOBAL PERSPECTIVES ON BEING A WOMAN

# ADVANCES IN GENDER RESEARCH

Series Editors: Marcia Texler Segal and Vasilikie Demos

Recent Volumes:

ADVANCES IN GENDER RESEARCH    VOLUME 21

# GENDER AND RACE MATTER: GLOBAL PERSPECTIVES ON BEING A WOMAN

EDITED BY

## SHAMINDER TAKHAR

*School of Law and Social Sciences,*
*London South Bank University,*
*London, UK*

Emerald

United Kingdom – North America – Japan
India – Malaysia – China

Emerald Group Publishing Limited
Howard House, Wagon Lane, Bingley BD16 1WA, UK

First edition 2016

Copyright © 2016 Emerald Group Publishing Limited

**Reprints and permissions service**
Contact: permissions@emeraldinsight.com

**British Library Cataloguing in Publication Data**
A catalogue record for this book is available from the British Library

ISBN: 978-1-78635-038-1
ISSN: 1529-2126 (Series)

ISOQAR certified
Management System,
awarded to Emerald
for adherence to
Environmental
standard
ISO 14001:2004.

Certificate Number 1985
ISO 14001

INVESTOR IN PEOPLE

For my mother, Avtar Kaur Takhar, a woman of courage

# CONTENTS

## PART II
## SEXUALITY AND GENDER SECURITY: INDIA AND AFRICA

## PART III
## WOMEN'S BODIES, NATION AND PERFORMANCE

# PART IV
## HAVING A VOICE: LITERATURE AND POETRY

# LIST OF CONTRIBUTORS

*Carole Boyce Davies*  African Studies and Research Center (ASRC), Cornell University, Ithaca, NY, USA

*Maria Martin de Almagro*  Department of Research and Teaching in International Politics/Relations, Faculty of Social and Political Science, Université libre de Bruxelles, Belgium

*Adrija Dey*  Department of Social Sciences, University of Hull, Hull, UK

*Jaya Gajparia*  School of Law and Social Sciences, London South Bank University, London, UK

*Hala Kamal*  Department of English, Cairo University, Giza, Egypt

*Priyasha Kaul*  Department of Social Sciences, School of Liberal Education, FLAME University, Pune, India

*Donatella Maraschin*  Division of Creative Technologies, School of Arts and Creative Industries, London South Bank University, London, UK

*Bev Orton*  Department of Social Sciences, University of Hull, Hull, UK

*Tara Povey*  SOAS, University of London, London, UK

*Kavyta Raghunandan*  Institute of Commonwealth Studies, University of London, London, UK

*Elaheh Rostami-Povey*  SOAS, University of London, London, UK

*Suzanne Scafe*        Division of Arts and Performance, School
                       of Arts and Creative Industries, London
                       South Bank University, London, UK

*Dorothea Smartt*      Writer, London, UK

*Shaminder Takhar*     Division of Social Sciences, School of Law
                       and Social Sciences, London South Bank
                       University, London, UK

*Jocelyn Watson*       Writer, London, UK

# ACKNOWLEDGEMENTS

I owe thanks to many people who have helped in the preparation and completion of this book. Firstly, I would like to thank Christina Irving at Emerald Books for the interest she showed in my paper on women's activism at the British Sociological Association (BSA) conference and for the enthusiasm she has shown throughout. It was a pleasure to work with a number of colleagues at Emerald Books and I would like to express my gratitude to the series editors of Advances in Gender Research, Vasilikie Demos and Marcia Texler Segal for their support and impeccable editing skills. I thank Emma Stevenson for her patience and professionalism throughout and for help in bringing the project to completion. I also thank the contributors of the chapters, without which this book would not exist and for their co-operation as I edited their work through to completion. The authors have shown inspiration and passion in their research on women's status globally and their efforts will hopefully find expression in global moves towards improving women's status. For the institutional support that I needed to complete the manuscript, I thank Professor Craig Barker and Cait Beaumont for last-minute research leave. Thanks to my other colleagues at London South Bank University, especially Elaine Bauer, Jaya Gajparia, Yvonne Robinson, Matthew Bond, Donatella Maraschin, Suzanne Scafe, Beverley Goring, Veronica Leacock and Ben Acquaah for their support in various aspects of university life. I am grateful to Professor Tracey Reynolds who invited me to present a paper at a symposium on higher education at Greenwich University, which helped me to fine tune my chapter on Bangladeshi women's experiences of university. Tam Sanger did a great job proofreading the manuscript. Thanks must also go to my family. Special thanks as always to Adrian Budd for his love, humour, musical interludes and support throughout.

# INTRODUCTION

We know of course there's really no such thing as the 'voiceless.' There are only the deliberately silenced or the preferably unheard.
— Arundhati Roy, 2004 Sydney Peace Prize lecture, activist and author of *The God of Small Things*

Arundhati Roy reminds us that through listening to the marginalised, valuable wisdom can be gained yet a large percentage of the world's population, women, have been systematically unheard. This makes the task of generating a fair and inclusive (global) society for women much more difficult. Gender inequality persists in most countries and although it appears that we have a long way to go, this collection contributes to a feminist scholarship that highlights a destabilising of established patterns of behaviour and gender relations. Indeed the drive for gender equality and social justice has featured in the work of the United Nations (UN), cited as occupying a central role for legislative change globally. Although discrimination and prejudice experienced by women vary from one country to another, it is the persistence of inequality that is of main concern. The UN has been at the forefront of campaigns and declarations which promote gender equality as a human right by establishing the Beijing Declaration and Platform for Action and the Convention on the Elimination of All Forms of Discrimination against Women (CEDAW). In 2010 the organisation, UN Women[1] was created by the United Nations General Assembly to monitor gender equality and empowerment of women. Over the last 20 years, many reports[2] have been published to highlight inequalities and injustice faced by women. The Global Gender Gap Reports since 2006 have measured inequalities by charting each country's performance in four major areas: health, education, economy and politics. Although progress had been made the struggle for equality and empowerment continues, and the existence of a political empowerment gap indicates severe lack of rights and opportunities for women.

This book presents different authors' work that demonstrate inequalities experienced by women and their empowerment through protest, cultural forms, activism and use of social media. Highlighting moments of agency is extremely important given recent events that have attracted global attention: the abduction of schoolgirls by Boko Haram in Nigeria in 2014,[3] the gang rape of a young woman in Delhi in 2012,[4] the treatment of women in public spaces such as Tahrir Square in 2011[5] and the increasing use of rape as a weapon of war.[6] At the Global Summit to End Sexual Violence in Conflict, held in June 2014, it was highlighted that global attitudes need to be changed. Yet as we know, changing attitudes and practices require raising awareness and proved to be a difficult task. This has been evidenced by the modest achievements of Millennium Development Goal 3 which sought to promote gender equality and empower women. Although the United Nations has the unenviable task of promoting awareness of women's issues, it has to be commended on, for example the 'He for She Campaign' launched in 2014.

The campaign for gender equality is a human rights issue that seeks to eradicate discrimination against women and promotes social justice by including men. As a concept, social justice holds a variety of meanings philosophically and politically. It has been associated with concepts such as (in)equality giving it a complexity which is rival only to the complexities of any given society. Equality is embedded in the following principle:

> Each person possesses an inviolability founded on justice that even the welfare of society as a whole cannot override. For this reason justice denies that the loss of freedom for some is made right by a greater good shared by others. (Rawls, 1971, p. 3)

The egalitarian conceptualisation of social justice above can also be found in the work of Miller (2001) who identifies four key principles of social justice: equal citizenship, the social minimum, equality of opportunity and fair distribution. This includes empowerment of women through equal access to education and employment *and* involvement in politics and decision-making. Statistics tell us that women continue to struggle for equal recognition in society from the global to the micro-world of gaining educational credentials and suitable employment. The contributors to this collection demonstrate an understanding of oppression and the initiatives taken to facilitate social change which includes resistance to patriarchal structures and hierarchies of power. However, what is required to overcome discriminatory practices that 'preserve patriarchy at the expense of women's rights' is the involvement of everyone (Raday, 2007, p. 70).

This collection uses a feminist analysis which sees women's involvement in activities that are empowering in a range of settings. Empowerment is an important concept to use particularly in the context of women's rights and involvement in decision-making processes, however, it is not the preserve of women in developing countries as the following example illustrates. Persistent inequality and sexism in British politics was played out in 2011 when David Cameron remarked, 'calm down dear', directed at a female MP during prime minister's questions and by the Secretary of State for Education David Willetts' negative assessment of the impact of feminism on male social mobility. It therefore comes as no surprise that there is under-representation of women in politics in a number of countries and is of deep concern with reference to policy making. Empowerment is a useful tool of analysis and is often used in connection with women and the gender gap highlighted above. It involves the contested term 'power' with theoretical debates revolving around its meaning (Lukes, 2005 [1974]). I propose that rather than using the 'power over' definition which implies control through overt coercion and subtle psychological processes *and* a perceived loss of power (by men), we should use the generative understanding. This can be used to improve women's position in society and can be thought of as relational and multiple, that is its existence relies on the moments it is exercised within social relationships. This form of empowerment provides women with a capacity for agency and self-definition. There is however a debate around the concept of empowerment because it draws on the different concepts of generative forms of power with some writers understanding it as psychological awareness of a woman's position in society (Takhar, 2013).

A feminist analysis enables us not only to look at power but how agency operates, that is consciousness of our position in society. Furthermore, the 'power to' (generative) understanding facilitates organised collective demands to transform society and to resist oppressive practices. The importance of feminism is eloquently expressed in the following statement by Judith Butler:

> Feminism is about the social transformation of gender relations [...] That it asks how we organize life, how we accord it value, how we safeguard it against violence, how we compel the world, and its institutions, to inhabit new values, means that its philosophical pursuits are in some sense at one with the aim of social transformation. (Butler, 2004, pp. 204–205)

This type of comprehension brings together an understanding that combines theory and action. Equality and rights through a feminist understanding challenges the victim status given to women who are oppressed by patriarchal structures, however, the eradication of structural inequalities associated with race and gender is not an easy task, conveyed by the writers in this collection. We live with risk, alienation, exclusion and conflict yet we strive for social justice that presents itself as a desire for 'conviviality' and a sense of belonging to a community (Gilroy, 2004). Conviviality 'is intimately related to a sense of becoming, and "becoming" occurs intersubjectively' (Wise & Velayutham, 2014, p. 1). All of this occurs in the context of globalisation, individualism, plurality and uncertainty so the answers are not simple or straightforward. Similarly the issues of a community and belonging come through as complex and contradictory. However, what we hear, are the voices of those who could easily be marginalised or excluded from society and how in an increasingly fractured world, strategies are employed at a micro level to facilitate social change. It acknowledges multiplicity of discrimination but locates women at the centre of a dialogue. It presents key interventions in gender and race matters through the inclusion of marginalised groups by giving them a 'voice' rather than silencing them. *Gender and Race Matter,* therefore, contributes to the study of women's agency and how their voices can be heard in the face of powerful discourses and ideology. One of the most powerful ways in which this can happen is through equal access to education. Although unequal access may be thought of as the preserve of developing countries, it is evident in most. This is illustrated by the contributions that explore inequality and marginalisation experienced at the intersection of race and gender in all societies:

> All cultures contain elements that disenfranchise women as well as ones that empower them. It is for us to recognize by whose machinations and for whose benefit the former become reified as tradition and the latter exiled to obscurity. As activists we need to salvage those parts of our culture that uplift women as a group. (Das Dasgupta, 2002, p. 10).

For the contributors, gender serves as an analytical framework and covers the experiences of women in different global settings related to education, political activism, corporeal violence, identity, sexuality, and poverty. The use of poetry and literature provides a powerful voice for women against exclusion and recognises their contribution to society. This collection hopes to be innovative in not only relating experiential evidence but also putting forward how women are able to challenge oppression through circumventing rules, roles, obligations and prejudice through a powerful agency.

Part I looks at activism and agency in Egypt and Iran as well as the diasporic experiences of Bangladeshi women in UK higher education institutions. In Egypt, women have been at the forefront of revolutionary aims and have displayed significant levels of agency. The Egyptian feminist movement has highlighted the struggle for equality in the public sphere, decision-making and constitutional rights in the post-2011 era illustrated in the chapter by Hala Kamal on women's empowerment and feminist activism. Kamal claims that Egyptian women have been involved in the struggle for spaces where their agency can be realised and which have been closely connected to revolutionary moments in national history. The chapter highlights key issues and socio-economic demands raised by women since the early twentieth century. She shows how agency, activism and empowerment amongst women have been promoted through CEDAW and solidarity with the international women's movement. Kamal plays particular attention to the current situation which focuses on constitutional rights and political representation in the wake of the 2011 revolution, and examines its impact on the Egyptian feminist agenda. Due to the global media attention given to the brutal handling of 'the blue bra woman' by the military, there is concern over the extent to which women's bodies have been subjected to physical and sexual violence.

Tara Povey's chapter looks at political activism of women in Iran, focusing on the strategies employed in a neo-liberal context. Through empirical research, she demonstrates how changes engendered by neo-liberal policies by successive governments, rather than religion, are shown to create difficulties and exclude people from mobilising politically. Povey suggests that women are in opposition to a neo-liberal state which poses interesting questions about the characterisation of Iran as an 'Islamic state'. The chapter offers an insight to Iranian women's struggle for liberation and contributes to an understanding of different forms of feminism globally.

Women globally have been shown to struggle with reference to inclusion in higher education institutions and the two chapters that follow are concerned with firstly, the diasporic experience of Bangladeshi women in the United Kingdom and secondly, Iranian women's struggles for freedom through progress made in higher education and employment. Shaminder Takhar's chapter addresses Bangladeshi female students' experiences of higher education in the United Kingdom through the race/gender trajectory. The chapter argues that statistically minority ethnic women invest heavily in education but they go on to face obstacles in the labour market. However, there is a strong desire to study which is evident in the increasing numbers of Bangladeshi women applying to university since 1994. Through qualitative research with young Bangladeshi students and graduates, the chapter demonstrates that they have claimed agency and show agentic behaviour/autonomy to negotiate access to higher education institutions despite structural inequalities.

Similarly in Iran, women have been successful in education and the number of women who are highly educated has been increasing yet they face gender inequality in employment and decision-making roles. Elaheh Rostami-Povey shows by using statistical evidence how Iranian women are actively involved in challenging gender oppression and through their recognisable agency demystify Western stereotypical understandings of Iranian and Muslim women. The chapter shows the importance of diversity in the production of feminist knowledge and through a geographical and historical contextualisation, it illustrates the complexities involved in women's liberation and hearing their voices.

Activism and agency of women are highlighted further in Part II which focusses on gender security in India, Burundi, Liberia, and South Africa. The chapter by Adrija Dey and Bev Orton examines how Indian feminist activists have organised to challenge oppression and have their voices heard on the reporting of sexual violence. The chapter applies intersectionality (class, caste, religion, geography) as a framework of analysis to understand the impact of the Nirbhaya (fearless) gang rape case (Delhi, December 2012), on the women's movement in India. Through a case study approach which analyses data from online news reports, videos, articles, blogs, and social media postings, the authors show how the protests in major Indian cities resulted in government action with reference to violence against women. In the following chapter, Maria Martin de Almagro uses the case study of the transnational advocacy campaign for the implementation of the UNSCR1325 on women, peace, and security to discuss gender security in Burundi and Liberia. Through the transnationalisation of local women activists, she shows how understandings of gender security affect advocacy for gender policies. Based on interviews conducted in both countries Martin de Almagro demonstrates how women's organisations in post-conflict contexts negotiate discourses and strategies to be used when advocating together for the implementation of international norms on gender security.

In her chapter, Bev Orton uses feminist theory and intersectionality to discuss gender security and sexuality in post-Apartheid South Africa where despite the existence of the Women's Charter and the Equality Act (2000), the justice system fails to protect children and women. Bev Orton discusses the normalisation of violence against women and presents the social reality of living in South Africa. Due to the increasing sexualisation of society and a masculine understanding of sexuality, sexual violence has increased and rape of heterosexual and homosexual women remains under reported in South Africa. Orton therefore puts forward that women's exclusion and isolation from security issues need to be challenged and points to female agency at grassroots level and protest to demand change.

If there is inadequate protection for women in the countries above, we have to ask the question why there is an assumption that oppressive practices and patriarchal structures can be challenged by appealing to human rights and the rule of law. After all this would imply full citizenship and rights. However if we look to the nature of citizenship and the relevance to challenging powerful patriarchal structures we can see that the concept itself is contested. Citizenship 'is therefore always inflected by power and by the commonsense assumptions of hegemonic cultural and political elites' (Werbner & Yuval-Davis, 1999, pp. 1–3) which is evident in Part III in the four chapters that look at the body of the woman, nation and performance. Although agency is characterised as ambiguous and contradictory, it emerges as an important part of micropolitics. The diversity of the nation is presented through the female body in this section which looks specifically at how citizenship does not necessarily result in equal representation of diverse groups of women. Jaya Gajparia's chapter on the poverty of being a woman demonstrates how the voices and agency of the women assumed to be victims, contribute to the debate on urban poverty. Gajparia's innovative use of a multi-methods approach that draws on participatory action research, participant observation and ethnography, provides a microanalysis of experiences and perceptions of gender and poverty in Mumbai, India. It puts forward new insights into everyday forms of agency, resistance and subversion while confronting Western ideas of development and colonial understandings of victimhood. The chapter reveals how agency can be acquired through bargaining and negotiation, deception, manipulation, subversion and resistance. This puts forward a more nuanced and complex approach to understanding agency and structural oppression.

Similarly despite the perceived lack of agency of indigenous Peruvian women who went through forced sterilization, Donatella Maraschin and Suzanne Scafe examine a range of media outputs that have raised this case as a violation of human rights. It has contributed to the women being transformed from digitally marginalised towards being considered networked subjects, that is empowered through a recorded public performance as part of the *Quipu Project*. The chapter investigates how media configure witness subjects, audiences and listeners. By drawing on theories of witnessing, Maraschin and Scafe use secondary data in the form of women's testimonies that have in most cases been edited by documentary filmmakers and campaigners, to analyse an experimental project such as the *Quipu Project*. They highlight the narrative potential of digital technology to make effective interventions into campaigns for justice and reparation, in particular the indigenous Peruvian women.

The sexuality and morality of the female body's involvement in the public performance of the carnival in Trinidad and Tobago is the subject of the third chapter in this section. It reveals the carnival setting as central to the role of race and gender in the national culture and psyche *and* highlights the agency of women involved in mas[7] performance. Based on ethnographic research in the form of interviews with young Indian Trinidadian women, Kavyta Raghunandan explores how gender and race highlight how agency, articulated as sexual liberation and 'free-up', is enabled and disabled in relation to mas performance. By problematising the mixed and multicultural image of carnival, this chapter contributes to an analysis of women's voices which do not typically feature in discourses of race, gender and the nation. The following chapter explores how gender has been an integral part of the nation building project in popular Hindi cinema (Bollywood) and focusses on the analysis of post-liberalisation mainstream popular Hindi films. Supported by data from interviews with prominent members of the film industry, Priyasha Kaul illustrates the contribution made by popular Hindi cinema to the mainstream discourse on post-liberalisation nationalism. It highlights gender as central to the tension between tradition and modernity that is played out in films. Although gender politics has been questioned, the resolutions proposed continue to fit an essentialised nationalist narrative.

The challenge to a woman's position in the world is evident in how she is (re)presented, therefore, it is important to consider how cultural forms not only convey important messages about gender inequality but also challenge oppression and marginalisation. Although cultural forms do not necessarily mean more freedom for women, they are important for challenging powerful discourses. It is with this in mind that Part IV of the book is concerned with women's voices expressed through literature and poetry. Carole Boyce Davies highlights how women have moved from the margin to the centre of African literature and as a consequence challenged the failures of the state. This chapter engages in literary and cultural analyses of selected texts, revealing how a range of current issues such as women's rights are discussed. Although women's rights were raised by the previous generation of writers, Boyce Davies contrasts this with the work of younger African writers such as Chimamanda Ngozi Adichie who are immersed in issues related to migration and the experiences of diasporic settlement. The theme of migration and diasporic experiences is evident in Jocelyn Watson's story about a young Syrian woman called Suha who flees Syria at the request of her family with her younger brother. Watson comments at the beginning of the chapter before the story starts that she was compelled to write this to highlight gender based violence that many women have to endure. The author of this story hopes that people's minds will be opened to the plight of refugees fleeing war torn countries against their will and the inhumanity they suffer as a consequence.

Although the writing of women may be regarded as 'emotional', the reflections they offer on sexual violence, unacceptable desire and exclusion indicates that emotions are moving, that we are moved by them, *and* that they connect us to our history, each other as collectivities, to our bodies and external structures (Ahmed, 2004). It can be seen so far that collective identities and the expression of agency are important for social change and challenging oppressive practices. It is often the case that control over women's sexuality is required especially when patriarchy is challenged. The negotiation of identity at a personal level is important with reference to female sexuality, especially when there is female transgression. Transgression is shown in Monica Ali's fictional work, *Brick Lane* (2003) which represents a (seemingly) passive diasporic woman who goes through a 'sexual awakening' and in Deepa Mehta's film *Fire* (1996) in which two married women become involved in a 'forbidden' relationship. Patriarchal discourse finds female desire unacceptable therefore women are expected to conform through self-sacrifice and denial of self-expression. Although disempowerment of women is variable, where such disempowering discourses exist for heterosexual women, it is equally important to consider how women who represent the 'other', that is lesbian become empowered and claim their agency. The contribution made by Dorothea Smartt, conveys a range of emotions about the desires associated with being a diasporic lesbian woman in the West.

The range of writing in this collection highlights a complex, uneven and contradictory matrix of discourses, institutional spheres and terrains which points to the need for a more nuanced conceptualisation of agency. Thus, the agency of women can be conceived as a dynamic space of manoeuvre within and between discourses, places, spaces and institutional and cultural forms regarded as a kind of work in progress. During the first decade of the twenty first century, the concepts of diversity, inclusion and equality attracted increasing attention, therefore, *Gender and Race Matter: Global Perspectives on Being a Woman* is a timely addition to the literature available on gender, social justice and political agency. However, the underlying question is whether we can generate a fair and inclusive society that takes into account that women make up half the world's population. The answer lies in promoting gender equality and social justice which strike at the heart of policy making. These are central to the work of the contributors in this collection.

Shaminder Takhar
*Editor*

# NOTES

1. The United Nations Entity for Gender Equality and the Empowerment of Women.

2. The World's Women 2010; Progress on the World's Women 2011–2012: In Pursuit of Justice; Global Gender Gap Reports since 2006.

3. Boko Haram kidnapped 276 schoolgirls from the northern village of Chibok sparking a worldwide campaign #bringbackourgirls. Although some girls managed to escape, the majority are missing or have been returned but are pregnant. This indicates that they have been raped — a stigma not easily dealt with in Nigerian society. Some are described as fighting for the Islamist group Boko Haram.

4. On 16 December, 2012, Jyoti Singh was gang raped in Delhi on a private bus by six men. She was transferred to a hospital in Singapore due to the severity of the attack, however she died from her injuries. This incident attracted global media attention and resulted in protests in many Indian cities. Before her identity was revealed, Jyoti Singh was known as *Nirbhaya* which means 'fearless' and she became a symbol for the women's movement in India who have struggled against blaming the victim.

5. A beating of a woman in Tahrir Square in Cairo by the military became the symbol for protesters in Egypt in 2011. A video recording showed how she was violently beaten and her clothes ripped off to reveal her torso and blue bra. A soldier is shown to stomp on her bare body. It provoked shock and international anger at the treatment of women in Egypt in public spaces. The Egyptian military was forced to apologise and the Supreme Council of the Armed Forces expressed regret to Egyptian women at their transgressions. Egyptian women want to be involved in the construction of the Constitutional Council that determines the future political system.

6. Rape is a prohibited weapon or tactic of war under the criteria set by the laws of war. Yet, despite the endemic use of rape as a weapon, no state has ever been held accountable for the use of rape as a prohibited weapon of war (Global Justice Center: Human Rights Through the Rule of Law).

7. Playing mas generally means to wear a costume during Carnival and perform a masquerade with one of the many mas bands which vary according to size: mini, small, medium or large.

# REFERENCES

Ahmed, S. (2004). *The cultural politics of emotion.* New York, NY: Routledge.

Ali, M. (2003). *Brick Lane.* London: Black Swan Books.

Butler, J. (2004). *Undoing gender.* New York, NY: Routledge.

Das DasGupta, S. (2002). Introduction. In S. Das DasGupta (Ed.), *A Patchwork shawl: Chronicles of South Asian women in America.* New Brunswick: Rutgers University Press.

Gilroy, P. (2004). *After empire: Melancholia or convivial culture?: Multiculture or postcolonial melancholia.* London: Routledge.

Global Justice Center: Human rights through the rule of law. Retrieved from http://www.globaljusticecenter.net/index.php/our-work/geneva-initiative/rape-as-a-weapon-of-war. Accessed on Febuary 28, 2016.

Lukes, S. (2005 [1974]). *Power: A radical view.* Basingstoke: Palgrave Macmillan.

Miller, D. (2001). *Principles of social justice.* Cambridge, MA: Harvard University Press.

Raday, F. (2007). Culture, religion, and CEDAW'S article 5(A). In H. B. Schöpp-Schilling (Ed.), *The circle of empowerment: Twenty five years of the UN committee on the elimination of discrimination against women.* New York, NY: The Feminist Press at the City University of New York.

Rawls, J. (1971). *A theory of justice.* Cambridge, MA: Harvard University Press.

Takhar, S. (2013). *Gender, ethnicity, and political agency: South Asian women organizing.* New York, NY: Routledge.

Werbner, P., & Yuval-Davis, N. (1999). Introduction: Women and the new discourse of citizenship. In N. Yuval-Davis & P. Werbner (Eds.), *Women, citizenship and difference.* London: Zed Books.

Wise, A., & Velayutham, A. (2014). Conviviality in everyday multiculturalism: Some brief comparisons between Singapore and Sydney. *European Journal of Cultural Studies, 17*(4), 406–430.

# FILMOGRAPHY

*Fire,* d. Deepa Mehta (1996, India/Canada, 108 mins).

# PART I
# WOMEN'S RIGHTS, ACTIVISM, EDUCATION AND EMPOWERMENT

# A CENTURY OF EGYPTIAN WOMEN'S DEMANDS: THE FOUR WAVES OF THE EGYPTIAN FEMINIST MOVEMENT

Hala Kamal

## ABSTRACT

Purpose — *This chapter offers a critical outline of the Egyptian feminist movement. It traces the forms of feminist activism and the demands raised by Egyptian feminists throughout the twentieth century and into the new millennium.*

Design/methodology/approach — *The study uses the tools of feminist theory and women's history in charting a critical outline of the Egyptian women's movement and feminist activism throughout a century of Egyptian history. The study attempts to identify the main features of the movement in terms of the demands raised by women and the challenges and achievements involved within the socio-political national and international contexts.*

Findings — *The Egyptian feminist movement is divided here into four waves, highlighting the intersections between feminist demands and*

Gender and Race Matter: Global Perspectives on Being a Woman
Advances in Gender Research, Volume 21, 3–22
ISSN: 1529-2126/doi:10.1108/S1529-212620160000021002

*national demands, as well as Egyptian women's struggle for their rights. The first wave is seen as focusing on women's right to public education and political representation. The second wave is marked by women's achievement of constitutional and legal rights in the context of state feminism. The third wave is characterised by feminist activism in the context of civil society organising. The fourth wave has extended its struggle into the realm of women's bodies and sexuality.*

Research implications/limitations — *The study limits itself to forms of women's agency and feminist activism in the public sphere.*

Originality/value — *This chapter is an original attempt at outlining the Egyptian women's movement based on the demands raised and challenges faced. The chapter also suggests the existence of a sense of continuity in the Egyptian women's movement.*

**Keywords:** Egypt; feminism; women's movement; revolution

# INTRODUCTION

The history of the Egyptian women's movement can be seen as an extended struggle for equal opportunities in the public sphere and justice in the domestic sphere. It is a struggle that is marked by both visibility and vocality, particularly throughout the twentieth century and into the new millennium. When we speak of the women's movement, as a mobilised action taking place in public against authority, one is reminded of the Egyptian women's first demonstration organised on 16 March 1919 as part of the Egyptian people's fight against British occupation, embodied in the Revolution of 1919. It is a demonstration that has not only been engraved in the official history of the Egyptian nation, but was also documented by the press and even praised in a poem by the Egyptian Poet of the Nile, Hafiz Ibrahim, in which he described the Egyptian women's march and the police forces' violent dispersion of the demonstration — an act of public dissent which led to the death of a woman and many being injured. The violence with which women protesters were met did not bring an end to Egyptian women's organising; on the contrary, it only led to further mobilisation, more organisation and political strategizing — a process that has continued to ebb and flow throughout the years. This historical incident still had reverberations in 2011, when Egyptian women joined the protesters in the streets of Egypt calling for bread, freedom, social justice and human dignity. The image of the demonstrators of 1919 has its contemporary equivalent in the masses of women whose dissent is violently confronted by the authorities — not only politically but socially as well. In addition to the typical methods of brutal assault, in the form of rubber bullets, tear-gas, and batons used by men in uniform, we have been witnessing additional forms of sexual assault, targeting women's bodies, not simply as human beings, but particularly as women. However, Egyptian women's struggle is, this time, being documented and illustrated through all forms of media, including social media, as well as by human rights and feminist non-government organisations. And again, as with the praise the women received in 1919 for their courageous act of protest, victims of physical violence and sexual assault today receive the support and admiration of many.

Although many acts of women's protests may not be directly feminist in terms of their demands, such as the demonstrations against the occupation or for social justice, any act of women's dissent, regardless of its demands, carries a feminist dimension. The process of women's mobilisation and public protest is in itself a struggle in the public sphere, an expression of women's visibility and agency. In spite of the fact that the women's demonstration in March 1919, as well as women's participation in the January 2011 protests, was not centred around feminist demands, the act of protest itself remains a feminist act. Nevertheless, since 1919 (and earlier) and up to the present, Egyptian feminists have been organising themselves, mobilising other women and protesting for women's rights. It is this struggle, and these demands, that I wish to explore here.[1] This essay, therefore, attempts to identify the main developments in the Egyptian feminist movement in the light of the demands it raised; and to organise the history of the movement within concrete phases based on the form and content of feminist activism in Egypt. I will identify the main features of the Egyptian feminist movement from the late 19th century to the present, with reference to the relationship between feminist activism and the state by tracing women's demands since 1910.

## THE EGYPTIAN FEMINIST MOVEMENT

One of the most common misrepresentations of the feminist movement is that of a group of prominent women figures demanding women's rights, very often at the expense of the family and society as a whole. At the same time, those supportive of women's rights often believe that women's rights should not be given priority over socio-political agendas since they claim that women would obtain their rights once democracy, liberalism or socialism is achieved — depending on their political stance. In Egypt, feminists have been repeatedly asked by their comrades to postpone women's rights demands and unite all power and energy towards ending colonialism, in the past, and implementing social justice, in the present. This essay, however, is grounded in the steadfast conviction that the feminist movement is a political movement based on women's subjugation to multiple forms of oppression, marginalisation and exclusion It is a movement that seeks to change women's conditions in line with social justice concerns.

The feminist movement is a political movement in the sense that it acknowledges the imbalance in the power structures and relations with respect to gender and in its intersection with other forms and categories of oppression. It places women at the centre and has struggled to empower women and improve their lives — a process which often involves confrontations with various forms and levels of authority: political, social, economic, religious and cultural, among many others. In all cases, a feminist movement is driven by its members' collective 'feminist consciousness' — the definition of which is perfectly articulated by feminist historian, Gerda Lerner:

> I define feminist consciousness as the awareness of women that they belong to a subordinate group; that they have suffered wrongs as a group; that their condition of subordination is not natural, but is societally determined; that they must join with other women to remedy these wrongs; and finally that they must and can provide an alternative vision of societal organization in which women as well as men will enjoy autonomy and self-determination. (Lerner, 1993, p. 4)

Feminist awareness thus involves knowledge and activism through intellectual realisation, solidarity and resistance, and action towards social change. In this light, the feminist movement, grounded in a feminist consciousness, emerges as a political movement that is aware of the socio-gender power structures that subjugate and marginalise women, and is involved in exposing and changing them.

The history of the Egyptian feminist movement is usually considered to go back to the Egyptian women's participation in the Revolution of 1919 against the British occupation of Egypt. Of particular significance is women's involvement in the March 1919 demonstrations which followed the British authorities' banishment of the Egyptian nationalist leader Saad

Zaghlool and his companions to the Seashell Islands. Moreover, the rise of the women's rights movement has often been attributed to the *nahda* (renaissance) male intellectuals such as Al-Afghani, Al-Tahtawi, Mohamed Abdou and Qassem Amin. It is only since the 1990s that feminist activists and academics have started highlighting the active role of women in raising feminist consciousness. Furthermore, feminist approaches to Egyptian history have revealed the role of Egyptian women since ancient Egyptian times and throughout Egyptian history (Elsadda & Abu-Ghazi, 2001). Yet, the earliest manifestations of a rising feminist consciousness, according to Gerda Lerner, can be identified in the work of Egyptian women intellectuals who have called for a revision of social norms and women's rights within the Egyptian renaissance/awakening/*nahda* project.[2] The Egyptian feminist movement has a long history and, similarly to western feminism, is characterised by waves. The following sections are devoted to the development of the feminist movement and provide a basis from which to understand women's contemporary and often dangerous activism.

## FIRST WAVE: EDUCATION AND SUFFRAGE (LATE 19TH CENTURY TO THE EARLY 1950s)

Women played a visible and effective role in the 1919 Revolution, yet Egyptian women's participation in the demonstrations of March 1919 does not mark a historical starting point in women's activism. However, there are historical accounts of Egyptian women's protests starting with their participation in the anti-French campaign in Egypt when French forces reached Egyptian land in Alexandria in 1798 and women took to the streets across the country against the French invasion. This political engagement must have alerted women to the multiple levels of oppression to which they were subjected, leading in 1799 to the Rosetta Women's Conference in which women discussed their gendered roles within Egyptian society in comparison to French women's positions in their families (Elsadda & Abu-Ghazi, 2001, p. 26). There is also mention of women's protests during Ottoman rule in Egypt, and particular mention is made of the organised protests of women in the Bab al-Sha'riya and Boulak districts against taxation and the rising cost of living (Elsadda & Abu-Ghazi, 2001, pp. 27−28). Historians also mention women's contribution to the popular resistance movement in Alexandria against the British navy's bombardment of the city prior to the fall of Egypt to British occupation in July 1882. Historical accounts refer to the Egyptian people's (men, women and children) resistance together with the role of the royal family's women in donating horses, medical supplies and money in support of the popular resistance movement against the British (Elsadda & Abu-Ghazi, 2001, pp. 39–41). Thus the earliest forms of women's political engagement documented by historians were directly related to the national cause, with the exception of the Rosetta Conference and its obvious gender dimension (Elsadda & Abu-Ghazi, 2001, pp. 81, 87; Sobki, 1986, pp. 26–27).

Although these early demonstrations did not carry feminist demands, it is worth noting that they still represent a stage in the development of feminist consciousness, perhaps not related to the content of these women's activism as much as to the form. Women organised themselves and took to the streets at a time when women were not even granted the right to education; this in itself is a political act with a feminist dimension. The feminism here does not lie in the slogans carried by these women, but in the fact that their act was an indirect rebellion against a general prevalent culture that kept middle class and upper class women confined within their homes and restricted to domestic concerns. Moreover, women's participation in the anti-colonial protests, led by the *Wafd* Party, consequently led to the formation of the The Wafd Women's Central Committee in December 1919. The party's initiative added to the liberal and national image of the *Wafd* Party as representing the nation, while at the same time it empowered women by allowing them a space for political activism within a powerful entity, whose leaders acknowledge women's rights.[3] Yet, it is also interesting to note that Egyptian women's struggle for their rights came hand in hand with national demands for independence – both in direct confrontation to the British occupation. For instance, women's demands for access to education were not only rejected by Egyptian conservative powers, but by the British authorities in Egypt as well (Ahmed, 1992; Baron, 1994).

In her book, *The Women's Awakening in Egypt*, Baron (1994) presents the role of Egyptian women's press (newspapers and magazines owned, established and edited by women), since the publication of the first women's newspaper *Al-Fatah* (*The Young Woman*) in 1892, followed by several others such as *Anis al-Jalees* in 1898, *Fatat al-Sharq* in 1906 and *Al-jins al-lateef* in 1908, among many others – all with the aim of defending women's rights and expressing their points of view. Baron points out that the rise of the national liberation movement encouraged reflections on the society and identity, leading to reconsiderations of socio-cultural and gender roles, as reflected in the press, which opened up the discussion of such issues as marriage, divorce, polygamy, custody, education and work, in addition to the veil and domesticity (Baron, 1994, p. 14ff.). In addition to the press, upper class women held literary and cultural salons, such as Princess Nazli Fadel's Salon and May Ziyada's Salon. These offered space for direct intellectual exchanges between women and men about social, political, cultural and gender issues, and salons that were frequented by prominent figures at the time. In 1914 the Women's Educational Association was formed, offering public lectures for women about women's issues, in response to women being prevented from joining the Egyptian University established in 1908.[4] Moreover, women were penetrating the public sphere through involvement in charity organisations, established and run by upper middle class women and funded by women of the Egyptian aristocracy. These offered medical services to poor women and children and provided shelters to homeless women and orphaned children.

Although these activities were not restricted to feminist activism, they played an important role in women's involvement in the public sphere. First, they allowed women a degree of mobility across the gender-restricted lines separating the public sphere from the private sphere. Second, although most of the roles taken up by women seemed related to the domestic sphere of nurturing and caring for others, this also involved breaking out of the confines of the home, and getting involved with offering solutions to social problems. Third, running newspapers, establishing organisations and holding salons required a development of management skills beyond the confines of domestic life, and helped these women acquire political tools of representation and negotiation alongside developing the skills of argumentation. Fourth, these activities offered women the opportunity to develop their networks among like-minded women as well as with other Egyptian intellectuals and collective entities. Egyptian women's active engagement in social and political issues was reflected in their efforts to include women's rights in the 1923 Constitution. However, as Mervat Hatem points out, women were prevented from accessing their political rights in the Constitution, highlighting Article 23 which states that the nation is the source of authority, with the nation defined in terms of maleness (Hatem, 1992, p. 35). Although women were allowed to attend lectures at the university as of 1908, it was in 1928 that they obtained equal enrolment opportunities which led to the graduation of the first batch of Egyptian University women graduates in 1933. It was the first step that enabled women to access academia and the public sphere of work − beyond the fields of nursing and schooling.

The systematic increase in the numbers of educated working women led to their rising awareness concerning their rights in the workplace, and mobilisation towards social change and legal reform. This is reflected in the establishment of the Egyptian Women's Party in 1942, which is the first entity that paid attention to gender equality in education, work, citizenship and political participation, with particular emphasis on working women's rights to paid maternity leave, in addition to its role in urging women workers to form unions in factories and other workplaces.[5] This trend was reinforced in 1946 by the establishment of the National Committee for Students and Workers, with women such as Latifa al-Zayyat and Inji Efflatoun elected to leading positions within the Committee, combining women's rights with national liberation demands (Abdel-Wahab, 1995, pp. 136–139). The 1940s also witnessed the establishment of the 'Daughter of the Nile Association', led by Doria Shafik, mobilising for women's political rights and leading the women's hunger strike in Cairo and Alexandria in 1954, demanding women's inclusion in the post 23 July Revolution constitutional process.[6]

## SECOND WAVE: STATE FEMINISM AND THE WORKING WOMAN (1950s INTO THE 1970s)

In her important study of Nasser's Egypt of the 1950s and 1960s from a gender perspective, Laura Bier highlights the connection between Nasser's national development project, Arab Socialism, and feminism in Egypt. In this respect, she states that Nasser's regime 'increasingly went from alternately ignoring and suppressing women's independent political initiatives to co-opting them into its own programme – a strategy it employed with other groups such as workers and peasants' (Bier, 2011, p. 55). It is this process that she, among other scholars, defines as a manifestation of state feminism. While the Egyptian legal system was on the whole secular, family law continued to abide by religious codes in the areas regulating marriage, divorce, custody, child support and inheritance. The paradoxical dimension of Egyptian state feminism highlighted the contradictions between the 'progressive framework' of women's rights in the public sphere stipulated in the constitution and labour laws and the 'conservative' personal status law governing women in the private sphere (Hatem, 1992, p. 232).

The state maintained its monopoly over the feminist realm in Egypt throughout the 1970s and into the 1980s. The Egyptian feminist struggle at that time directly addressed the State, demanding legal reforms of the family and personal status law. The two main issues raised at the time were those related to women's obedience (*al-ta'a*) and divorce laws. *Al-ta'a* refers to the husband's right to resort to legally proving his wife's 'disobedience' if she leaves home and having her forcibly brought back to the marital house, 'bayt al-ta'a' (obedience house). Feminist lawyers, academics, journalists and social reformers such as Aziza Hussein led the campaigns towards personal status law reforms, challenging bayt al-ta'a and the man's unilateral right to end the marriage by divorcing his wife. Women demanded that courts certify divorce, that child custody decisions be based on court rulings, that taking a second wife be conditioned by court permission, that divorced women receive fair compensation, and the abolition of obedience verdicts (abolished in 1967) (Bier, 2011, p. 112).

The 1956 Constitution and National Charter recognised women's equal status as citizens in building the new socialist nation, while Article 52 of the Constitution committed the state to providing work to all citizens. Compulsory primary education, the expansion in health services, nationalisation of industries and consolidation of state institutions required and encouraged female employment. Although women worked in education, health care and social services, the judicial, diplomatic and ministerial positions continued to exclude women (Bier, 2011, p. 66). At the same time, women's work in the public sphere was encouraged through family planning policies. Family planning became a national policy implemented nationwide as contraceptive methods were distributed free of charge in clinics, health centres and health units across the country. The nuclear family, composed of parents and a maximum of three children, became the model, and this was reflected in child-care laws. Similar to the case with legal reform of the family and personal status law, the campaigns propagating these reforms relied on secular discourses relying on modern values, while at the same time adopting modernised religious discourses based on reinterpretations of women's rights in Islam, in order to confront religious conservatism.

# THIRD WAVE: CIVIL SOCIETY
# FEMINISM (1980s—2011)

The state's grip on civil society began to loosen with the assassination of President Sadat and the coming to power of Mubarak in 1981. More importantly for women, Egypt continued seeking international support, and ratified CEDAW in 1981, thus committing itself to the elimination of

discrimination against women. At the same time, changes in the law of
association opened the door for the establishment of human rights and
feminist organisations – the earliest of which are the New Woman
Foundation and the Alliance of Arab Women, in addition to law centres
offering legal assistance to women, such as CEWLA (Center of Egyptian
Women's Legal Assistance), among many others. The International
Conference on Population and Development (ICPD) held in Cairo in 1994
was another milestone in placing women's rights on the national agenda,
with Egypt hosting the conference and the Egyptian civil society organisations emerging as the most knowledgeable and concerned about women's
rights. They campaigned for women's reproductive rights, including the
formation of female genital mutilation (FGM) task forces, among many
other issues directly related to women's bodies and sexualities. It was during the ICPD that the human rights movement and the rising feminist
movement cooperated to create networks, pressure groups and campaigns
nationally and internationally. The aim was to highlight continuing gender
discrimination against women despite the enforcement of international
women's rights and human rights conventions.[7]

During this phase in the history of the Egyptian feminist movement we
can identify feminist activism within three general frameworks. First, the
most obvious and formal was the formation of women's committees in
political parties. Although these committees were concerned with women's
issues, they were more interested in the role of the family than in women's
rights as such. Moreover, their agendas were generally designed to fit
within party agendas rather than promoting feminist goals. Second, these
three decades witnessed the emergence of feminist concerns that manifested
themselves as initiatives – both independent initiatives and others within
human rights organisations which established women and gender programmes within their institutions. The most visible and vocal initiatives
were the FGM Task Force and the Media Watch Group. The FGM Task
Force focused on the eradication of female genital mutilation in Egypt,
using tools garnered from UN efforts to improve women's lives within the
framework of women's health and reproductive rights. Similarly, the
Media Watch Group was formed of independent women researchers and
activists with the purpose of exposing gender-stereotyping and highlighting
its role in maintaining and reinforcing discriminatory images and representations of women in the media and school curricula. Third, similar to these
initiatives, independent groups of women came together around various
issues related to women's lives and rights. Yet, these groups decided
to make use of the change in the government's attitude to freedom of

association, and to establish themselves as legal entities. It is within that framework that several women's organisations and centres were established from the late 1980s onwards, while the early years of the millennium witnessed the establishment of Nazra for Feminist Studies in 2005.[8]

With reference to political participation, the introduction of a quota system led to 64 seats reserved for women (518 total seats) in the parliament of 2010, the majority of whom were senior state figures, and members of the ruling party and the National Council of Women. It was this state manipulation of the women's quota in the 2010 parliamentary elections that developed skepticism of the system among Egyptian feminist activists. This was obvious immediately following the 2011 Revolution, when Egyptian feminist activists raised the issue of parity during the parliamentary elections of 2011 and the formation of the Constitution Assembly, but were more concerned about the presence of feminist representation in the constitution-writing process.

During this time CEDAW became a battle ground for the Egyptian feminist movement, where the non-government sector proved to be more knowledgeable and more involved in the struggle for the elimination of discrimination against women – as unequivocally manifested during the 1994 ICPD in Egypt. It was the international visibility and vocality of the Egyptian feminist movement at that time that led the state to revive its State Feminism policy by establishing the National Council for Women to counter civil society representation of Egyptian women's issues, and gain the support of the international agencies and organisations that were developing a serious interest in cooperation with Egyptian feminist legal non-government entities. Another area of joint campaigning went beyond feminist issues and was linked to the State's realisation of the growing power and credibility of those non-government organisations, legal assistance centres and human rights institutions proliferating throughout the 1990s. Thus the state introduced legal changes in the form of the Law of Association in 1999, which enforced legal frameworks restricting freedoms of association. An organised campaign proved this law unconstitutional, which led again to the State issuing the new Law of Association in 2002, and further restrictions are continually introduced. The most recent was implemented in 2014, forcing all civil society organisations, institutions and centres to register and gain governmental approval via the Ministry of Social Solidarity. This led several civil rights entities to either freeze their work or modify their statuses, among ongoing threats of the imposition of further restrictions through yet another Law of Association.

Since the 1990s, and into the first decade of the millennium, one notices a rise in the number of feminist groups and human rights NGOs including sexuality rights on their agendas and directing marked efforts towards confronting traditional practices such as honour killings and virginity tests in addition to FGM and reproductive rights. Moreover increasing attention was given to domestic violence, sexual harassment and the human rights of LGBTQ citizens. This can be seen as a development of the issues raised in Cairo during the 1994 United Nations International Conference on Population and Development (ICPD, 1994) when the term 'sexual rights' appeared on the agenda and the ICPD Program of Action included 'several allusions to sexual rights' (Ilkkaracan, 2008, p. 5). The issue of women's bodies was ranking among the most important human rights concerns in Egypt, and has continued to be the main component of feminist and human rights activism.

## FOURTH WAVE: WOMEN'S BODIES AND WOMEN'S RIGHTS (2011 ONWARDS)

It is perhaps too early to claim the ability to analyse the consequences of the 2011 Revolution on women's rights in Egypt. However, one cannot deny that the past few years have witnessed major developments in Egyptian women's relationships to the public sphere. As an Egyptian feminist, I will attempt in the following to identify what seem to me the most visible shifts in women's agency, particularly in relation to the struggle for space in the public sphere. In this respect, I will be reflecting on the way in which the revolution empowered women, and the feminist struggle to insert women's rights into the post-revolution society. Since 2011 two main issues have received the most attention: sexual violence against women and including women's rights in the new constitution. Egyptian women's participation in the revolution was spectacular but not at all exceptional. Women of all classes have managed to carve themselves various spaces across the past few decades, as peasants, street vendors and domestic workers, as well as teachers, doctors, lawyers, civil servants, academics and political activists, among many other women occupying the workplace and public space. This was the outcome of the struggles of several generations of women to enter and then maintain that space — a struggle that continues to the present day. Together with Egyptian women's spectacular presence in the anti-Mubarak protests, confronting the police and army forces, women journalists and activists were beginning to face an additional form of violence – sexual violence.

The earliest sexually violent targeting of women activists goes back to the anti-Mubarak demonstration on 25 May 2005, when for the first time women protesters were sexually attacked in public by men in civilian clothes standing next to the police. They were part of the civilian clothed thugs who have been regularly accompanying the police in the last decade, known among the protesters as 'the karate squads'. On that day in May, and for the first time, the demonstrators came face-to-face with an obviously new batch of police-supported thugs: the sexual harassment squad. This developed during the 2011 Revolution and onwards into organised squads, as well as sexual violence and gang rape groups targeting women activists and journalists during demonstrations. This direct targeting of women was not only restricted to women participants in political protests. Throughout the past decade, there has been a growing phenomenon of sexual harassment, violence and rape incidents during national holidays at crowded recreational city centre spots, such as in public parks and at cinemas.

For several years no action was taken by the government to confront these attacks against women. There have even been reports of women who feared reporting the incidents to the police because of the mistreatment received at police stations. Similarly, sexual violence against women activists was dismissed by the media and often blamed on the protesters, if not the women themselves. Consequently, the past few years witnessed the formation of various civil society independent anti-harassment groups which organised themselves, making sure they were present in key positions during protests and holidays. These include women and men who are trained to handle the sexual attack situation by rescuing the victim, then offering her medical, psychological and legal assistance.[9] This anti-sexual harassment movement has been developing and gaining much credibility throughout the past few years, to the extent that Cairo University has established a unit to combat sexual harassment and violence against women on campus.[10] Similarly, the Egyptian Ministry of Interior has established a unit within the ministry to combat violence against women, including sexual harassment. This issue of sexual harassment against women has been repeatedly addressed in the media, and several Egyptian feminist activists have written about it in the press.[11]

The other area of visible organised feminist activism took place during the constitution-writing process. A group of members of Egyptian feminist organisations got together as early as May 2011, forming the Women and

Constitution Group, which included feminists from feminist NGOs and human rights organisations as well as independent feminist activists and researchers. The group's involvement with the constitution-writing process was carried out in three consecutive stages and addressed several groups involved in the actual drafting of the Islamist constitution of 2012 and then the post 30 June 2013 constitution issued in 2014. These stages involved examining Egyptian constitutional history and exploring articles related to women, gender and the family in several international constitutions; drafting a list of women's demands to be included in the new constitution and phrasing them in constitutional language; and finally campaigning and mobilisation of political powers and constitution-writing committees to adopt these demands and include them in the body of the new constitution.[12] Yet, the final struggle was led and conducted by the feminist members of the constitution-writing 50-Committee, engaged in the negation process, particularly around Article 11, known as 'the women's article' in the 2014 Constitution (Constitution of the Arab Republic of Egypt, 2014).[13]

During the process of drafting the Egyptian post-revolution constitution feminist activism addressed two issues: women's representation on the constitution-writing committees and the demands that needed to be included in the process. The first constitution-writing assembly included very few women, and there was an unwillingness to fight for the preservation of Egyptian women's constitutional rights, not to mention raising the ceiling of these rights. Thus, the Constitution of 2012 came as a major blow to Egyptian women, threatening to deprive them of the rights they had obtained throughout the history of Egyptian feminist activism. When the Islamist president was removed from power in July 2013 following the massive demonstrations that started on 30 June and continued till 3 July, the new road map set included a revision of the constitution. A new process of constitutional amendments lead to issuing the Constitution of 2014 that granted women rights in several of its articles. Although, the committee of 50 members that drafted the constitution included only five women, feminist activists did not undermine the committee due to its 10% women's representation. It was deemed important to acknowledge that these five women had a long history of involvement in the struggle for women's rights across at least the past two decades. Moreover, there were many male members on the constitution committee who were known for their support for women's rights. This was a concrete incident when feminist activists decided to work with the feminist and women's rights supporters within the committee, instead of demanding a greater representation of women who would not necessarily be supportive of women's rights.

Another important feature of the feminist struggle since January 2011 is the issue of political representation. This manifested itself at three main levels: parliamentary elections, membership of the constitution-writing bodies, and within the emerging post-revolution political parties. At the level of political parties, it is noticeable that most of the new political parties shared an interest in including women in top party positions, leading to the appointment of prominent figures such as Hoda Elsadda as vice-president of the Egyptian Social Democratic Party, Hala Shukrallah as president of the Dustoor Party, and Karima El-Hefnawy as secretary general of the Egyptian Socialist Party, not to mention other visible women figures in various parties. Even the Muslim Brotherhood's Freedom and Justice Party chose to place a few of its women members in the limelight, although their commitment to women's rights has completely failed during their year in power under the Islamist president Morsi. It is worth noting that while women are penetrating the public sphere of party politics, this phase in the history of the Egyptian women's movement is also witnessing a remarkable involvement of men in the movement.

We are currently witnessing the gradual realisation of gender-mainstreaming, not only within state, party, and bureaucracy politics and policies, but the younger generations of Egyptians are coming to age now in a post-revolutionary setup that acknowledges women's rights to the public sphere and tries to safeguard these through civil society initiatives as well as government policies and media discourses. We seem to be moving from the stage of women's rights to that of gender equality within the framework of social justice − one of the main slogans of the 2011 Revolution. We are still in this process of change, and the success or failure of this phenomenon still needs to stand the test of time.

# CONCLUSION: A CENTURY OF EGYPTIAN FEMINIST DEMANDS

The Egyptian feminist movement has a long history of its own that dates back to the end of the 19th century. This chapter has traced the development of the movement in the light of the demands it has raised throughout over a century of feminist activism in Egypt. Several features can be identified in this process. First, the Egyptian feminist movement has been constantly closely connected to its national political contexts, while at the same time being responsive to the international feminist agenda. Egyptian women have attended international feminist conferences since 1923, with the Egyptian delegation participating in the Women's Congress in Rome in 1923. It is therefore noticeable that the Egyptian feminist agenda has always worked to enhance women's position from an international feminist perspective, while remaining deeply rooted in the national context with all its internal struggles. Second, Egyptian feminist activists have been aware of the importance of legal reform towards socio-cultural change in gender discrimination. Egyptian feminists have addressed parliaments, constitution-writing committees and legislators with their demands, and have, by and large, gradually succeeded in inserting their rights within the Egyptian constitutions. Feminists have mobilised for changes in labour law as well as the personal status and family law across the decades. Third, Egyptian feminists have been aware of the importance of political representation in enhancing women's condition in society. From the right to suffrage articulated as early as 1909 in the Egyptian feminist, Malak Hifni Nassef's demands to the parliament,[14] up to today's women's demands for quotas in parliament and party leadership as well as in judiciary and decision-making positions. Fourth, women have been addressing issues related to their bodies and sexuality, both directly and indirectly, since the early 20th century. Women's repeated demands to raise the age of marriage since the early 20th century are a manifestation of women's control of their bodies and reproductive rights. Women's campaigns against FGM, virginity tests, honour crimes, domestic and sexual violence mark a further development in women's struggle for sexual rights. Fifth, throughout the history of the Egyptian feminist movement, we notice an insistence on women's rights to education, higher education, work and independence. Even though women's right to education was a battlefield in the early 20th century and is currently taken for granted, feminists continue to push this right by maximising girls' access to school and university education. They have done this by legally raising the age of marriage to force parents to keep their daughters in schools rather than marry them off at an early age, and insisting on the protection of free higher education to provide young women with more access to national universities.

Finally, the Egyptian feminist movement has used the tools of political activism. Across the decades, they have implemented the tactics and strategies of national liberation and international solidarity as well as human rights activism to develop their own agendas and campaign to impose change. To achieve their goals, they have resorted to various forms of political protest, including issuing statements, marching in demonstrations, forming coalitions and organising occupational and hunger strikes, in addition to using the media to create supportive public opinion. Feminists, having been involved in party politics and civil society organising throughout the history of the Egyptian feminist movement, have combined awareness with agency, deeply rooted in 'feminist consciousness'. Egyptian feminists have continually exposed and fought socio-economic and cultural forms of gender discrimination. They have worked together towards building national, regional and international networks and alliances among individual women and women's organisations. Their solidarity and cooperation has led to designing feminist agendas that seek to gain, ensure and maintain women's rights at various levels and in different contexts. Living in a post-revolution Egypt today, where we wish to think of the 2011 Revolution as an ongoing political, social, cultural and economic period of change, I can also see the Egyptian feminist movement as an ongoing process, an ongoing revolution.

# NOTES

1. The study of the Egyptian feminist movement can be approached from various perspectives through: the study of women's press (Baron, 1994); the study of Egyptian women and legal structures within the Islamic tradition (Ahmed, 1992; Mir-Hosseini, Larsen, Vogt, & Moe, 2013; Sonbol, 1996; Tucker, 1985); the study of particular periods (Bier, 2011; Khalifa, 1973; Sobki, 1986); the study of women's writing (Ashour, GHazoul & Reda-Mekdashi, 2008; Booth, 2001; Elsadda, 2012) and the study of prominent feminist figures and their auto/biographies (Lafranchi, 2012; Shaarawi, 1981, 1987; Nelson, 1996); while the two most prominent accounts of the movement itself focused on its organisational goals, activities and structures (Abdel-Wahab, 1995; Al-Ali, 2000).

2. For more on the role of Egyptian women in conceptualising and mobilising for women's rights and gender reforms, particularly during the early years of the twentieth century, in the context of the Egyptian national movement and socio-cultural enlightenment, see Baron (1994), Elsadda (2012) and Sobki (1986).

3. According to Makdisi (2001), the women's anti-colonisation movement was at its beginnings a popular movement that engaged women from all classes of the Egyptian society, but was later transformed into an elitist movement involved in party politics.

4. When the Egyptian university was opened in December 1908, women demanded access to university education. Some women joined the university and attended its lectures, while others from the upper and more conservative rungs of the society demanded the inclusion of lectures open to women only. These pressures led to the establishment of the Women's Section at the Egyptian University (1909–1912), with lectures restricted to women on Wednesdays and Fridays, given by prominent women figures. For more on the Women's Section, see Kamal (2001).

5. The agenda of the Egyptian Feminist Party, established by Fatma Ne'mat Rashed, can be found in Amal El Sobki's book on the women's movement in Egypt (1986, pp. 120–121).

6. The agenda of the Union can be found in Sobki (1986, pp. 122–123), while more on Doria Shafik's role in the Egyptian feminist movement can be found in Nelson's (1996) biography of Doria Shafik.

7. The Cairo ICPD 1994 Programme of Action can be found at the following link: http://www.unfpa.org/sites/default/files/event-pdf/PoA_en.pdf

8. More information can be found via the following links: New Woman Foundation (http://nwrcegypt.org/), Alliance for Arab Women: AAW (http://www.theallianceforarabwomen.org/), Center for Egyptian Women's Legal Assistance: CEWLA (http://www.cewla.org/), The Women and Memory Forum: WMF (http://www.wmf.org.eg/), and Nazra for Feminist Studies (http://nazra.org/).

9. For more information about Egyptian anti-harassment initiatives, visit the following links: HarassMap (http://harassmap.org/ar/), OpAntiSH (http://www.gsrc-mena.org/successstories/SuccessStoryEgypt.pdf), Shoft Ta7rosh (I Saw Harassment) (https://www.facebook.com/Shoft.Ta7rosh/info?tab = page_info).

10. For more on the Cairo University Anti-Harassment Unit, see http://cu.edu.eg/anti-harassment

11. For example, Zaki and Abd Alhamid (2014), originally published in Arabic in two parts on 8 January 2014 and 10 January 2014.

12. For a detailed description of the process, see Kamal (2015).

13. Elsadda (2015) gives a detailed account of the negotiation process within the 50-Committee in her article entitled 'Article 11: feminists negotiating power in Egypt'.

14. The Egyptian feminist, Malak Hifni Nassef, submitted a list of 10 demands to the Egyptian parliament in 1909. She presented them within a public lecture which she gave at the *Umma* Liberal Party, and that was later published in *Al-Jareeda* newspaper, as well as in Nassef's book *Al-Nisa'iyyat* (Women's Issues) (1998 [1910], p. 147).

# REFERENCES

Abdel-Wahab, N. (1995). Al-haraka al-nisa'iya fi misr. [The women's movement in Egypt.] In N. Abdel-Wahab & A. Abdel-Hady (Eds.), *Al-haraka al-nisa'iya al-arabiya* [*The Arab Women's Movement*] (pp. 127–170). Cairo: New Woman Research Center.

Ahmed, L. (1992). *Women and gender in Islam: Historical roots of a modern debate*. New Haven, CT: Yale University Press.

Al-Ali, N. (2000). *Secularism, gender and the state in the Middle East: The Egyptian women's movement*. Cambridge: Cambridge University Press.

Ashour, R., GHazoul, F. J., & Reda-Mekdashi, H. (2008). *Arab women writers: A critical reference guide (1873–1999)*. Cairo: American University in Cairo.

Baron, B. (1994). *The women's awakening in Egypt: Culture, society, and the press*. New Haven, CT: Yale University Press.

Bier, L. (2011). *Revolutionary womanhood: Feminism, modernity and the state in Nasser's Egypt.* Stanford, CA: Stanford University Press.

Booth, M. (2001). *May her likes be multiplied: Biography and gender politics in Egypt.* Berkeley, CA: University of California Press.

Constitution of the Arab Republic of Egypt – 2014. (2014). Retrieved from http://www.sis. gov.eg/Newvr/Dustor-en001.pdf. Accessed on July 30, 2015.

Elsadda, H. (2012). *Gender, nation, and the Arabic novel: Egypt, 1892–2008.* Edinburgh: Edinburgh University Press.

Elsadda, H. (2015). Article 11: Feminists negotiating power in Egypt. *Open Democracy,* January 5. Retrieved from https://www.opendemocracy.net/5050/hoda-elsadda/article-11-feminists-negotiating-power-in-egypt. Accessed on July 30, 2015.

Elsadda, H., & Abu-Ghazi, E. (2001). *Significant moments in the history of Egyptian women (H. Kamal, Trans.).* Cairo: National Council for Women.

Hatem, M. (1992). Economic and political liberation in Egypt and the demise of state feminism. *International Journal of Middle East Studies, 24,* 231–251.

ICPD. (1994). *ICPD Programme of action: Adopted at the international conference on population and development,* Cairo, September 5–13, 1994. Retrieved from http://www.unfpa. org/sites/default/files/event-pdf/PoA_en.pdf. Accessed on July 30, 2015.

Ilkkaracan, P. (2008). Introduction: Sexuality as a contested political domain in the Middle East. In P. Alkkaracan (Ed.), *Deconstructing sexuality in the Middle East: Challenges and discourses* (pp. 1–16). Burlington, VT: Ashgate Publishing.

Kamal, H. (2001). Muhadaraat al-far' al-nisa'i fi al-gami'a al-misriyya, 1909–1912 [The women's section at the Egyptian University, 1909–1912]. In H. Elsadda (Ed.), *Min ra'i-daat al-qarn al-'ashreen: shakhsiyyat wa qadaaya [Women pioneers of the twentieth century: Individuals and issues]* (pp. 177–199). Cairo: The Women and Memory Forum.

Kamal, H. (2015). Inserting women's rights in the Egyptian Constitution: Personal reflections. *Journal for Cultural Research, 19*(2), 150–161.

Khalifa, I. (1973). *Al-haraka al-nisa'iyya al-misriyya.* [The Egyptian Women's Movement.] Cairo: Al-matba'a al-haditha.

Lafranchi, S. S. (2012). *Casting off the veil: The life of Huda Shaarawi, Egypt's first feminist.* London: I.B. Tauris.

Lerner, G. (1993). *The creation of feminist consciousness: From the Middle Ages to eighteen seventy.* Oxford: Oxford University Press.

Makdisi, J. S. (2001). liqa'aat wa riwayaat: Huda Sha'rawi wal mu'tamar al-nisa'i fi Roma 1923. [Meetings and accounts: Huda Sha'rawi and the Women's Conference in Rome 1923.] *Al-nisaa' al-'arabiyat fi al-'ishreenaat: huduran wa hawiyya* [Arab Women in the 1920s: Visibility and Identity] (pp. 387–422). Beirut: Al-Bahithat.

Mir-Hosseini, Z., Larsen, L., Vogt, K., & Moe, C. (2013). *Gender and equality in Muslim family law: Justice and ethics in the Islamic legal tradition.* London: I.B. Tauris.

Nassef, M. H. (1998 [1910]). *Al-nisa'iyyat* [Women's issues] (2nd ed.). Cairo: The Women and Memory Forum.

Nelson, C. (1996). *Doria Shafik: Egyptian feminist, a woman apart.* Cairo: American University in Cairo.

Shaarawi, H. (1981). *Muthakkirat Huda Sha'rawi: Raida-t al-mar'a al-'arabiyya al-hadeetha [Memoirs of Huda Sha'rawi: Modern Arab pioneer].* Cairo: Dar Al-Hilal.

Shaarawi, H. (1987). *Harem Years: The Memoirs of an Egyptian Feminist (1879–1924) (M. Badran, Trans.).* New York, NY: The Feminist Press.

Sobki, A. (1986). *Al-haraka al-nisaa'iya fi misr ma bayna al-thawratayn 1919–1952* [The women's movement in Egypt between the two revolutions 1919–1952]. Cairo: General Egyptian Book Organisation.

Sonbol, A. (1996). *Women, the family and divorce law in Islamic history*. Syracuse, NY: Syracuse University Press.

Tucker, J. (1985). *Women in nineteenth-century Egypt*. Cambridge: Cambridge University Press.

Zaki, H., & Abd Alhamid, D. (2014, July 9). *Women as fair game in the public sphere: A critical introduction for understanding sexual violence and methods of resistance*. Retrieved from http://www.jadaliyya.com/pages/index/18455/women-as-fair-game-in-the-public-sphere_a-critical. Accessed on July 30, 2015.

# THE WOMEN'S MOVEMENT AND NEO-LIBERALISM IN IRAN: BETWEEN ACCOMMODATION AND RESISTANCE

Tara Povey

## ABSTRACT

Purpose — *This chapter analyses the strategies employed by women and youth political activists in Iran in the context of changes engendered by the neo-liberal policies pursued by successive governments since the end of the Iran-Iraq war.*

Design/methodology/approach — *The analysis in this chapter is based on semi-structured interviews conducted by the author with women and youth activists in Iran in 2015. This qualitative data is contextualised within a theoretical discussion of the nature of the Iranian state, the impact of neo-liberal policies, and debates surrounding gender and neo-liberalism.*

Findings — *Contrary to the view of politics in Iran as a battle between hard-line religious fundamentalists and moderates, this chapter argues that it is not the religious nature of the state but its neo-liberal policies that have made it more difficult for women and youth activists to*

Gender and Race Matter: Global Perspectives on Being a Woman
Advances in Gender Research, Volume 21, 23–40
ISSN: 1529-2126/doi:10.1108/S1529-212620160000021003

*mobilise against the exclusionary policies of the state. In response acti-
vists in Iran have developed and articulated strategies of resistance to
and accommodation with the Islamic Republic's neo-liberal project.*

Originality/value — *The chapter breaks with prevailing socio-cultural
analyses of women's rights in Iran and provides a critique of prevalent
ideas of women's rights as innately connected to liberal and specifically
neo-liberal forms of politics and governance.*

**Keywords:** Iran; women; liberalism; neo-liberalism; activism;
political change

# INTRODUCTION

In this chapter I argue that a dominant discourse in western countries views
women's rights as part of the liberal project and thus constructs a world-
view in which liberalism is the best political system for women. This presentation of the superiority of western 'liberal' values means that the problems
of states like Iran, which are viewed as 'non-liberal', are seen as stemming
from their religious and/or revolutionary nature. In particular, the problems facing Iran's political system are portrayed by many western media
commentators and academics as arising from its nature as an 'Islamic
state'. Those who oppose the state's policies, such as women's rights activists, are conversely defined in terms of their adherence, or not, to liberal
values and as either anti-Islamist or pro-regime. This analysis both simpli-
fies and obscures the political situation inside the country and the diverse
strategies of women activists. This chapter will argue in opposition that the
anti-democratic and exclusivist nature of the state stems from its nature as
a neo-liberal state and confounds the idea that liberalism, particularly in its
current guise as neo-liberalism, is the best political system for women.
Those who oppose the state, such as many in the women's movement, are
engaged in finding strategies of accommodation with aspects of the neo-
liberal project as well as opposing a neo-liberal global order.

# THE RESEARCH

My analysis is to a large degree based on informal conversations, as well as
more formal interviews I conducted with activists in women's movements,

artists, film makers and democracy activists in Iran. In April 2015 I travelled to Iran and interviewed six women and three men about what they thought of the changes taking place in the country. My rationale for conducting these interviews was not to gain a 'representative sample' but to utilise semi-structured interview techniques in order to gain knowledge from participants who had experience of being active in specific movements. In this sense these were 'elite interviews' with women and men who were included on the basis of their experience of working in democracy movements and women's movements. Four of the women and two men were activists in women's organisations and were veterans of previous political administrations and movements including the 1979 revolution and the reform movement of the 1990s. They identified with a range of political opinions such as Islamic reformist, leftist and nationalist. Although they held a range of heterogeneous political opinions, these activists were broadly sympathetic to the goals of the 1979 revolution and the reformist project of the Khatami administration in the 1990s. I also interviewed three young activists working in the arts who had been active in more recent movements including the Green movement of 2009.[1] They also held diverse political views, however all expressed frustration with both the exclusionary nature of the state and aspects of its economic and social policies. In utilising these interviews I do not make claims about what 'ordinary Iranians' or 'Iranian women' think. Nor do I think that it is possible to homogenise the views of such a diverse population. However the interviews do help us to gain insight into the knowledge and experiences of specific activists, which I argue should be valued.[2]

## LIBERALISM AND WOMEN'S RIGHTS

In this chapter I will analyse the nature of the Iranian state and broadly outline the changes that have taken place since 1979. I will introduce debates about neo-liberalism from within the country utilising interviews. Finally I will examine the impact of neo-liberalism on gender relations. I view gender as a social construct but most crucially one in which the meanings attributed to masculinities, femininities and sexed bodies are not static but are continually shifting in response to changing socio-economic and political contexts, giving rise to complex and often contradictory intersections of race, class and gender. Experiences of women are therefore not homogenous but diverse and can be linked to their class position, ethnic and religious identity, age, living situation and life experiences. It is important not to homogenise women's varied experiences, political affiliations and strategies. However it is also important to analyse the broader material conditions and relations of power that interlink with women's struggles. In this chapter I utilise the methodology proposed by Chandra Talpade Mohanty of 'reading up' from women's specific and varied subjective experiences to the local and global layers of power at work (Mohanty, 2003). In particular, this chapter focuses on the changing nature of the state. A number of frameworks have been articulated in recent years which move the focus of social science away from the state and on to social movements or politics from below, engendering a critique of 'statist' approaches (Mitchell, 1991). I argue on the contrary that the state remains an important arena for politics. However I view the state not as a neutral arbiter occupying a place above society but as a set of institutions and networks which encompass both state and non-state actors such as corporations and NGOs, which are deeply enmeshed in the relations of power present in society. Finally I see focussing on the state as a way of 'reading up' from the specific experiences of women and a nexus at which we see most clearly the intersection of local and global power relations and forces.

In April 2015 the Iranian president Hassan Rouhani appointed the experienced foreign office spokeswoman Marzieh Afkham as ambassador to East Asia. A number of journalists, such as Saeed Kamali Dehghan writing in *The Guardian* newspaper, hailed this as a 'breakthrough for women in Iran' (Dehghan, 2015, p. 1). The appointment drew the attention of the western media[3] and due to the nature of the coverage it received, proves useful when reading the current western gendered and racialised discourse on women's rights in Iran. The appointment of women to high office in Iran is not after all a rare event, although more men occupy positions of power in the country, as in most western countries. It is also notable that historically women's participation in politics has been important in Iran. Throughout the nineteenth and twentieth centuries, women participated in and led movements for gender rights, democracy and social justice *and* opposed colonialism and dictatorship (Paidar, 1995). Millions of women played a major role in the Iranian revolution of 1979 which overthrew the Shah's dictatorship and since the 1990s a diverse women's movement has been at the forefront of achieving legislative and political change in the country (Rostami-Povey, 2012). Coverage which heralds the appointment of a female ambassador as a breakthrough for women obscures this history of women's participation in politics and presents a familiar picture of Iran in which gender relations are static and uniformly bad for women.

However, it is also based on the premise that liberalism is the best political system for women and sees gender equality as essentially tied to 'liberal' values. Several authors have criticised the 'teleology of emancipation' inherent in ideas of liberal feminism (Abu-Lughod, 2002; Mahmood, 2001, p. 210). However the focus of this chapter is not on liberalism as a set of historically constituted ideas, but on the notion that liberal political systems are the most favourable for women.

The terms liberalism and neo-liberalism can be used to encompass a range of political systems and give rise to competing and contradictory ideas about politics. Not only are they contested concepts but the relationship between them has also been the subject of academic debate (Harvey, 2005, p. 19). According to Luckham and White (1996, pp. 2–4), liberalism, as a political system, consists of 'open political competition, multi-party elections, civil and political rights guaranteed by law and electoral representation'. Interestingly it also encompasses concepts such as 'participation, social empowerment and popular sovereignty'. The relationship between liberal political systems, social empowerment and participation is complex and often contradictory. Iran is a country with historically high levels of political participation and much higher electoral turn-outs than in western countries with non-mandatory voting systems. But Iran is not commonly perceived as a 'liberal' political system, nor does it claim to be one. Some adherents of neo-liberalism have attributed its origins to the classic liberal ideas of individual liberty and freedom of choice. Freedom from state intervention in the market, for example, makes possible more individual choice and competition. However as Harvey (2005, p. 19) points out, neo-liberalism, as the dominant economic ideology of the past 30 years, can be seen not as a utopian plan but as primarily economically driven, and a project that enables the 'restoration of the power of economic elites'. In this chapter, I argue that perceptions of neo-liberalism, both within Iran and outside of the country, link neo-liberal policies, and in particular the roll-back of the state, with increasing political participation. Thus they conflate certain normative aspects of liberalism with neo-liberal economic policy.

In the remainder of this chapter I argue that there is no innate link between gender equality and liberalism. Najmabadi (2000) has argued against the presumed 'natural association' between women's rights and secularism. She contends that in Iran women's rights became associated with secularism through the violence of a secular westernising state, that of Reza Shah Pahlavi, who in 1936 banned the hijab and introduced some limited gender reforms while severely repressing independent women's organisations. The dominance of secular, westernised state feminism continued until it was disrupted by the revolution and the women's movement of the 1990s which won significant legislative and political victories and in which religious women activists invited secular women to join them in campaigns (Najmabadi, 2000). Therefore in Iran as elsewhere the presumed link between secularism and women's rights was in fact the result of particular historical processes. Using this model, I see the links between liberalism and gender reforms or progressive movements not as universal but as the result of specific historical processes. This analysis stands in contrast to the ways in which modern social movements are imagined which I argue are both gendered and racialised, as are ideas around gender equality and women's movements (Povey, 2015a).

Many analyses of Iranian society and women's positions see a major change taking place in 1979 and then view the following period as static. It is commonly argued that the Iranian people chose to return to an 8th century religious 'theocracy' which was bad for women until recent reforms. In contrast to this chronology, I see an enormous shift taking place between 1979 and 2015. During this period a revolutionary welfarist state brought about by a popular revolution in which women participated in their millions has almost completely abandoned its ethos and goals. In the 1980s the Islamic Republic of Iran introduced mass social legislation that lifted a generation of women out of poverty and enabled their participation in the economic, social and political life of the country. However successive postwar governments introduced neo-liberal reforms which have privatised the public sector, cut subsidies on essential items such as food, medicines and fuel, and rolled back welfare programmes. Iran today is therefore very different from the Iran of the revolution and in the following sections I explore some of the ways in which these differences have impacted on women.

## NEO-LIBERALISM AND THE IRANIAN STATE

The nature of the Iranian state has been a subject of debate since the revolution that removed the Shah's regime in 1979 and two major approaches have emerged. One, dominant in the western media and sections of the academic world, sees the revolution as having created an exceptional religious, theocratic and 'medieval' state. Other approach gives primacy to the political and economic features of the state following the revolution and has contended that far from being exceptional, the post-revolutionary state bears resemblance to other populist or republican states (Abrahamian, 1991).

The way that the nature of the state is conceptualised is important as it connects to wider questions of the state's legitimacy and basis of support, as well as views on where power lies in the state and the role and nature of religious authority. Frameworks that view power as stemming from the religious nature of the state also tend to view the Iranian state as exceptional and posit that religious authority forms the basis of its popular legitimacy. This framework also stresses continuity since 1979, with power continuing to be invested in the office of the Supreme Leader. This is an argument that is proposed by those analysts who see the office of the Supreme Leader and the unelected institutions of the *Velayat-e Faqih*[4] as being the principle obstacles to the democracy movement in Iran (Alehossein, 2013). The Iranian state is viewed primarily as a religious dictatorship – although some would argue that this is due to the state's interpretation of religion rather than being indicative of religion itself.

A focus on the political and economic nature of the state disrupts this chronology. In this view the post-revolutionary state was a populist or welfarist state that owed its legitimacy to the massive welfare programmes that were enacted by the Islamic Republic in the 1980s – including social welfare, health programmes including availability of contraception, a school in every village and free education up to tertiary level (Povey, 2015a, p. 66). These programmes led to an increase in the standard of living for the majority of the population and provided much of the state's legitimacy in the 1980s. The eight-year-long war with Iraq was also crucial in creating a strong centralised state with an anti-imperialist foreign policy and repressive domestic policy (Povey, 2015a, p. 70).

In the post-war period every government, whether identified as reformist or conservative, has enacted neo-liberal reforms. These have led to a transformation of the welfarist ethos of the state that has impacted on the relationship between society and the different sectors of the state. In 1989 the Rafsanjani government introduced a programme of structural adjustment as part of its post-war reconstruction programme. This consisted of privatisation and the removal of subsidies, tariffs and price controls. In 1991 the World Bank provided Iran with a loan of US$250 million and a further US$850 million in 1994 (Rostami-Povey, 2010, p. 98). In 1997 a reformist government led by Mohammed Khatami was elected with an unprecedented majority on a platform of empowering 'civil society', ending Iran's international isolation and enacting social reforms. Women, youth, national minorities and Islamic reformers voted for Khatami in their millions. However, Iranian reformists also enacted neo-liberal reforms and both those within the Khatami government (1997–2005) and some major reformist intellectuals outside it supported privatisation and lauded neo-liberal economic policies. For example, the dissident journalist Akbar Ganji's 'Republican Manifesto' argued for a free market economy as a precondition to democracy in Iran (Povey, 2015a, p. 88). Many reformists believed that neo-liberalism would lead to the shrinking of the state and empower civil society, leading to increased venues for democracy movements in the country. The Khatami administration's enacting of neo-liberal reforms was thus supported by a number of women's groups and organisations. However, increasing poverty and unemployment levels led to opposition to these policies among the poor and working class. An activist in a women's organisation who I interviewed in Tehran argued:

> Under Khatami, more attention was given to political and democratic issues and economic issues were forgotten. As a result people's grievances increased. (Simin, female activist, Islamic reformist and women's organisation, 60+)

Dissatisfaction with Khatami's economic policies was one of the factors which led to the election of Mahmoud Ahmadinejad who came to power with a populist message, highlighting his humble origins as the son of a blacksmith and promising to 'put the oil money on the tables of the poor' (Povey, 2015a, p. 89). However, privatisation increased in pace as the Ahmadinejad government (2005–2012) dismantled subsidies on gasoline, water, electricity, rice, flour, bus fares and university tuition. These policies caused an enormous rise in inflation and the cost of living, particularly affecting food. In addition the welfare programmes of the state were cut back and the country's revolutionary constitution was amended to allow full privatisation of the public sector. The current government, elected in 2012 and led by Hassan Rouhani, has continued these policies and despite criticising Ahmadinejad's economic policies has implemented a second stage of subsidy reforms in accordance with IMF demands that Iran remove remaining subsidies on energy, food and medicine.

The social impact of neo-liberalism has been extensive in Iran as elsewhere. Reforms have led to increasing unemployment and a rise in the cost of living among the middle class and working class.[5] Removal of labour protections has led to an increase in casualised, underpaid employment, and this, alongside rising unemployment, has caused the growth of the informal sector of the economy. Women activists I spoke to in Tehran commented on the changes during the Ahmadinejad period:

> The living standard of the people was reduced enormously; the poor got poorer but the rich got richer. According to the labour law workers should receive wages above the rate of inflation; although wages were increased to some extent, the increases did not

reach the high level of inflation. (Tala, female activist, Islamic reformist and women's organisation, 60 +)

However, other social groups have benefited from privatisation and the selling off of billions of dollars of state assets:

Many became rich through the black market, a black market which imported not just goods and services but also arms and ammunitions. Those who entered this new system benefited and those who did not enter the new system were the losers. Our neighbour entered the system and became rich and we did not. They travelled around the world, while we could not afford it. Very fast, the poor got poorer and the rich got richer. (Simin, female activist, Islamic reformist and women's organisation, 60 +)

Other forms of social impact are harder to quantify but were equally significant for the women and men I interviewed. Five of the interview participants (three women and two men in their sixties who had worked for both reformist and women's organisations and who came from the generation that remembered the revolution) spoke of how economic policies since the 1980s have meant that some of the key demands of the revolution of 'freedom from global capital and imperialism' have been forgotten. In their place a new consumerist culture has arisen which stresses the importance of the 'good life', 'looking good' and 'wearing nice clothes'.

Women argued that turning back the goals and accomplishments of the revolution has an important gender dimension. As one interview participant described, women were some of the main beneficiaries of the revolution and their mass participation meant that they felt that they had a prominent role to play in public and political life:

Despite many restrictions and limitations, women in Iran are much more present in society than women in many other countries. This is because of our history, we see in our history women's struggle for the vote, for education, employment etc. [...] We also have been through revolution and war, Iranian women have been out of the home and when a woman is out of the home, it is difficult to put her back in the home. (Firouze, female director, producer and screen writer, 40 +)

Despite state repression, the reforms of the 1980s meant that for the first time working class women and those from rural areas were able to become educated and play an important role in society. These women fought to preserve their rights after the revolution and to challenge patriarchal laws and male-dominated institutions. Interview participants stressed that the presence of women in politics and the advances in gender equality were due to their own work and struggles:

[Women] are present in all aspect of life, not just the elite women like myself, but also in rural areas, young women do not see themselves as second class citizens. Men also do not look at them as the second class citizens; this is because we have worked hard to achieve this level of awareness and consciousness. (Firouze female director, producer and screen writer, 40 +)

Some activists from the generation of particularly religious women who were empowered by the revolution and the reforms that followed argued that neo-liberal reforms have led to a worsening situation for women:

A society which went through the revolution and eight years of war where one million people were killed and many injured and became disabled suddenly changed. The ideals of the revolution changed. Instead a section of society began to think only of themselves and how to benefit from the new system. (Simin, female activist, Islamic reformist and women's organisation, 60 +)

Ironically the 'winners' in the neo-liberal reforms originated from those very groups that had suffered the most during the Iran-Iraq war. A process thus occurred where the working class and popular dimensions of the Revolutionary Guard and *basij*[6] were either coopted or stifled. One activist described this process:

The veterans of the Iran-Iraq war who had physically and psychologically suffered questioned what is happening. Why have people suddenly changed and only think of their own interests and getting rich quick. In Shiraz, Mashhad, Qazvin [regional capitals] there were demonstrations by people who were part of the Revolutionary Guard and who went to war but they were suppressed. They were thrown out of the Revolutionary Guard and many of them were isolated. Others were given the opportunity to become part of the new privatised Foundations which owned and controlled the capital under the control of the state and soon became millionaires. For example, Transport and Communications went under the ownership and control of Janbazan, the disabled from the war. (Simin, female activist, Islamic reformist and women's organisation, 60 +)

Other women welcomed some aspects of neo-liberal reforms. In particular younger artists and film makers argued that freedom from state censorship and centralised funding of the arts enabled more creative freedom and gave artists the opportunity to criticise government policy. A female film maker described the work of her private film company:

My work is concentrated within the private company that I have set up. This gives me the opportunity to work independent of the state ideology. In this context [the private sector] is positive. I work within the rules and regulations and I understand the limitations. Within this framework, I work, I write, I produce and I direct and I have been successful. I have been able to attract investment in my work without the state's intervention. We have learnt how to push the barriers without allowing the state and its institutions to stop our work. (Firouzeh, female director, producer and screen writer, 40 +)

Similarly, a musician and producer argued that state investment in the arts is seen as 'an instrument for political propaganda' and that privatisation is therefore a benefit to artists who want to work outside of the state system. However people working in the arts also criticised what they saw as the negative impacts of privatisation such as advertising, fashion, and the rise of celebrity culture and conspicuous consumption. They saw this as an outcome of the creation of new political and economic elites particularly during the Ahmadinejad presidency, and their investment in the arts:

> In the last ten years, especially under Ahmadinejad's second term in office, a new class has been created which have become millionaires over night, they benefited from the money market and the property market, corruption, sanctions and rising prices. Some of them invested in art. They promote consumerism. They promote popularism in art. They have created art for business. (Siamak, male music producer and participant in the Green movement, 30 +)

The impact of neo-liberal reforms in Iran has been uneven and contradictory. On the one hand it has led to a worsening economic situation, particularly for the young, women, the working class and middle class. On the other hand it has been supported by some sections of the left and reformist movements as an alternative to state intervention in social life. In the next section I will examine some of these debates in more detail in the context of theoretical approaches to gender, neo-liberalism and Islamism, and raise the question of whether there is an alternative to neo-liberalism in Iran.

## GENDER AND NEO-LIBERALISM IN IRAN – DEBATES AND ALTERNATIVES

Since the 1990s gender and 'women's empowerment' have become major parts of mainstream development discourses and a wide range of literature has emerged which has examined the effect of neo-liberal reforms on women. The impact of neo-liberalism has been analysed at both a sociological and a discursive level and a number of authors have criticised claims that neo-liberalism would empower women, lift them out of poverty and free them from the patriarchal and 'traditional' social structures of their own societies (Cornwall, Gideon, & Wilson, 2008). Neo-liberalism has been theorised to have produced the end of the 'family wage' and thus to have undermined women's economic dependence on men – a central plank of the patriarchal structure of society, as theorised by socialist feminists among others. Not dependent on men for economic survival, women have become workers and consumers in their own right. However critics have argued that rather than leading to women's empowerment, the process known as the 'feminisation of labour' has resulted in women being employed in casualised and precarious work with no rights, non-existent contracts and low wages. At the same time neo-liberalism has arguably strengthened existing patriarchal social relationships. As the welfare state has been rolled back, women are expected to care for the young, the sick, the mentally ill and the old. This means that women have become caught in a double-bind where they are expected to be both autonomous workers and full time carers.

Far from challenging patriarchal structures in the developing world, the policies and language of development agencies originating in western countries has re-produced them by celebrating women as responsible community-oriented carers and mothers (Molyneux, 2006). This kind of gendered development discourse is apparent when micro-credit loans are extended to women on the basis that they are more family and community-oriented, better business women and responsible citizens (Chakravarti, 2008). Even in the area of sexual health, which is presumed to be a distinctive feature of the 'liberal' and sexually enlightened West, a gendered discourse dominates. Contraception education programmes run by international agencies in the developing world, for example, stress the idea that having fewer children makes you a better and more responsible mother (Ali, 2002). In both cases it is argued that framing gender equality in terms of 'traditional' gender roles and language appeals to conservative religious families − an argument that relies heavily on orientalist and static notions of what constitutes 'traditional culture' and re-produces a conservative, neo-liberal gender discourse.

Neo-liberalism can thus be seen to have re-produced existing patriarchal arrangements as well as producing new ideas of the 'good woman' who is at once a part of community and family and at the same time an empowered worker and consumer. Despite these criticisms, in writing on neo-liberalism in the Middle East it is still often assumed that one of its strengths is its ability to free women from traditional societies and give them access to new resources, and in this way neo-liberalism is seen as counter to or separate from existing patriarchal structures. Valentine Moghadam, for example, makes the claim that what she calls a 'fundamentalist Islamic movement' emerged parallel to neo-liberalism as two dominant ideologies of the 1980s (Moghadam, 2005, p. 22). The presumed separation between neo-liberalism and religious movements has been questioned in other contexts by authors who see the emergence of religious movements as connected to the social dislocations brought about by neo-liberalism and the rollback of the state. There are also ideological and material links between Islamic movements and neo-liberalism (Beinin, 2005; Mitchell, 2002). These perspectives are beneficial in that they go beyond the 'traditional' versus neo-liberal dichotomy and could usefully be applied to theorising gender and neo-liberalism in the Middle East. The limits of such approaches are their tendency to view both religious movements and neo-liberalism as conservative or reactionary forces in society. In particular presentations of Islamism as small-business-oriented and a movement of the middle class that is unconcerned with questions of social justice fail to explain the mass support of women for Islamic movements. They also fail to explain the complex attitudes to economic reform in Iran, a country in which neo-liberal reforms were associated with a reformist Islamic administration and social movement. My research demonstrates that there is a debate about neo-liberalism in Iran which connects to questions of the legacy of the revolution, the role of reformism and what contemporary challenges to the state and its policies should look like. Given the complex effects of economic reform on gender relations, it is not surprising that different groups of women and different sections of the women's movement are concerned with articulating strategies of accommodation or resistance to neo-liberalism.

A major debate hinges on the question of whether neo-liberalism in Iran is a distorted version of neo-liberal theory and practice elsewhere in the world. Some women pointed out that the neo-liberal policies of the past 20 years have become problematic when instituted by an undemocratic state:

> Privatisation needs a degree of freedom. Therefore, in my view the idea of the reform and the reform movement came to existence under Rafsanjani. But a real democracy never took shape, because our constitution gives absolute power and right to the Supreme Leader. All institutions are under the control of the Supreme Leader. And the Supreme Leader is above the law. (Tala, female activist, Islamic reformist and women's organisation, 60+)

The fact that neo-liberalism has empowered existing local elites connected to sections of the state has led to the view that its power has strengthened, not diminished. As one participant stated, 'we have never had an independent economy from the state, a state which is totalitarian and dictatorial'. However, others pointed out that neo-liberal reforms have been instituted by US-educated ministers such as Mohammad

Nahavandian, President Rouhani's chief of staff, and are therefore indicative of foreign policy prescriptions on other developing countries:

> Under Khatami, many of the theoreticians were/are western educated and have very little knowledge about developing countries' economies. They follow western global economic policies. We cannot simply follow the global economy, we have to have a more national understanding and reduce the amount of corruption. (Arang, male activist in reformist and women's organisation, 60 +)

Other debates raise the question of whether having a large state, particularly a large public sector, is good for women:

> The state run economy or state intervention works in the interest of women. For example, a woman teacher, nurse, or office worker in the state sector is paid equal to a man, or at least theoretically should be paid equal to a man for performing an equal type of job. But in the private sector, women are paid one tenth of the men, in many industries women are paid half of what men are paid for performing equal types of jobs. (Simin, female activist, Islamic reformist and women's organisation, 60 +)

Some women argued that governments that undertook mass privatisation of the public sector also strengthened gendered discourses – particularly those which portray women as occupying the domestic realm as mothers and carers:

> In particular in Iran, women's work is considered as helping the family, because men are considered as the bread winners. Under Ahmadinejad these became important arguments – the titles of women's organisations which were promoting women's socio-political positions changed to 'women and family organisations' promoting women's reproductive roles. He argued that women can work from home and extended maternity leave to six months. This way 45,000 women lost their jobs and became unemployed. (Simin, female activist, Islamic reformist and women's organisation, 60 +)

At the same time the economic situation of many women worsened:

> We have two million women who are the bread winners. There is very little financial protection for them; we have many homeless women who live in cardboard boxes. There are many women who are sex workers or drug dealers and drug addicts. There are many women who have escaped from their families because of domestic violence. 15% of the society is super rich and control the wealth of 85% of the society. (Simin, female activist, Islamic reformist and women's organisation, 60 +)

Despite the presence of these debates and criticisms, many of the participants felt that the only alternative to neo-liberal privatisation was a strong state that was also not in women's interests as it was undemocratic:

> The alternative is totalitarianism. We do not have any alternatives. We have no other models to follow. Even in terms of co-operatives, we have co-operatives, but they are owned and controlled by the state and the Revolutionary Guard. We are fast moving

towards branding and creating chains, supermarket chains, restaurant chains, coffee shops chains etc. [...] but all under the ownership and control of the state. (Siamak', male music producer and participant in the Green movement, 30+)

The view that there is no alternative to economic reform is also a product of the fact that historically, neo-liberalism has been supported by sections of the democracy movement and women's movement in Iran. Despite the problems associated with these policies, women argued that they continue to support the Rouhani administration in the hope that the removal of sanctions and the ending of Iran's isolation would benefit the economy and allow civil society organisations to operate:

We voted for Rouhani for two reasons: Firstly to resolve the nuclear issue and open the way for removal of sanctions and secondly to resolve some of the economic issues and corruption. Because we believe that if these issues are resolved, there is a chance for civil society and social movements to grow and fight for the democratic rights of the people. (Arang, male activist in reformist and women's organisation, 60+)

These interviews demonstrate that women and men are very aware of the limitations of the current administration and are critical of neo-liberal policies in Iran. However in the absence of alternatives women are finding strategies of accommodation with neo-liberalism and taking advantage of the opportunities afforded to them to pursue activities that challenge the state and patriarchal social relations. At the same time they expressed a desire for a genuine alternative, as one participant argued:

We also need a movement such as the one which led to the 1979 revolution, and the one before for oil nationalisation and before that, the constitutional movement, to change this culture. But at the moment there is no sign for creation of such a movement in Iran. (Arang, male activist in reformist and women's organisation, 60+)

## CONCLUSION

In this chapter I have argued that the case of Iran confounds the presumed links between campaigns for gender equality or women's rights, and liberalism. In Iran, the reforms of a post-revolutionary welfarist state enabled the participation of millions of women in the political life of the country. This included for the first time working class, rural women and religious women, whose participation had been discouraged by the dictatorial regime of the Shah. These women, through their own efforts, have challenged the undemocratic and patriarchal nature of state institutions and have won significant victories since the 1990s. Neo-liberal reforms of the past 30 years have worsened the economic situation for the majority of women in the country as well as leading to the strengthening of certain patriarchal discourses and the introduction of new ideas of the 'good woman'. At the same time, privatisation and neo-liberalism have been supported by sections of the women's movements as an alternative to state intervention and control over areas of civil society.

We need to move beyond frameworks that view the struggle over women's rights as one carried out by moderate 'liberals' against religious hardliners. This presentation is in itself part of the gendered and racialised way that movements in non-western countries are viewed and relies on notions of the superiority of western liberal values. Indeed, despite espousing concern for women's rights in the Muslim world, the policies of international agencies and of western governments which have isolated Iran have hurt middle class and working class Iranians. This may erode the ability of a new generation of women to participate in politics in Iran. Thus, instead of viewing women's struggles as unconnected, we should recognise the impact of the international economic and political system on women in Iran and elsewhere as well as the diversity of responses and strategies that women develop.

# NOTES

1. The largest popular movement since the revolution of 1979, the 'green movement' consisted of demonstrations in major Iranian cities and was sparked by the disputed election results of June 2009 in which the incumbent president, Mahmoud Ahmadinejad, was declared winner after the first round of voting.

2. I have changed the names of all the participants in the interviews quoted in this chapter.

3. For example of the coverage of the appointment see: Dehghan (2015), 'Iran to appoint first female ambassador since Islamic revolution', http://www.theguardian.com/world/2015/apr/14/iran-marzieh-afkham-first-female-ambassador-since-islamic-revolution, and http://www.telegraph.co.uk/news/worldnews/middleeast/iran/11537058/Iran-to-appoint-first-female-ambassador-since-1979-Islamic-Revolution.html, https://theconversation.com/ambassadors-post-is-the-latest-step-on-a-long-and-winding-road-for-women-in-iran-40417

4. The *Velayat-e Faqih* (Government of the Jurist) is a theory of Islamic governance formulated by Ayatollah Khomeini which provided the theoretical basis for the foundation of the Islamic republic in Iran.

5. There is a debate about the level of poverty in Iran. While some sources claim that poverty has risen in the last 10 years to almost 40% of the population — see for example, http://www.ft.com/cms/s/0/4d017b7a-3cc2-11e3-86ef-00144feab7de.

html#axzz3eXLJObrc, others maintain that there is very little real poverty in the country — see for example, Salehi-Isfahani (2009), and this is supported by the UN Economic and Social Council report from 2013. Most analysts agree however that unemployment, particularly among youth and women, has risen and the cost of living has increased exponentially due to sanctions and economic policies. Youth unemployment is estimated at 28.3% and female unemployment is among the worst in the region (Bahramitash, 2013, p. 17).

6. The Islamic Revolutionary Guard Corps or 'Revolutionary Guard' is a military organisation formed as a volunteer paramilitary force during the 1979 revolution. They are increasingly involved in economic and commercial activities. The '*basij*' (mobilisation) organisation was created as a volunteer paramilitary organisation during the 1979 revolution. Its social base is traditionally the urban and rural poor, particularly the generation who fought in the Iran-Iraq war.

# REFERENCES

Abrahamian, E. (1991). Khomeini: Fundamentalist or populist? *New Left Review, 1*(186), 102—119.

Abu-Lughod, A. (2002). Do Muslim women really need saving? Anthropological reflections on cultural relativism and its others. *American Anthropologist, 104*(3), 783—790.

AFP. (2015). Iran to appoint first female ambassador since 1979 Islamic revolution. *The Telegraph*, April 15. Retrieved from http://www.telegraph.co.uk/news/worldnews/middleeast/iran/11537058/Iran-to-appoint-first-female-ambassador-since-1979-Islamic-Revolution.html.

Alehossein, A. (2013). Could Iran's Rouhani soon face the 'deep opposition' that Egypt's Morsi encountered? *Open Democracy*, August 6. Retrieved from https://www.open-democracy.net/ahmad-alehossein/could-irans-rouhani-soon-face-deep-opposition-that-egypts-morsi-encountered

Ali, K. A. (2002). *Planning the family in Egypt: New bodies, new selves*. Austin, TX: University of Texas Press.

Bahramitash, R. (2013). *Gender and entrepreneurship in Iran: Microenterprise and the informal sector*. New York, NY: Palgrave Macmillan.

Beinin, J. (2005). Political Islam and the new global economy: The political economy of an Egyptian social movement. *CR: The New Centennial Review, 5*(1), 111—139.

Bozorgmehr, N. (2013). Inflation and weak rial push Iran's middle class towards poverty. *The Financial Times*, October 25. Retrieved from http://www.ft.com/cms/s/0/4d017b7a-3cc2-11e3-86ef%2000144feab7de.html#axzz3eXLJObrc.

Chakravarti, U. (2008). Beyond the mantra of empowerment: Time to return to poverty, violence and struggle. *IDS Bulletin, 39*(6), 10—17.

Cornwall, A., Gideon, J., & Wilson, K. (2008). Introduction: Reclaiming feminism: Gender and neoliberalism. *IDS Bulletin, 39*(6), 2—9.

Dehghan, S. K. (2015). Iran to appoint first female ambassador since Islamic revolution. *The Guardian*, April 14. Retrieved from http://www.theguardian.com/world/2015/apr/14/iran-marzieh-afkham-first-female-ambassador-since-Islamic-revolution.

Harvey, D. (2005). *A brief history of neoliberalism*. Oxford: Oxford University Press.

Luckham, R., & White, G. (1996). Introduction: Democratizing the south. In R. Luckham & G. White (Eds.), *Democratization in the south: The jagged wave* (pp. 1–10). Manchester: Manchester University Press.

Mahmood, S. (2001). Feminist theory, embodiment and the docile agent: Some reflections on the Egyptian Islamic revival. *Cultural Anthropology, 16*(2), 202–236.

Mitchell, T. (1991). The limits of the state: Beyond statist approaches and their critics. *The American Political Science Review, 85*(1), 77–96.

Mitchell, T. (2002). McJihad: Islam in the world order. *Social Text, 20*(4), 1–18.

Moghadam, V. M. (2005). *Globalizing women: Transnational feminist networks.* Baltimore, MD: The John Hopkins University Press.

Mohanty, C. T. (2003). 'Under western eyes' revisited: Feminist solidarity through anticapitalist struggles. *Signs, 28*(2), 499–535.

Molyneux, M. (2006). Mothers at the service of the new poverty agenda: Progresa/ Oportunidades, Mexico Conditional Transfer Programme. *Social Policy and Administration, 40*(4), 425–449.

Najmabadi, A. (2000). (Un)veiling feminism. *Social Text, 18*(3), 29–45.

Paidar, P. (1995). *Women in the political process in twentieth century Iran.* Cambridge: Cambridge University Press.

Povey, T. (2015a). *Social movements in Egypt and Iran.* London: Palgrave Macmillan.

Povey, T. (2015b, April 19). *Ambassador's post is the latest step on a long and winding road for women in Iran.* Retrieved from https://theconversation.com/ambassadors-post-is-the-latest-step-on-a-long-and-winding-road-for-women-in-iran-40417

Rostami-Povey, E. (2010). *Women, work and Islamism, ideology and resistance in Iran* (2nd ed.). London: Zed Books.

Rostami-Povey, E. (2012). The Iranian women's movement in its historical context. In T. Povey & E. Rostami-Povey (Eds.), Women, power and politics in 21st century Iran (pp. 17–33). Farnham: Ashgate Publishing.

Salehi-Isfahani, D. (2009, January 29). *Iran: Poverty and inequality since the revolution.* Retrieved from http://www.brookings.edu/research/opinions/2009/01/29-iran-salehi-isfahani

United Nations Economic and Social Council. (2013, May 7). *Concluding observations on the second periodic report of the Islamic Republic of Iran, adopted by the Committee at its fiftieth session.* Retrieved from http://tb.ohchr.org/default.aspx?country = ir.

# BANGLADESHI FEMALE STUDENTS IN HIGHER EDUCATION: 'AGENTIC AUTONOMY' AT THE RACE/GENDER TRAJECTORY

Shaminder Takhar

## ABSTRACT

Purpose — *This chapter addresses Bangladeshi female students' experiences of higher education in the United Kingdom through the race/gender trajectory. Research shows that although minority ethnic women invest heavily in education, they go on to face obstacles in the labour market. However, there is a strong desire to study which is evident in the increasing numbers of Bangladeshi women applying to university since 1994. The chapter draws on empirical research with women who have claimed a kind of 'agentic autonomy' to pursue education in the face of structural inequalities.*

Design/methodology/approach — *The chapter is based on research conducted with a sample of Bangladeshi women studying at or recently*

Gender and Race Matter: Global Perspectives on Being a Woman
Advances in Gender Research, Volume 21, 41–62
Copyright © 2016 by Emerald Group Publishing Limited
All rights of reproduction in any form reserved
ISSN: 1529-2126/doi:10.1108/S1529-212620160000021004

*graduated from university. Qualitative research was carried out in the form of semi-structured interviews with 13 participants.*

Findings — *The study finds that Bangladeshi women are undeterred by structural inequalities in higher education and employment. Although they expect to face some difficulty finding suitable employment, they are optimistic about the future. They represent a group of women who have been able to achieve their objectives to study at degree level and show aspirations towards achieving similar objectives after graduation.*

Originality/value — *Bangladeshi women show agency and agentic behaviour to negotiate access to higher education institutions. This will, in the future have a knock-on effect in employment.*

**Keywords:** Bangladeshi women; higher education; agency; agentic autonomy; race; gender

# INTRODUCTION

I know a degree doesn't guarantee a job but I wanted to do a degree. For me it's an achievement because a degree is worth a lot.

— Fatima, graduate

The above quote is from one of the women in my research which captures the desire and determination to achieve in education and employment. It is indicative of a trend over the last two decades or so of minority ethnic groups exceeding expectations to gain educational qualifications. Although the Indian, Chinese and Black African groups have consistently performed as well or better than their white counterparts, groups such as Bangladeshi women have made the most progress (Broecke & Nicholls, 2007; Richardson, 2008). This has been reflected in newspaper articles that reported on research conducted by the Centre on Dynamics of Ethnicity (University of Manchester) in sensational headlines such as 'White British adults "less qualified" than ethnic minorities' (*The Telegraph*, 2014). Ahead of the above research being presented at the House of Lords, newspaper reports highlighted that there is a long way to go for minority ethnic groups to fulfil their aspirations (*The Guardian*, 2014). Given the contradictory nature of reports, this chapter explores higher education experiences of Bangladeshi women who are positioned at the race/gender trajectory.

Overall, research shows that although minority ethnic women invest heavily in education, they go on to face obstacles in the labour market (Heath & Cheung, 2006). However, there is a strong desire to study which is evident in the increasing numbers of minority ethnic women applying to universities over the last 25 years in the United Kingdom. The chapter draws on research specifically with Bangladeshi women who have claimed a kind of 'agentic autonomy' to pursue education in the face of structural inequalities. The women's agentic behaviour includes taking advantage of opportunities in order to have control over their lives and activities. Therefore, they represent a group of women who have been able to achieve their objective to study at degree level and show aspirations towards achieving similar objectives after graduation in the labour market.

The racialised gendering of labour markets is not a new phenomenon yet it persists. Although progress has been made with reference to educational qualifications since the publication of the Report *Moving on Up: Ethnic Minority Women at Work* in 2007 (EOC), Bangladeshi, Pakistani and Black Caribbean women face obstacles in their efforts to participate in the labour market. Once in the labour market they struggle to compete with other workers with reference to work that is commensurate with qualifications, promotion and pay. This is despite them having the same aspirations as other minority ethnic groups (Black African, Chinese, Indian). It demonstrates that young minority ethnic women have invested heavily in their education and shown determination to overcome the obstacles they face in employment such as lower glass ceilings, racism and sexism (Dale, 2002; Dale, Lindley, & Dex, 2006; Heath, Fuller, & Paton, 2008; Lindley, Dale, & Dex, 2006). This is borne out by the quote at the beginning by one of the participants and statistics that demonstrate increasingly high levels of participation in higher education by minority ethnic women[1] (Ball, 2003). Furthermore, according to calculations made of HESA data from 2006 by Niven, Faggian, and Ruwanpura (2013) show that:

> Bangladeshi women were better represented at 'old' universities (pre-1992) than young British-Bangladeshi men. This result is even more surprising if we consider that young British Bangladeshi women are often subjected to strict parental control and not allowed to attend higher education institutions too far away from the parental domicile, which considerably restricts their choices. (Niven et al., 2013, p. 121)

Given the context above and how structural inequalities operate, the first part of the chapter shows the women's awareness of structural inequalities whilst maintaining a strong desire to study and work, which flies in the face of stereotypical expectations of certain minority ethnic women

(Heath & Brinbaum, 2007). It explores how agency is operationalised by Bangladeshi women despite the varying constraints and social restrictions imposed on them by the family (Bhopal, 2010; Hussain & Bagguley, 2007). It will be shown that agency is involved in the desire for higher qualifications through 'agentic autonomy'.

## AGENCY AND EDUCATION

The implication of increasing numbers of Bangladeshi women entering higher education institutions is that they are actively engaged in attempting to secure a better future. The operationalisation of agency and 'agentic autonomy' indicates how a generation of women is actively involved in a type of social transformation which has implications for future gender relations. This chapter departs from the many studies carried out on the relationship between social/ethnic capital and acquisition of educational credentials (Crozier & Davies, 2006; Modood, 2004; Shah, Dwyer, & Modood, 2010; Thapar & Sanghera, 2010). Although they provide a good explanatory framework, they tend to focus on the family and the acquisition of social capital by the younger generation. As a result, the agency or agentic autonomy of young women is overlooked and it is with this in mind that I have utilised these concepts as a framework of analysis.

Furthermore, agentic autonomy and its relationship to social capital has been taken up by some writers who recognise the potential of such an alliance to transform gendered relations (Bruegel, 2005; Lister, 2005). It has been shown by some feminists that there are advantages in utilising social capital as an analytical concept to understand how gendered power structures are reproduced in society and how they can be challenged (Kovalainen, 2004; Lowndes, 2004). The feminist critique takes into account the existence of structural inequalities relating not only to social deprivation but also to gender, race and class. If social capital raises questions about its applicability and explanatory power, the conceptualisation of agency is not straight forward either. The question of agency is fraught with difficulties and embedded in ambiguity; it remains a hotly debated issue. Viewed as operating through the race/gender trajectory, we can see how agency 'is embedded in women's lifecycles, everyday practices and cultural expectation' (Ciotti, 2009, p. 113). In *Gender and Agency*, Lois McNay proposes that agency needs to move away from the 'dialectic of freedom and constraint' to its contextualisation within power relations

(McNay, 2000, p. 2). This would provide a way to understand acts of resistance in the face of constricting social sanctions. It is particularly relevant to the women in my research as they grapple with gender, class, race and generational inequalities. McNay puts forward the following:

> A more precise and varied account of agency is required to explain the differing motivations and ways in which individuals and groups struggle over, appropriate and transform cultural meanings and resources. This in turn, indicates the necessity of contextualizing agency within power relations in order to understand how acts deemed as resistant may transcend their immediate sphere in order to transform collective behaviour and norms. (McNay, 2000, p. 4)

The ideas of collective behaviour and norms are applicable within the context of social change which young Bangladeshi women are involved in with regard to education. If we accept that education is a causal factor in social change then we also need to look at the relationship between agency and autonomy. Judith Butler has argued that the female subject is constituted through processes of 'exclusion', 'differentiation' and 'repression', which are obscured by illusory notions of autonomy (Butler, 1990). These processes serve to position women as the subordinate Other, rendering them invisible. To an extent this is applicable to Bangladeshi women and their experiences of the labour market in which they are under-represented. Although the women are excluded from the labour market to a greater extent than other minority ethnic groups, they show the ability to use their agency in order to pursue goals and aspirations.

Human agency or agentic behaviour includes taking advantage of opportunities and to have some control over one's life and activities (Meyers, 2004). It also involves the use of autonomy, however, people's autonomy levels vary in different situations with some people having considerable control over others. Thus in South Asian families, parents exert more control over their daughters when entry into higher education is being considered (generational inequalities) (Niven et al., 2013). There are obvious difficulties in connecting agency with autonomy as autonomy can be compromised (Takhar, 2006; Weinreich, 2002). Agentic autonomy and the ability to act, in the context of this chapter, refer to Bangladeshi women pursuing their goals. For Meyers (2004), it seems the acts of choosing, deciding and valuing are central to being an autonomous subject. The actual content of the choices one might make does not seem of importance, therefore one can 'choose' from the various means to achieve a range of goals and act intentionally. Intentional action is based on the women's assessment of whether they have the agentic capacity to carry this through.

From the evidence of statistics of young Bangladeshi women in higher education, it shows that they do have agentic capacity, capability and relative autonomy, which is expressed by one of the participants:

> I know a degree doesn't guarantee a job, but I know I'm capable of a lot more. I know there are some people don't want to do a degree, they think they won't be able to cope, some people are just not bothered. But I wanted to do a degree, for me it's an achievement more than if I was to do ten little courses here and there − you know the ones that you can do at college. For me, a degree is worth a lot more, it's valued a lot more. (Yasmina, undergraduate student)

The high value placed on the acquisition of a degree uncovers the 'agentic self' which refers to how people discover their own capabilities and identity. It relates to a process that 'contributes to an integrated sense of personal agency' (Little, 2002, p. 226). The concepts 'agentic self' and 'agentic autonomy' are used within psychology to explain the processes that are similar to those experienced by young Bangladeshi women in the pursuit of education and work. It is worthwhile to remember also that the 'agent' is located within social and cultural contexts and has to negotiate within set parameters, something that Bangladeshi women have done with reference to education. What they have done through a self-realised agency is to bring about gradual social change by refusing to comply with dominant discourses. When we desire something we try by different means to get what we want and need in order to arrive at a self that is acceptable to us. The following captures what it means to do what you desire and arrive at a position that is acceptable:

> Achievement is down to the individual and with determination and finding the right resources, you can get into any field. (Rowena, graduate)

The resources referred to here are not only material but realising her own capability to assert what she desired, that is her agency enabled her 'to act in one's best interest' (hooks, 1990, p. 206). Doing what one desires and what is in one's best interest is also applicable to family and community interests, therefore young Bangladeshi women have been able to draw on a range of sources to satisfy their desire to study and work.

## METHODOLOGY

Qualitative research in the form of case study interviews was carried out with a sample of Bangladeshi (13) women studying at a post-1992 university. They were recruited through advertising for participants through posters at the university and due to the timing of the research, some had recently graduated. The sample group consisted of women between 19 and 23 years, a range of subject areas of the university. All have ethnic origins in Bangladesh and are Muslims, none live on campus, all are single and come from what would be described as working class backgrounds. All of the participants were born in the United Kingdom and four had recently graduated. The aim of the research was to analyse their aspirations concerning education, employment and career development. Their experiences of higher education were explored in connection with negotiating routes, managing their desires and frustrations and how universities can aid in their progression to a career. The interviews provided the women with a space from which they not only spoke about their experiences, but were also able to explore their own thinking about particular issues and reflect on decisions they had made. The individual case studies give voice to women who often simultaneously form part of a highly visible/invisible group. During the interview a range of areas were covered from their family background to specific experience, family support, careers and employment, and structural inequalities such as sexism and racism. The aim was to provide useful insights to the experiences of this group of women in university in the context of their ability to use agency. The objective of the research was to make recommendations regarding the role of the careers service, work experience schemes and the establishment of links with potential employers. It is to the link between educational attainment, employment and social mobility that we turn to in the next section.

## NEGOTIATING EDUCATIONAL DESIRE[2]

The desire to study among minority ethnic women is evident in the increasing numbers applying to universities since 1994. The highest growth in applications has been amongst Bangladeshi and Pakistani young women (HESA, 2006 cited in Niven et al., 2013). Previous research has shown that there have been marked differences amongst minority ethnic groups in terms of applying to and getting into university. Amongst the Bangladeshi and Pakistani groups in the past, more young men applied to university than young women indicating a gender gap (Connor, Modood, & Hillage, 2004; Modood & Shiner, 1994; Shiner & Modood, 2002). In addition to this, despite the increase in the number of minority ethnic students staying in full-time education, they were disadvantaged with reference to the non-traditional route followed into higher education. It has been shown that disadvantage experienced by Black Caribbean, Bangladeshi and Pakistani women begins at entry point to higher education institutions, that is access and type of institution (Broecke & Hamed, 2008). It has resulted in lower acceptance levels into higher education institutions and had a knock-on effect of disadvantage at the shortlisting stage by graduate recruiters (Taylor, 1993). Although new universities have operated admission policies that are more flexible, Connor, La Valle, Tackey, and Perryman (1996) found in their study conducted in 1993 that Bangladeshi women were under-represented. Indeed Bangladeshi women who attended universities and acquired a degree during the first half of the 1990s have been referred to as 'pioneers' who struggled to overcome barriers to their education. They asserted their agency and negotiated with their parents to allow them to study in opposition to expectations of the parents and community, that is marriage as a priority (Bhopal, 2010; Hussain & Bagguley, 2007). The Bangladeshi women in the research are subjected to racialised gendered identity and have 'struggle[d] for educational inclusion in order to transform their opportunities and in doing so subvert racist expectations and beliefs' (Basit, 1997; Mirza, 2009, p. 153; Shain, 2003). Projecting into the future benefits of a degree qualification is highlighted by their narratives below:

> In this modern age everyone is studying, even all the girls, not like in my sister's time when the girls were getting married rather than studying. (Farida, undergraduate student)

> I've always wanted to come to university and graduate, and my family wanted me to come to university as well. I'm like the first person in my family to come to uni so it's like a big accomplishment for them. I just thought getting a degree and stuff would help me in getting a better job I knew I could use my degree to my advantage. (Yasmina, undergraduate student)

> My parents saw my uncles and aunties graduate and they got good jobs, so they got something out of their degrees and that was a great influence. Another thing is that I have to influence my sisters, I have to be a role model to them and encourage them. If I do well, then they do well. (Jahanara, undergraduate student)

> I am definitely ambitious in the sense that I need to work and be independent. I don't want to be dependent on anybody. That's the one thing my parents − my dad, well actually both my parents − they wanted me to get a degree and do my own thing rather than depend on anyone. (Jasmine, undergraduate)

Over a number of decades, minority ethnic communities have been engaged in a struggle in connection with access to educational opportunities, which as Mirza (2009, p. 153) states is 'a struggle for humanity [and] for a black person to become educated is to become human'. The latter part of the quote informs us how certain minority ethnic groups are only assigned the 'human' status once they have acquired language and education. This 'putting on of the white world' (Fanon, 1986, p. 36) brings to the fore the colonial encounter whereby the colonised subject through acquisition of language and behaviour of the 'civilised' simultaneously reassures and threatens. Although minority ethnic women are positioned as subordinate through stereotyping and dominant discourses, they are actively engaged in transformation from the 'margin' (Bhabha, 1990). Being located at the margin does not imply a position of weakness or a 'marginality which is imposed by oppressive structures' (hooks, 1992, p. 22), rather it has been regarded as a site of resistance. The margin has also been referred to as the 'third space' where 'everything comes together':

> Subjectivity and objectivity, the abstract and concrete, the real and imagined, the knowable and the unimaginable, the repetitive and the differential, structure and agency, mind and body, consciousness and the unconscious, the disciplined and the transdisciplinary, everyday life and unending history. (Soja, 1996, pp. 56–57)

The 'third space' has been used to demonstrate that although racism and sexism are experienced in educational institutions by minority ethnic women, they demonstrate a resistance which has the resources of the centre (Mirza, 2006, 2009; Mirza & Reay, 2000; Takhar, 2013). Despite being considered as 'out of place' (Puwar, 2004, p. 51), the third space is where a type of disruption and coming together of history and identity occur. Although the women may have 'a sense of one's place which leads one to exclude oneself from places from which one is excluded' (Reay, Davies, David, & Ball, 2001, p. 864), the process of applying to university has continued. Women in the research demonstrated determination to enter university based on the high value attached to education, evident amongst all minority ethnic groups. Indeed in terms of attainment, 'women from the British Bangladeshi community have recorded a threefold increase in higher educational attainment' (Niven et al., 2013, p. 121). Although education is popular, some young women, however, were and still are restricted to higher education institutions that are closer to home. This does not detract from the determination to succeed, rather it indicates a process of negotiation that involves compromise to achieve what they desire, that is to fulfil their aspirations (Bhopal, 2010; Dale, Shaheen, Kalra, & Fieldhouse, 2002; Hussain & Bagguley, 2007). The young women understand that restrictions are imposed on them in response to their possible corruption by western influences if they studied away from home. Within South Asian communities, women are carriers of the family's honour (*'izzat'*) and must avoid shame (*'sharam'*) (Patel, 1997; Siddiqui, 2000; Wilson, 2006). However, as a consequence of the restrictions imposed on them they are placed at a disadvantage by their relative geographical immobility when attempting to find suitable employment (Equality Challenge Unit [ECU], 2010; Hussain & Bagguley, 2007; Women and Equality Unit, 2006). Studying, therefore, involves agency through negotiation with parents but living away from home would require a considerable amount of negotiation, which some have done successfully and gone on to enter older universities. The ability to move geographically in turn has a positive effect on employment opportunities (Ahmad, 2005; Niven et al., 2013). Given the above, it is also important not to present women as victims rather we can present them as having agency or 'agentic autonomy' in connection with education (Housee, 2004; Mirza, 2009; Tyrer & Ahmad, 2006).

## THE UNAVOIDABLE LINK: EDUCATION AND WORK

Research has shown that minority ethnic students are clustered in post-1992 universities which provide a challenge particularly with reference to employment (Curtis, 2006; Modood, 2006). There are exceptions to the rule such as King's College, LSE and Imperial College. It is also becoming evident that the widening participation *and* equality and diversity agendas do not take into consideration the expected discrimination and marginalisation of these groups in universities and employment. However, it is precisely the existence of admissions policies, widening participation and outreach work of the 'old' universities that has resulted in the gradual increase in minority ethnic students studying at degree level (Reay, David, & Ball, 2005). Despite the increase in numbers in higher education institutions, evidence indicates that institutional racism, stereotyping and tokenism continues into employment (Bhavnani & Mirza, 2005; Jones, 1993; Mason, 2003; Moosa, 2008; Peach, 2006). Although widening participation has encouraged the inclusion of previously marginalised groups, one of the participants stated the following about the Bangladeshi community and being a Muslim female:

> As an ethnic community, we have the potential to do better however, the word 'Bengali' is at the bottom of the pile. It conjures up a sense of failure among others. Bengalis have potential and hidden talent. Bengali students should work hard to

challenge these negative views and they should be given the opportunity to show off their talents. (Fatima, graduate)

There is complexity to how certain minority ethnic communities are seen with the overlapping of factors such as socio-economic status, class background, migration and possession of capital. The difficulties associated with being Muslim expressed by Fatima above is similar to Mirza (2006) commenting on her daughter having to change her Muslim name to secure a job interview. Given that widening participation (David, 2009; Weekes-Bernard, 2010) has been at the forefront of educational policies to increase the numbers of marginalised students into higher education in pre- and post-1992 universities, the Bangladeshi community continues to be seen as the most disadvantaged. If we accept that education moulds and prepares individuals for employment, it would be expected that due to race relations legislation (1965, 1968, 1976, 2000) and the Equality Act (2010) that the economic environment would have improved over time. Instead findings from research show that occupational segregation for minority ethnic women is severe, therefore they find it 'difficult to fulfil their potential' (EOC, 2007, p. 4; Platt, 2002). The occupational segregation of minority ethnic women has been well documented in the past (Afshar, 1989, 1994; Brah, 1994; Brah & Shaw, 1992; Breugel, 1989; Bryan, Dadzie, & Scafe, 1985). Yet it is their less favourable positioning in the labour market that has compounded structural inequalities and lead to segregated labour market patterns. Whilst earlier research displays a more straight forward picture of inequalities, the 1990s presented evidence of a more varied and diverse nature which offered hope in the form of better job prospects (Dale et al., 2002; Joly, 1995; Lindley, 1994).

## *Discrimination*

Furthermore by problematising reductionist discourses of 'modern' and 'traditional' that are used to describe Muslim women (particularly since the London bombings in 2005) challenges universities and employers to accept them as a resource rather than a burden (Crozier & Davies, 2006; Tyrer & Ahmad, 2006). The importance of religion (Islam) was expressed by the participants and they were aware of the challenges ahead but were not open to compromise on the issue of Islamic dress:

Religion is very important to me because I am a practising Muslim and I pray five times a day and in terms of the university, I am grateful that there is a prayer room. (Henna, graduate)

I wear a headscarf and if for a job or something, I was told that I couldn't wear my scarf or I had to dress in a particular way that I felt uncomfortable with, that didn't follow the way that Muslims dress ... I wouldn't take up that job. I wouldn't do anything that was considered wrong by Islam — drink alcohol or drugs or anything. (Yasmin, undergraduate)

Employers will think twice about employing you. (Jahanara, undergraduate)

I wouldn't go to those kinds of jobs anyway where I would feel out of place, where everyone's wearing suits or whatever and I'm the only odd one out wearing this (Islamic dress). I'd look for a place where I'd feel comfortable wearing what I wear. (Ameera, undergraduate)

The last response is from a woman who recognises that she is at a disadvantage with reference to dress and has thus focused on working in a hospital located in an area with Sylhetti speakers. She is therefore able to use her language and professional skills in an environment where she feels comfortable. Most of the women commented on the negative portrayal of Muslims in the media (Macdonald, 2006) and worried that if they did find suitable employment, they may not progress up the career ladder:

I am optimistic but sometimes all this Islamophobia stuff doesn't help. Sometimes you just think oh my God how are they viewing me? Do they think that I'm a terrorist? All the Islamophobia is worrying me about what's going to happen to us Muslims getting employment. (Maryam, graduate)

Similarly in education, it has been noted that although minority ethnic women have struggled for inclusion, they have taken opportunities and continue to aspire to upward social mobility and have underlying adherence to the concept of meritocracy (Mirza, 2006, 2009; Reynolds, 1997). Although minority ethnic women have improved their marketability through acquiring qualifications, it is interesting to note that Baroness Valerie Amos only recently took charge of SOAS thereby becoming the first female black woman to do so (THES,[3] 2015). In politics there are currently twenty minority ethnic female MPs representing a small minority in the House of Commons. However, the women I interviewed were undeterred by such statistics and continued in their ambitions to lead a better life through acquiring educational credentials. It demonstrates minority ethnic women's, and Bangladeshi women in particular, desire to be successful at university and in employment. Indeed the increasing numbers of these young women entering universities and gaining higher education qualifications show they are able to negotiate routes into education and promote social change. They were also acutely aware of discrimination:

Certain industries are looking for independent career women ads because employers have this stereotypical view of Asian women, they would rather employ a white woman.

Searching for jobs is hard if you have a Muslim name. You will be placed at the bottom of the pile. Employers view Asian women as risky so there is sexism and Asian women suffer multiple forms of discrimination. (Fatima, graduate)

I know women in general do face discrimination and regardless of what your background is, women face discrimination. So it doesn't help that I'm a woman, it doesn't help that you know that I'm a Muslim, all those things that are possible barriers. (Latifa, undergraduate)

Three of us, two Bangladeshis and one Indian did a SWOT analysis. The threat for all of us was our background – our ethnicity. I mean that is our threat once we get into employment. That is a barrier, so I have concerns about that as well. I think having no experience and then having that ethnicity as an issue when finding a job would be both a problem. (Jahanara, undergraduate)

Due to the possible difficulties the work placement appeared to find resonance amongst the women interviewed:

I think it's such a great idea. Everyone talks about the fact that graduates don't find themselves a job as soon as they leave. Work placements help employers to actually accept you because you've got that from the university, the knowledge, as well as the experience. You can get a good reference as well. (Latifa, undergraduate)

It would have been very helpful to have a work placement in terms of getting employment, developing experience. (Maryam, graduate)

## *Valuing Education and Its Consequences*

It would be short-sighted at this stage to state that Bangladeshi Muslim communities have been left untouched by external influences due to young women currently in universities and in employment. Muslim communities have been presented as lacking resources, living in segregated communities and leading 'parallel lives' but in doing so avoids looking at structural inequalities along the lines of class, race and gender (Cantle Report, 2001). The failure 'to recognise the significance of wider social and economic forces and the inequalities they produce' (Franklin, 2001, p. 2) questions how empowerment and demands for resources can occur (Campbell, 2001; Goulbourne & Solomos, 2003). Finney and Simpson (2009) refute the claim of segregation arguing that media perpetuate the myth of certain communities as a burden. Although there is recognition of structural inequalities and institutional racism, which could make a community look inwards, the women in the research continued to aspire to work in professional settings (Mirza, 2009). It is evident from the responses given by some of the participants that going to university was a parental expectation. There was also reliance on family members who had attended university for advice although one participant was guided by her school teacher into university. The choices made by the women represent a cross over between the 'contingent chooser' (encouragement and expectation) and the 'embedded chooser' (knowledge of league tables, no financial worries):

> The contingent chooser is typically a first generation applicant to higher education whose parents were educated outside of the UK. Their parents are working class and have low incomes. [...] The process of information gathering and choice is left to the student, who will often act on the basis of very limited information. [...] The embedded chooser has parents who attended university and often other relatives and friends with experience of university, although not necessarily in the UK. [...] Not to go on to higher education is virtually unthinkable and certainly unacceptable to parents. (Reay et al., 2005, pp. 113–119)

Both aspects of choosing are evident in the narratives of the women I interviewed:

> My dad said to me you don't have to rely on people. You know, after marriage one of the issues he used to tell my mum was that 'she doesn't have to fall back on anyone after marriage, she's got her stuff, she's got her education, she's got her job, she doesn't have to rely on anyone'. The influence my father had on me was so great, it was like now I understand what he means. I think I'm happy because without dad's encouragement I wouldn't have been here. I probably would have been in some local job, doing something and probably getting married soon [..] I wanted to go to university. (Jahanara, undergraduate)

> My dad and my sisters are my role models. My dad gives me positive advice and support. He is a good role model for me because he had a difficult start when he came to Britain thirty years ago with nothing and then opened his business. (Fatima, graduate)

> I have three brothers and four sisters, I am the youngest. Although my brothers went to university, my sisters didn't so I am the first daughter to go to university [...] Going to university wasn't up for discussion ... my parents, my father wanted and encouraged me to study at university. He had very high expectations. Education is highly valued in the Asian community. My father wanted me to study IT which is highly valued in the Asian community. I am keeping teaching as an option as youth work is not viewed as 'high ranking' or 'respectable'. (Joshna, undergraduate)

> They [parents] always wanted me to study so they wanted me to go to college. My dad has always said that he wanted me to do something with my life like become something ... just do something different to what everyone else has done. He's really happy and he wants me to carry on the way I am. That's like motivated me but I wouldn't call that pressure or anything. (Yasmina, undergraduate)

In order to arrive at a self that is acceptable through a self-realised agency, the women were not necessarily involved in negotiating terms for attending university. Despite the university being 'local', the positive attitude of parents and fathers in particular, towards education challenge the stereotype of Muslim fathers as oppressive. Instead they are central to their daughters' academic achievements as it brings not only economic capital but 'prestigious capital' (Ahmad, 2005, p. 275) alongside a liberal and educated status to the family as a whole. Indeed 'this pursuit of "educational prestige" is not simply a middle-class strategy' (*ibid*., p. 276). Research therefore flies in the face of the stereotype of the Muslim family as patriarchal and the women as oppressed and subservient. Therefore, located in family and community networks there are young people who have succeeded and are considered to be role models.

A subsequent effect of the high value placed on female education is the effect it has had on negotiating marriage. Therefore, families were also aware of the value of a qualified woman in terms of earning power and this increased the chance of finding a more suitable husband (Ahmad, 2005). Social change and changes in attitudes towards education and marriage have occurred gradually over the last two decades. If 'agentic autonomy' is evidenced through women's successful negotiation regarding education and work, I have argued that it is also present in negotiating marriage (Takhar, 2013). One of the women stated that her aunt who is in her early thirties is not married which is uncommon and that her own parents encouraged her to find herself a suitable partner. She is engaged to a Muslim man and commented that:

> My family is very liberal and there is no pressure for me to get married. I have not set a date to get married because I am not ready. I plan to focus on my career first and gaining another qualification would require time and commitment. (Fatima, graduate)

Liberal attitudes and negotiating marriage is something that has developed over time within the Asian community (Bangladeshi, Indian and Pakistani communities) (Bhopal, 2000; Gardner & Shukur, 2004; Ramji, 2003). For Bangladeshi women 'the opportunity to go to university was used to defer and negotiate the timing of marriage' (Hussain & Bgguley, 2007, p. 91). Furthermore, liberal attitudes, the ability to build links with different people through university and work, and discussions between parents and their daughters are also evident amongst the women interviewed:

> My parents do get worried, though they say 'oh don't do this, don't do that'. But I say that I have more non-Muslim friends than Muslim friends and they understand and when they don't understand they ask me. My friends are mainly white and there is one homosexual Pakistani guy. (Jasmine, undergraduate)

Although the quote above is one example of evidence that indicates a shift in friendship and support networks for minority ethnic women, the friendships are weaker than those with whom they can experience a level of support, belonging and security (Bhopal, 2010). Friendship networks are based on feelings of exclusion, marginalisation and sometimes racism (Bhopal, 2010; Hussain & Bagguley, 2007; Puwar, 2004; Shain, 2003). Working within an Islamic framework with reference to friendship and socialising is exemplified by the following narrative:

> I still go out with my friends I go out in the evening – my parents are really good with that, they're really good, obviously I've got a deadline ... time out kind of curfew, it is better than most Bengali and Pakistani girls I know. So my parents are quite liberal. I mean they're strict in the sense that they think that we should follow Islam and pray, wear the head-scarf us being girls and things like that. I think we should follow that because that's what Islam says, that's what Islam is about, it's not complicated. (Joshna, undergraduate)

Religion has been shown to act as a positive leverage for young women who have drawn on the importance placed on education by Islam for both men and women. Through this mechanism, religion has acquired the status of being more progressive than culture and the cultural community (Takhar, 2013). Furthermore, some women have also been able to appease the 'cultural community' by ensuring that they adhere to wearing Islamic dress. For these women, dress codes act as symbols of attachment to Islam and therefore facilitate more freedom to study and socialise. This can be conceptualised as an inventive way of building social capital amongst the young women within a framework that is acceptable for the community and the family.

# CONCLUSION

This chapter has shown through empirical evidence that the educational and employment aspirations of young Bangladeshi women remain intact with a high value placed on educational qualifications. Although previous research indicates low levels of participation in higher education and employment amongst this minority ethnic group, the situation has changed dramatically over the last two decades. It has been accompanied by changes in attitudes towards the education of girls and young women amongst the Muslim community. Participation does not correspond with their relatively disadvantaged positions in British society yet despite encountering structural inequalities there has been a gradual increase in educational attainment. The research is not a representation of Bangladeshi women, however, the results support that education is regarded highly and that negotiations are occurring between the young women and their parents. The success of young women is also dependent on their ability to strike the right balance between educational attainment and protecting their family's honour. The process of entering higher education institutions requires from young women a more complex level of negotiation in comparison to young men. Their ability to carry through the negotiation, the young women have demonstrated that they have the determination to arrive at a self that is acceptable to them. Through a self-realised agency and the refusal to comply with dominant discourses, they have exhibited 'agentic autonomy' in their decision to enter higher education and to act in their own interest. It also challenges the stereotype of Muslim fathers as oppressive. Instead they are central to their daughters' academic achievements as it brings prestige and status to the family as a whole. Through presenting a liberal and educated status, the women are able to negotiate marriage to a more suitably educated man who is already in employment. Although patriarchal oppression varies between and amongst South Asian communities, the increasing numbers of Bangladeshi women in higher education institutions in the United Kingdom challenges the perception of the Muslim family as only patriarchal.

## NOTES

1. This would appear to go against the idea that students who gain educational credentials possess more cultural capital. For an examination of Bourdieu's theory of cultural capital performance in school examinations see Sullivan (2001).
2. See Mirza and Reay (2000).
3. *Times Higher Educational Supplement.*

## REFERENCES

Afshar, H. (1989). Education: Hopes, expectations and achievements of Muslim women in West Yorkshire. *Gender and Education, 1*(3), 261–272.
Afshar, H. (1994). Muslim women in West Yorkshire: Growing up with real and imaginary value amidst conflicting views of self and society. In H. Afshar & M. Maynard (Eds.), *The dynamics of 'race and gender': Some feminist interventions* (pp. 127–147). London: Taylor and Francis.

Ahmad, F. (2005). Modern traditions? British Muslim women and academic achievement. In C. Skelton & B. Francis (Eds.), *Feminist critique of education: Fifteen years of gender development* (pp.269–285). New York, NY: Routledge.

Ball, S. J. (2003). *Class strategies and the educational market: The middle classes and social advantage*. London: Routledge Falmer.

Basit, T. (1997). 'I want more freedom', but not too much: British Muslim girls and the dynamism of family values. *Gender and Education, 9*(4), 425–439.

Bhabha, H. (1990). The third space: An interview with Homi Bhabha. In J. Ruthertford (Ed.), *Identity: Community, culture and difference* (pp. 207–221). London: Lawrence and Wishart.

Bhavnani, R., & Mirza, H. S. (2005). *Tackling the roots of racism: Lessons for success*. Bristol: Policy Press.

Bhopal, K. (2000). South Asian women in East London: The impact of education. *European Journal of Women's Studies, 7*(1), 35–52.

Bhopal, K. (2010). *Asian women in higher education; Shared communities*. Stoke-on-Trent: Trentham Books Limited.

Brah, A. (1994). 'Race' and 'culture' in the gendering of labour markets: South Asian young Muslim women and the labour market. In H. Afshar & M. Maynard (Eds.), *The dynamics of 'race' and gender: Some feminist intervention* (pp. 151–171). London: Taylor and Francis.

Brah, A., & Shaw, S. (1992). *Working choices: South Asian young Muslim women and the labour market*. London: Department of Employment. Research Paper No. 91.

Breugel, I. (1989). Sex and race in the labour market. *Feminist Review, 32*(Summer), 49–68.

Bruegel, I. (2005). Social capital and feminist critique. In J. Franklin (Ed.), *Women and social capital*. London: London South Bank University.

Broecke, S., & Hamed, J. (2008). *Gender gaps in higher education participation: An analysis of the relationship between prior attainment and young participation by gender, socio-economic class and ethnicity*. DIUS Research Report 08-14. London: Department for Innovation, Universities and Skills. Retrieved from http://dera.ioe.ac.uk/8717/1/DIUS-RR-08-14.pdf. Accessed on January 20, 2016.

Broecke, S., & Nicholls, T. (2007). *Ethnicity and degree attainment*. DfES Research Report RW92. DfES, London.

Bryan, B., Dadzie, S., & Scafe, S. (1985). *The heart of the race: Black women's lives in Britain*. London: Virago Press.

Butler, J. (1990). Gender trouble, feminist theory and psychoanalytical discourse. In L. Nicholson (Ed.), *Feminism/postmodernism* (pp. 324–340). London: Routledge.

Campbell, C. (2001). Putting social capital in perspective: A case of unrealistic expectations? In V. Morrow (Ed.), An appropriate capital-Isation? Questioning social capital. London: LSE Gender Institute. Research in Progress Series, Issue 1, pp. 1–10.

Cantle, T. (2001). *Community cohesion: A report of the independent review team*. London: Home Office.

Ciotti, M. (2009). The conditions of politics: Low-caste women and political agency in a northern Indian city. *Feminist Review, 91*, 113–134.

Connor, H., La Valle, I., Tackey, N., & Perryman, S. (1996). *Ethnic minority graduates: Degrees of difference*. Institute for Employment Studies. IES Report 309.

Connor, H., Modood, T., & Hillage, J. (2004). *Why the difference: A closer look at higher education minority ethnic students and graduates*. DfES Research Report 552. Nottingham: DfES Publications.

Crozier, G., & Davies, J. (2006). Family matters: A discussion of the Bangladeshi and Pakistani extended family and community in supporting the children's education. *The Sociological Review, 54*(4), 678–689.

Curtis, P. (2006). Black students failing to get into to top universities. *The Guardian*, January 3. Retrieved from http://www.guardian.co.uk/uk/2006/jan/03/highereducation. race. Accessed on January 25, 2016.

Dale, A. (2002). Social exclusion of Pakistani and Bangladeshi Women. *Sociological Research Online, 7*(3). Retrieved from http://www.socresonline.org.uk/socresonline/7/3/dale.html. Accessed on January 26, 2016.

Dale, A., Lindley, J. K., & Dex, S. (2006). A life-course perspective on ethnic differences in women's economic activity in Britain. *European Sociological Review, 22*(3), 323–337.

Dale, A., Shaheen, N., Kalra, V., & Fieldhouse, E. (2002). Routes into higher education and employment for young Pakistani and Bangladeshi women in the UK. *Ethnic and Racial Studies, 25*(6), 942–968.

David, M. (Ed.). (2009). *Improving learning by widening participation in higher education*. London: Routledge.

Equal Opportunities Commission (EOC). (2007). *Moving on up: Ethnic minority women at work*. Equal Opportunities Commission. Manchester: EOC.

Equality Challenge Unit. (2010). *Equality in higher education: Statistical report 2010*. London: ECU. Retrieved from http://www.ecu.ac.uk/publications/equality-in-he-stats-10. Accessed on January 25, 2016.

Fanon, F. (1986). *Black skin, white masks*. London: Pluto Press.

Finney, N., & Simpson, L. (2009). *'Sleepwalking to segregation'? Challenging myths about race and migration*. Bristol: Policy Press.

Franklin, J. (2001). Women and social capital. In J. Franklin. (Ed.), *Women and social capital* (pp. 2–3). Families and Social Capital ESRC Research Group Working Paper, 12. London: London South Bank University.

Goulbourne, H., & Solomos, J. (2003). Families, ethnicity and social capital. *Social Policy and Society, 2*(4), 329–338.

Heath, A., & Brinbaum, Y. (2007). Explaining ethnic inequalities in educational attainment. *Ethnicities, 7*(3), 291–305.

Heath, A. F., & Cheung, S. Y. (2006). *Ethnic penalties in the labour market: Employers and discrimination*. Leeds: Department for Work and Pensions. Research Report No. 341. Published for the Department for Work and Pensions by Corporate Document Services. Retrieved from www.dwp.gov.uk/asd/asd5/rrs2006.asp. Accessed on January 25, 2016.

Heath, S., Fuller, A., & Paton, K. (2008). Networked ambivalence and educational decision making: A case study of 'non-participation' in higher education. *Research Papers in Education Special Issue on Challenges of Diversity for Widening Participation in UK Higher Education, 2*(2), 219–231.

Higher Education Statistics Agency (HESA). (2006). *C05018 Introduction: Target response rates*. Retrieved from http://www.hesa.ac.uk/index.php/content/view/329/233/#target. Accessed on January 25, 2016.

hooks, b. (1990). *Yearning: Race, gender and cultural politics*. Boston, MA: South End Press.

hooks, b. (1992). *Black looks: Race and representation*. Boston, MA: South End Press.

Housee, S. (2004). Unveiling South Asian female identities post September 11: Asian females' sense of identity and experiences of higher education. In I. Law, D. Phillips, & L. Turney (Eds.), *Institutional racism in higher education* (pp. 59–70). Stoke on Trent: Trentham Books.

Hussain, Y., & Bagguley, P. (2007). *Moving on up: South Asian women and higher education.* Stoke on Trent: Trentham Books.

Joly, D. (1995). *Britannia's crescent: Making a place for Muslims in British society.* Aldershot: Ashgate.

Jones, T. (1993). *Britain's ethnic minorities.* London: PSI.

Kovalainen, A. (2004). Rethinking the revival of social capital and trust in social theory: Possibilities for feminist analyses of social capital and trust. In B. L. Marshall & A. Witz (Eds.), *Engendering the social: Feminist encounters with social theory* (pp. 155–170). New York, NY: Open University Press.

Lindley, J. K., Dale, A., & Dex, S. (2006). Ethnic differences in women's employment: The changing role of qualifications. *Oxford Economic Papers, 58.*

Lindley, R. M. (1994). *Labour market structures and prospects for women.* Manchester: Equal Opportunities Commission.

Lister, R. (2005). Feminist citizenship theory: An alternative perspective on understanding women's social and political lives. In J. Franklin (Ed.), *Women and social capital* (pp. 18–26). Families and Social Capital ESRC Research Group Working Paper, 12. London: London South Bank University.

Little, T. D. (2002). Agency in development. In W. H. Hartup & R. K. Silbereisen (Eds.), *Growing points in developmental science: An introduction* (pp. 223–240). East Sussex: Psychology Press.

Lowndes, V. (2004). It's not what you've got, it's what you do with it: Women, social capital and political participation. In B. O'Neill & E. GIdengil (Eds.), *Gender and social capital* (pp. 213–240). New York, NY: Routledge.

Macdonald, M. (2006). Muslim women and the veil: Problems of image and voice in media representations. *Feminist Media Studies, 6*(1), 7–23.

Mason, D. (2003). Changing patterns of ethnic disadvantage in employment. In D. Mason (Ed.), *Explaining ethnic differences: Changing patterns of disadvantage in Britain* (pp. 69–86). Bristol: Policy Press.

McNay, L. (2000). *Gender and agency: Reconfiguring the subject in feminist social theory.* Malden, MA: Blackwell.

Meyers, D. T. (2004). *Being yourself: Essays on identity, action, and social life.* Lanham: Rowman & Littlefield Publishers.

Mirza, H. S. (2006). 'Race', gender and educational desire. *Race Ethnicity Education, 9*(2), 137–158.

Mirza, H. S. (2009). *Race, gender and educational desire: Why Black women succeed and fail.* London: Routledge.

Mirza, H. S., & Reay, D. (2000). Spaces and places of black educational desire: Rethinking black supplementary schools as a new social movement. *Sociology, 34*(3), 521–544.

Modood, T. (2004). Capital, ethnic identity and educational qualifications. *Cultural Trends, 13*(2), 87–105.

Modood, T. (2006). Ethnicity, Muslims and higher education entry in Britain. *Teaching in Higher Education, 11*(2), 247–250.

Modood, T., & Shiner, M. (1994). *Ethnic minorities and higher education: Why are there differential rates of entry?* London: Policy Studies Institute.

Moosa, Z. (Ed.). (2008). *Seeing double: Race and gender in ethnic minority women's lives.* London: Fawcett Society.

Niven, J., Faggian, A., & Ruwanpura, K. N. (2013). Exploring 'underachievement' among highly educated young British-Bangladeshi women. *Feminist Economics, 19*(1), 111–136.

Patel, P. (1997). Third wave feminism and black women's activism. In H. S. Mirza (Ed.), *Black British feminism: A reader* (pp. 255–267). London: Routledge.

Paton, G. (2014). White British adults 'less qualified' than ethnic minorities. *The Telegraph*, March 10. Retrieved from http://www.telegraph.co.uk/education/educationnews/10688017/White-British-adults-less-qualified-than-ethnic-minorities.html. Accessed on January 20, 2016.

Peach, C. (2006). Islam, ethnicity and South Asian religions in the London 2001 census. *Transaction of the British Institute of Geographers, 31*(3), 353–370.

Platt, L. (2002). *Parallel lives? Poverty among ethnic minority groups in Britain.* London: Child Poverty Action Group.

Puwar, N. (2004). *Space invaders: Race, gender and bodies out of place.* New York, NY: Berg.

Ramji, H. (2003). Engendering diasporic identities. In N. Puwar & P. Raghuram (Eds.), *South Asian women in the diaspora* (pp. 227–242). Oxford: Berg.

Reay, D., David, M. E., & Ball, S. J. (2005). *Degrees of choice: Class, gender and race in the higher education choice process.* Stoke on Trent: Trentham Books.

Reay, D., Davies, J., David, M., & Ball, S. (2001). Choices of degree or degree of choices? Class, 'race' and the higher education process. *Sociology, 35*(4), 855–874.

Reynolds, T. (1997). (Mis)representing the black superwoman. In H. S. Mirza (Ed.), *Black British feminism: A reader* (pp. 97–112). London: Routledge.

Richardson, J. T. E. (2008). The attainment of ethnic minority students in UK higher education. *Studies in Higher Education, 33*(1), 33–48.

Shah, B., Dwyer, C., & Modood, T. (2010). Explaining educational achievement and career aspirations among young British Pakistanis: Mobilizing 'ethnic capital'? *Sociology, 44*(6), 1109–1127.

Shain, F. (2003). *The schooling and identity of Asian girls.* Stoke-on-Trent: Trentham Books Limited.

Shiner, M., & Modood, T. (2002). Help or hindrance? Higher education and the route to ethnic equality. *British Journal of Sociology of Education, 23*(2), 209–332.

Siddiqui, H. (2000). Black women's activism: Coming of age? *Feminist Review, 64*, 83–96.

Sidghi, A. (2014). Ethnic minorities, employment and social mobility: See the research findings. *The Guardian*, June 12. Retrieved from http://www.theguardian.com/news/datablog/2014/jun/12/ethnic-minorities-employment-and-social-mobility-see-the-research-findings. Accessed on January 20, 2016.

Soja, E. W. (1996). *Thirdspace: Journeys to Los Angeles and other real-and-imagined places.* Oxford: Blackwell.

Sullivan, A. (2001). Cultural capital and educational attainment. *Sociology, 35*(4), 893–912.

Takhar, S. (2006). South Asian women, social capital and multicultural (mis)understandings. *Community, Work and Family, 9*(3), 291–307.

Takhar, S. (2013). *Gender, ethnicity and political agency: South Asian women organizing.* New York, NY: Routledge.

Taylor, P. (1993). Minority ethnic groups and gender in access to higher education. *New Community, 19*(3), 425–440.

Thapar, S., & Sanghera, G. (2010). Building social capital and education: The experiences of Pakistani Muslims in the UK. *International Journal of Social Inquiry, 3*(2), 3–24.

Tyrer, D., & Ahmad, F. (2006). *Muslim women students' experiences of higher education, equal opportunities and graduate employability*. Liverpool: Liverpool John Moores University. Retrieved from http://www.aulaintercultural.org/IMG/pdf/muslimwomen.pdf. Accessed on January 22, 2016.

Weekes-Bernard, D. (Ed.). (2010). *Widening participation and race equality*. London: Runnymede Trust. Retrieved from http://www.runnymedetrust.org/uploads/publica tions/pdfs/WideningParticipation.pdf. Accessed on January 25, 2016.

Weinreich, P. (2002). *Identity structure analysis*. London: Pergamon Press.

Wilson, A. (2006). *Dreams, questions, struggles: South Asian women in Britain*. London: Pluto Press.

Women and Equality Unit. (2006). *Engaging with Muslim women: A report from the Prime Minister's Event*. London: HMSO.

# WOMEN'S EDUCATION AND EMPLOYMENT IN IRAN

Elaheh Rostami-Povey

## ABSTRACT

Purpose — *This chapter demonstrates that women challenge oppressive gender relations by engaging in active agency at different levels. Iranian women's struggles for gender equality show a critical consciousness of the politics of local male domination and an indigenous contestation of the cultural practices which sanction injustices against women.*

Design/methodology/approach — *This chapter is based on the findings and analysis of the book,* Women, Power and Politics in 21st Century in Iran. *It is the result of the political and personal experiences of a number of Iranian women academics, journalist and activists who live and work in Iran.*

Findings — *Based on the updated findings and new statistical data, this chapter argues that women, despite their high level of education and activism, continue to face gender inequality, in particular in the sphere of employment.*

Social implications — *This chapter is intended to counter the often inaccurate and misleading impressions put forward by the media, politicians and some academics in the West when they talk about Iranian women.*

**Gender and Race Matter: Global Perspectives on Being a Woman**
Advances in Gender Research, Volume 21, 63–83
ISSN: 1529-2126/doi:10.1108/S1529-212620160000021005

*Within the broader feminist theoretical positioning, the aim of this chapter is to contribute to the debate on essentialism and the stereotype of Iranian women as submissive Muslim women without agency.*

Originality/value — *Feminist knowledge production is diverse. Nonetheless, consideration of the historical and geographical locations of feminist knowledge production is vital to our understanding of the complex processes of women's liberation. Thus, Iranian women's voices are important to what is traditionally understood as feminism.*

**Keywords:** Gender; education; employment; feminism; patriarchy; agency

## INTRODUCTION

In the second decade of the twenty-first century women's level of education is high in most countries. In the Middle East and North African (MENA) countries education has expanded faster than in other regions, especially for women, who in recent years have overtaken men in this respect (HDR in MENA, 2010).

In the Middle East the percentage of women in universities is high and in some countries, including Iran, the majority of university students are women (Aryan, 2012; Rostami-Povey, 2010a, pp. 46—51). The age of marriage is also high, ranging from the mid- to late-twenties for both women and men. The fertility rate has also declined substantially across the region, with the lowest rate in Iran. Micro- and macro-level studies have historically demonstrated that education and fertility rates are important indicators for women's participation in the workforce. Economic development, industrialisation and urbanisation in this region have also contributed to increases in women's participation in the economy. However, women's participation in the formal workforce in this region is lower than in any other region (HDR in MENA, 2010).

In Iran, since the 1980s, the number of women entering universities has increased dramatically, and since the early-2000s the numbers of female students and graduates have exceeded those of males. However, despite their high level of education and socio-economic and political activism, they face gender inequality, in particular in the sphere of employment.

This chapter will first discuss the implications of the rise in the number of highly educated women, in relation to their own lives, the shift in women's position in society, the reaction of the patriarchal state and society to this phenomenon, and the challenges that women continue to face. It will then discuss women's employment and argue that, despite women's high level of education and low fertility rate, their access to the formal economy is limited. Women remain concentrated in the informal economy and the process of economic development and patriarchal gender relations limit their access to their areas of expertise, and in particular to decision-making positions.

Since the early 1990s, however, Iranian women have been challenging gender inequalities. Their struggle for gender justice, including in the economic sphere, has resulted in reforms to education and employment laws in favour of women. Thus, this chapter will argue that women's contribution to the economy as a whole, including their work in the informal economy, is important as the analysis of the whole economy reveals gender contestation. The period under investigation is that following the 1979 revolution and the Islamisation of the state and society. In this context, some comparisons will be made with the pre-1979 period under the secular pro-West state of Mohammad Reza Shah (1941–1979).

The aim is to challenge the dominant orientalist view that women's subordinate positions result solely from Islamic ideologies on women's issues. This view ignores two important issues: firstly, the main reason for women's low participation in Iran's formal economy, as elsewhere in the region, is that economic development is disproportionately based on oil production and revenues in comparison with other regions. This important subject has been debated widely (Razavi, Pearson, & Danloy, 2004; Ross, 2008 amongst others), and this chapter will therefore concentrate on the second important issue, namely the impact of patriarchal gender relations, together with a conservative interpretation of gender rules and regulations, on women's participation in the formal workforce. Gender relations are not static, however, and changes in material circumstances (including socio-economic and political developments) and the dynamic nature of women's struggle are constantly changing the male-dominated state and society.

## WOMEN AND EDUCATION

The process of socio-economic development under the secular state of the Shah was uneven. As a consequence of women's struggle for gender equality, by 1979, 31% of university students were women, yet the majority of people were excluded from socio-economic and political developments, with poverty and political repression alienating the majority of the population. The modernisation of the state and society that did take place was part of the Shah's process of Westernisation, was not based on an indigenous model and was estranging for the majority of the population, who regarded the culture of modernity based on the Western model as inappropriate for them, especially the change in women's position in the family and wider society. In the 1970s the opposition — consisting of the secular left and nationalists, and liberal and conservative Islamists — to the Shah's dictatorship intensified. The secular left and nationalists pursued liberation and socialism in purely formulaic ways and failed to consider class, gender and ethnic inequalities except in an abstract way. As a result the majority of the population related more to the liberal Islamists than to the secular left and the nationalists (Rostami-Povey, 2010b, pp. 46—80).

The majority of women of different social classes and with different levels of religiosity participated on a mass scale in the 1979 revolution which ended the Shah's pro-Western dictatorial regime. The Islamic Republic was founded on the slogan of democracy, independence from imperialism, an end to the monarchy and the Shah's client state of the West. In contrast to the Shah's secular state, which served to enrich the small elite and did little to develop the rest of the country, the state now distributed wealth and provided social welfare to the majority of the population.

The Islamic state, however, soon suppressed the secular movements, including the secular women's movement which believed that the Islamic state was reproducing a new form of patriarchal order. The state favoured only religious women's organisations and actions and in the eyes of Islamist women activists it provided measures for their empowerment, thereby encouraging their participation in Islamic state building (Rostami-Povey, 2010b, pp. 22—80).

At a global and regional level, the 1979 revolution threatened the economic and strategic interests of the United States and its allies in the region. In 1980 Saddam Hussein, the president of Iraq and at that time an ally of the West, invaded Iran and provided the West with an opportunity to replace the Islamic state with a more amenable regime. However, the subsequent Iran-Iraq war (1980—1988) created a state of emergency which led to a far more centralised, authoritarian Islamic state. Women were the first to bear the brunt of repression as the state reinforced patriarchal structures: it imposed compulsory *hijab*, a rigid sexual division of labour, and laws and regulations around women's education and employment based on a conservative traditional interpretation of *Sharia* (Islamic law) (Rostami-Povey, 2012, pp. 17–35).

As Table 1 shows, by 1986 the population grew by 3.9%. The state introduced quotas which resulted in a sharp decline in women's presence in universities. The percentage of female students decreased from 31% in 1979 to 29% in 1989 (Aryan, 2012, pp. 35–52). Other minimal advances women had made under the secular regime of the Shah were reversed: men's exclusive right to divorce and to take four permanent and an unlimited number of temporary wives (*sighe*)[1] without the first wife's permission were reintroduced. Further indications of the reversal of some of the advances of earlier years included: a husband's right to forbid his wife to take employment; the requirement that a woman obtain permission from her male kin to work, travel, study and change her place of residence; in the case of divorce, the father's right to custody of female children over seven and male children over two and the banning of contraception and abortion; and women were forbidden to work as judges. This was a serious affront to the millions of women who had supported the 1979 revolution (Rostami-Povey, 2010a, pp. 77–94).

The imposition of *hijab* and sex segregation promoted women's reproductive role within the family and limited their participation in the sphere of economy and society. However, the Iran-Iraq war changed the conservative Islamic ideology as the state had no choice but to encourage women's voluntary work to support men at the war fronts. The demand for women's paid labour also increased in areas where the supply of male workers decreased. Furthermore, women were encouraged politically to participate in the daily anti-imperialist street demonstrations and against Iraq's invasion of southern part of the country. This combination of women's economic and political participation on a mass scale increased gender consciousness (Rostami-Povey, 2001, pp. 9–17, 2010a, pp. 44–77).

***Table 1.*** A Comparison of Population Growth Rates since 1976.

| Year | Growth Rate (%) |
| --- | --- |
| 1976 | 2.7 |
| 1986 | 3.9 |
| 1996 | 1.9 |
| 2006 | 1.6 |
| 2009 | 1.2 |

*Source*: Extracted and calculated from Iran Statistical Yearbook (2009, 2011).

Despite the marginalisation of secular women's activism, throughout the 1980s the debate over women's issues and women's responses to patriarchal gender ideology continued. Many women, despite their diverse forms of religiosity and secularity, began to challenge the state gender ideology. Although in the 1980s the Islamists and secular women were a world apart, by the 1990s a form of unity had come about. Despite their diverse socio-economic, cultural and political stances, especially among the new generation of women, a unity was achieved to fight for women's rights, in particular on the terrain of women's education and employment.

### The Post-War Reconstruction Era, 1989–1996

In this period, a greater degree of industrialisation, development and urbanisation took place in comparison with the pre-revolutionary era. Under the premiership of Akbar Hashemi Rafsanjani there was a move towards integration into the global economy, neo-liberalism, privatisation and NGO-isation.[2] However, under pressure from civil society activism, especially the women's movement, the state invested in public services, particularly education (Povey, 2015, pp. 75–79). Education became an important part of reconstruction and development, while attempts were also made to promote women's participation in society. The Office of the Presidential Advisor for Women's Affairs was established, and Shahla Habibi appointed as the first such advisor. Population and birth control and education became important priorities for the government. Some restrictions on women's higher education were removed and the number of female students increased in many programmes of study (Aryan, 2012, pp. 35–52). As indicated in Tables 1 and 2, the rate of population growth diminished dramatically and has continued to do so. Similarly the literacy rate increased, a trend which has also persisted.

In this period, young women and men demanded access to higher education en masse, as having a high school diploma was no longer considered sufficient. Even families in rural areas sent their sons and daughters to towns and cities for higher education, and in most large urban centres two or three branches of various universities were established. Since then, every year the demand for higher education has exceeded supply. Students crisscross the country, commuting from the capital city Tehran to small towns and vice-versa, to access appropriate institutions. Higher education is no longer solely for the middle and upper classes of the major urban centres. This has increased the level of gender, class and cultural diversity

***Table 2.***   A Comparison of the Literacy Rate amongst Young People since 1976.

| Year | Male (%) | Female (%) |
| --- | --- | --- |
| 1976 | 59 | 35.5 |
| 1986 | 71 | 52 |
| 1996 | 95 | 90.5 |
| 2006 | 98 | 97 |
| 2012 | 98 | 98 |

*Source*: Extracted and calculated from Iran Statistical Yearbook (2009, p. 606, 2012, p. 661).

throughout the country and women in particular have demanded gender equality in education.

Since the early 1990s all governments, whether conservative or liberal Islamists, have encouraged the establishment of private universities. Distance learning, evening courses and semi-attendance courses are offered by both private and state universities, which are popular with female students who work and have child-care and family responsibilities. At the same time, the state allocates university quotas to the people disabled in the Iran-Iraq war, the ex-prisoners of this war, and the sons and daughters of those who died in the war. This includes millions of students, as one million Iranians died in the Iran-Iraq war and hundreds of thousands were injured and disabled. The allocation of quotas extends to Olympic athletes and those who have gained first-grade status in scientific contests. These students are given the opportunity to enter universities without undertaking the competitive *Concour* (the university entrance examination) as a reward for their achievements (Aryan, 2012, pp. 35–52). These factors have contributed to the increasing number of students in higher education.

As Khosrokhavar argues (2009, pp. 211–246), significant advances have been achieved in scientific research and activity and a new scientific community mainly comprising young men and women has been created. Despite the dominant conservative gender ideology placing obstacles on the path of women's education, the rising number of women in higher education has led to a large number of women specialising in science and technology. In 2014, the hi-tech award-winning *Tabiat* (Nature) bridge, connecting two large parks, was completed in Tehran. This 270 metre structure was designed by Leila Araghian, a 31-year-old young woman architect who was one of the winners of the Architizer A + award, a global architectural competition based in New York (Dehghan, 2015).

## The 'Reform Era', 1997–2005

Throughout the 1990s many people identifying themselves as secular left, liberal and nationalist, alongside liberal Islamists, echoed the unfinished business of the 1979 revolution and called for democracy. A democracy movement called 'Reform Movement' was created which led to the election of Mohammad Khatami (1997–2005). During this period civil society organisations were set up to defend the rights of women, workers and students, the media reflected the aspiration of the democracy movement, and social movement activism played a major role in the process of social and political change and called for a massive expansion of democracy (Povey, 2015, pp. 72–96). The Islamist modernists, including a large number of women's rights activists, were and still are a vital part of this movement. Women's participation in the reform movement demonstrated, and continues to demonstrate, that gender has become an important force in the shaping of politics in Iran. Women's magazines and journals played an important role as a forum for the views of both religious and secular women activists. These publications were set up by Islamist women, but they invited secular women to contribute to the debate on women's issues. Shahla Sherkat, editor of journal *Zanan* (Women) and Faezeh Hashemi the editor of daily newspaper *Zan* (Woman) emphasised the diversity of women's rights activism (Farhadpour, 2012, pp. 91–106). Critical tensions remained within the women's movement, ranging from secularising tendencies to voices searching for a way to articulate women's rights and gender equality. But the growing overlap and unity between secular and religious women produced reforms in family law, employment and education legislation, and constitutional law that have favoured women. For example, although women are still excluded from working as judges, many women study law, work as lawyers and specialise in woman and family law. As a result, the legal system has been reformed to employ women judicial advisers, with judicial status, to be consulted by the male head of the courts before the final ruling on divorce is issued. A new clause in marriage law gives women the right to divorce, to retain custody of children, and the right to forbid the husband to marry a second wife (subject to these rights being written on the marriage certificate). Female headed households receive a pension and are eligible to receive loans, and under certain medical conditions abortion is approved. Iranian women who are married to foreign men are now able to pass on their nationality and citizenship rights to their children if the children are born in Iran or have lived in Iran for 18 years or more (Rostami-Povey, 2010a, 2010b, pp. 71–75, 2012, pp. 1–17).

In this period the increasing participation of women in society and the rise of the women's movement led to the establishment of different women's centres which promoted women's positions, especially women's education and employment. Hence women entered higher education in great numbers (Aryan, 2012, pp. 35–52).

### The Conservatives' Position on Women in Higher Education

The unprecedented rise in the number of women in higher education was alarming to conservative policy makers. The authorities became particularly concerned by the number of young women who were leaving their family and home towns and moving from one corner of the country to another to study in higher education institutions. As a result, a quota system limited the entry of female students to some courses, and the practice of allocating university places to young women only in their home towns emerged. These limitations raised many criticisms as women's choices were significantly reduced.

The conservatives have long believed that the increasing number of female students will lead to a social crisis within the family and wider society — men staying at home and women working outside of the home, and a further rise in the age of marriage and divorce. During the conservative government of Mahmoud Ahmadinejad (2005–2013) more restrictions and quotas were imposed. Despite the quotas, the number of female students in higher education continued to rise. In response, in 2007–2008 the state imposed another quota system, offering 60% of university places to male students and 40% to female students, even if female students' grades were higher than those of male applicants. This positive discrimination in favour of male students is the opposite of the positive discrimination in favour of women which is practiced in some other societies and the gender quota system negatively affected women's education and employment. Since then, female students have been challenging this discriminatory practice by campaigning and lobbying members of the parliament and through the media, especially social media, which is popular with young people, as Iran is ranked third in the world for blogging (Rostami-Povey, 2010a, 2010b, pp. 50–51).

Despite attempts by the conservatives to limit women's access to higher education, Tables 3 and 4 demonstrate women's presence in higher education and their success in obtaining higher degrees.

***Table 3.*** Female Proportion of Students Enrolled at State and Private
Universities, 1996—2013.

| Academic Year | State Universities (%) | Azad Private University (%) |
|---|---|---|
| 1996—1997 | 43 | 44 |
| 2001—2002 | 52 | 50 |
| 2006—2007 | 50 | Figures not available |
| 2008—2009 | 54 | Figures not available |
| 2009—2010 | 50 | 37 |
| 2010—2011 | 52 | 38 |
| 2011—2012 | 52 | 39 |
| 2012—2013 | 47 | 37 |

*Source*: Extracted and calculated from Iran Statistical Yearbook (2012/2013, pp. 703—704).

***Table 4.*** Percentage of Degrees Obtained by Female
Students, 1996—2013.

| Academic Year | All Degrees (%) | Under-Graduate (%) | Post-Graduate (%) | Doctoral (%) | Post-Doctoral (%) |
|---|---|---|---|---|---|
| 1996—1997 | 36 | 39 | 18 | 33 | 32 |
| 2001—2002 | 50 | 55 | 25 | 48 | 24 |
| 2006—2007 | 58 | 63 | 43 | 56 | 34 |
| 2008—2009 | 58 | 63 | 44 | 59 | 32 |
| 2009—2010 | 56 | 62 | 46 | 59 | 34 |
| 2010—2011 | 56 | 62 | 48 | 60 | 37 |
| 2011—2012 | 56 | 61 | 49 | 60 | 38 |
| 2012—2013 | 53.5 | 60 | 50 | 59 | 39 |

*Source*: Extracted and calculated from Iran Statistical Yearbook (2012/2013, p. 705).

These statistics demonstrate that female students are concentrated in state universities as they cannot afford the high fees charged by private universities. Additionally, 68% of students at the distance learning university are women, as many young women students are also part-time workers or have child-care and family responsibilities (Aryan, 2012, pp. 35—52).

Despite conservatives' attempts to exclude women from higher education, they now make up a higher proportion of successful doctoral candidates and under-graduate students than men. It is possible to conclude that their exclusion from the formal economy prevents them from continuing to post-doctoral and further specialisation.

The election of President Hassan Rouhani in June 2013 ended the conservative era (2005–2013) and brought hope to many Iranians, as he stood for relaxing social restrictions and political repression and paving the way to resolve the nuclear issues in order to end the economic sanctions imposed by the West since 1979, and in particular the sanctions throughout the last decade. These economic sanctions have caused enormous suffering for the majority of the people, and in particular, as discussed by Olmsted (2011, pp. 25–52), sanctions have had negative effects on women's education and employment.

## WOMEN AND EMPLOYMENT

### *Women in the Formal Economy*

According to the latest statistics 15% of Iran's economically active population are women. The formal economy is divided into the private sector (employers, self-employed, wage and salary earners, unpaid family workers) and public sector wage and salary earners. 87% are male workers and 13% are female workers. Out of the 15% economically active female population 26% of women work in agriculture, 25% in industries and 49% in services. The majority of workers (83%) work in the private sector (Iran Statistical Yearbook, 2012–2013, pp. 165, 194, 196, 203).

As indicated in these statistics, the formal economy absorbs a small percentage of women. Women are more visible as 'government employees' (35%) working in various ministries. Despite the dominant conservative gender ideology, Table 5 shows a relative increase in female participation in this form of employment since the 1979 revolution and the Islamisation of state and society in comparison with the pre-1979 period under the secular state of the Shah. This suggests that the structure of the economy, not Islam, is at fault.

Similarly, as shown in Table 6, within the manufacturing sector, women workers are a minority, but there has been a small increase in this form of employment since the early 2000s.

**Table 5.**   Female Government Employees.

| Year | Male (%) | Female (%) |
|------|----------|------------|
| 1971 | 71 | 29 |
| 1981 | 71 | 29 |
| 1991 | 70 | 30 |
| 2001 | 69 | 31 |
| 2006 | 66 | 34 |
| 2008 | 66 | 34 |
| 2010 | 65 | 35 |

*Source*: Extracted and calculated from Iran Statistical Yearbooks (1977/1978, p. 66, 1986/1987, p. 86, 1996/1997, p. 89, 2002/2003, pp. 88–127, 2008/2009, pp. 183–187, 2012/2013, pp. 203, 341).

**Table 6.**   Female Labour Participation in Manufacturing Industries, Mainly in the Private Sector.

| Year | Male (%) | Female (%) |
|------|----------|------------|
| 1972 | 92 | 8 |
| 1996 | 94 | 6 |
| 2001 | 92 | 8 |
| 2006 | 90 | 9 |
| 2011 | 89 | 10 |

*Source*: Extracted and calculated from Iran Statistical Yearbook (2002/2003, pp. 88–127, 2008/2009, 2012/2013, p. 341).

As discussed above, women in Iran are highly educated but are not fully absorbed into the formal labour market and have not occupied decision-making employment positions according to their educational expertise. Nevertheless they have systematically and imaginatively challenged the patriarchal state and society and have succeeded in removing some of the obstacles in the way of achieving gender equality. As a result of women's struggle since the 1990s a small minority have occupied high positions such as vice-presidents, deputy ministers, regional governors and regional deputy governors. Under President Khatami (1997–2005) Massoumeh Ebtekar was the vice-president and Head of the Department of the

Environment, and Zahra Shojaee was the president's advisor on women's affairs and head of the Centre for Women's Participation (1997–2005). This important centre emphasised women's high educational level and their potential contributions to the economy (Ebtekar, 2012, pp. 153–168). In this period, women's NGOs were born out of the women's movement and acted as civil society organisations, creating an autonomous space between the family, state and market. Their struggle represented an unprecedented transformation, responding to profound changes in women's and men's consciousness. Many families and many men have realised that they have nothing to lose and everything to gain by supporting legislation to improve women's education and employment. Many men argue that struggle for democracy is not separated from the struggle for gender equality. However, the creation of autonomous spheres of social activity for women has constantly been undermined by a patriarchal social order.

Nevertheless, even under the conservative government of Ahmadinejad (2005–2013), women's relative presence was visible as a few women occupied decision-making positions. Fatemeh Javadi was vice-president and the head of the Department of the Environment (2005–2009) and Marzieh Vahid Dastjerdi was the health minister from 2009 to 2013. Nasrin Soltankhah was vice-president (2005–2009) on women's affairs and the head of the Centre for Women and Family Affairs, and in 2009 she was replaced by Maryam Mojtahedzadeh. In this period, the name of the institution, Centre for Women's Participation, was changed to the Centre for Women and Family Affairs. This change of name was significant as it indicated an emphasis on the role of women within the family. New laws encouraged women to work fewer hours and part-time and to take early retirement. The taxing of the *mahr*,[3] bride price, was introduced in this period and worked against women's interests, especially poorer women. Attempts were made to pass laws to encourage polygamy, by reversing the law which made it necessary for the first wife to give her husband permission to marry a second wife. These conservative laws and regulations were designed to weaken women's position in society and to promote women's reproductive role within the family (Kadivar, 2012, pp. 121–136; Koolaee, 2012, pp. 137–152).

This period ended in 2013 when the moderate president Rouhani came to power. In this administration there are three women in decision-making positions: Elham Aminzadeh, the vice-president on law; Shahindokht Mollavardi, vice-president on Women and Family issues; and Massoumeh Ebtekar was re-appointed as the head of the Head of the Department of the Environment. The *Zanan* magazine which had been closed down under

Ahmadinejad was re-opened in 2014. This important journal and its chief editor Shahla Sherkat employ women journalists and challenge unequal gender relations. The first issue of this journal was devoted to women and employment. According to its statistical analysis, despite the conservatives' hostility to women's employment throughout the period of 2005—2013, modern industries such as animal husbandry and dairy products have had no choice but to employ women specialists in these 'men's jobs' (Zanan, 2014).

Also, while there are 4,500 recognised/registered women traders who have trade cards, only three of them are members of the Iran Traders Representatives (Otaghe Iran, or Iran's Room), which shows the unequal representation of women in the Iranian economy, especially in high positions. In 2007, the Iranian Women's Economic Society was established. Its aim is to raise women's profile in international trade and cooperate with women traders in other Muslim majority societies. The council, which has 1,000 active members, is setting up websites and publishing journals for distributing information and knowledge to women. It is the largest women's council whose members are engaged in different economic fields (Nejadbahram, 2012, pp. 73—90).

Hundreds of thousands of women write books, make films and work as high-level sportswomen. The majority of journalists who work as political correspondents are women and women blog intensely, contributing to an increasingly feminised media (Farhadpour, 2012). Art education and working as an artist have become a front for demonstrating resistance. A large number of women artists use art to challenge the patriarchal gender rules and roles (Honarbin-Holliday, 2012, pp. 53—72).

## Women in the Informal Economy

The informal economy in Iran is large, diverse and feminised, ranging from unpaid work to low paid work in small enterprises, and to highly paid or high earning work within the money market and the property market. Some home-based carpet weavers and other handicraft workers, mainly women, are amongst the low paid workers who may also work in small workshops. There are also the self-employed such as the petty traders, selling goods in the streets and in the metros, a large number of whom are women whose earnings are low to medium range. There are also various types of unpaid family labour, exclusively women at home producing dried herbs, pickles, puree, jam, blankets, sheets, cloth, etc., who sell their goods to earn a living (Rostami-Povey, 2010a). Social media and networking are particularly popular with female informal sector workers who use Facebook, Instagram and Pinterest to sell their products online (Zanan Journal, 2014).

Another aspect of women's informal employment in Iran is to be found in the increasing numbers of modern coffee shops where a large number of young women university graduates work. Many of them are not registered workers, as entry to and exit from these businesses is easy for women. Although there are disadvantages to this form of employment as there is no job security, for many women it has the advantage of flexibility, allowing them to study or work elsewhere. Women in this sector are low to middle range earners. Many women welcome the presence of female waitresses and argue that this phenomenon makes it easier for young women to sit in a coffee shop without being harassed by men. Also the character of these coffee shops is changing from the traditional *ghahvekhanehs* (coffee houses) which were and still are totally male institutions, where men are served by men (Rostami-Povey, 2013a, 2013b).

The culture of work within another male-dominated profession is also changing. A large number of female home-based workers are engaged in the property and money markets. The majority of those who are formally engaged in this profession are men. However, increasing numbers of young women educated as home-based workers are entering this male-dominated profession. This is a profitable business for these women and demonstrates that informal workers are not necessarily poor. These different categories of women's work amount to millions of invisible hours of work, and their monetary value remains unknown as they are not counted in the statistics or the national income accounts. The work of this large and growing female workforce is essential for the functioning of the economy and the well-being of their families and communities. These women are fully aware of their contribution; they are empowered by working and earning money in these informal economies and are confidently engaged, alongside the women in the formal economy, in changing gender relations within the home and in wider society. Together, as purposeful agents, they devise work and other strategies to renegotiate aspects of gender relations within the patriarchal household, the state, the market and other institutions (Beneria, 2003, p. 39).

Thus, the dynamic of women's struggle for gender equality is changing gender relations. As discussed above, women's success in winning the reform of family law, education and employment law has had a relatively positive impact on women and work. These reforms have affected the work of women in both the formal and informal economies. No doubt women who have access to the formal economy have greater bargaining power and are able to directly challenge gender relations by engaging in active agency at different levels of economic, social, political and cultural life. While the majority of women may not directly confront gender equality their contribution to the economy and society as a whole has proved to be empowering for them. Thus, different factors affect women's bargaining strength, including their participation in the informal economy. This case study of Iran contributes to the debate on women's work in the formal and informal economy. As is argued by Pearson (2004) and Beneria (2003, pp. 116–152) the focus should be on recognising the importance of informal workers, mainly women, and their location within the larger economy.

*Obstacles in the Path of Women*

As discussed above, women throughout their life cycles experience rigid gender divisions of labour, both within the family and in wider society. Women are placed in a subordinate position to men and this subordinate position is treated as the norm and has a negative impact on their lives. The family does not facilitate the right circumstances for women's full participation in the economy. Only in a minority of cases are women encouraged by their family to participate in decision-making and participate in political leadership (Nejadbahram, 2012, pp. 73–90).

For many women, even those who can afford to hire domestic helpers, domestic responsibility is an important obstacle to their goal to achieve high positions in employment. Many women feel that they have to work harder and longer hours in order to prove to their male counterparts that they are as good as them in the workforce, and that society will only accept them if they perform their household duties equally well. Thus, women's hours of work are much longer than men's (Rostami-Povey, 2010a, pp. 122–156).

As discussed above, women's high level of education was a crucial factor in creating the right circumstances for them to enter their field of expertise in workplaces. However, the education system does not prepare young women to participate in decision-making positions and to seek political leadership and power. The media largely emphasises the centrality of women's role in the family and ignores women's contribution to wider society, especially with regard to employment. Nevertheless, women are clearly present in the media as journalists, writers, film makers, directors, and actresses, and use the media to challenge the unequal gender rules and regulations. Although women constantly struggle to change the dominant gender roles, the power of the media profoundly strengthens the institutionalisation of conservative gender roles (Farhadpour, 2012, pp. 91–106).

The constitution and the civil legal system treat women and men relatively equally. The constitution recognises the equality of citizenship: according to articles 19 and 20 all citizens are equal. The law states that conditions must be created to develop women's potential. The reformed family laws of the late-1990s and early-2000s, and in particular the law that grants insurance for women who do not work outside of the home work in women's favour. However, in many instances family law, employment law, and laws with regard to judgement and punishment are discriminatory to women. In some cases women are not identified as independent beings but as part and parcel of the family (Hoodfar, 2000).

Many women believe that the *urf*, whose meaning can encompass aspects of local custom and customary law, is the foundation of barriers to women's progress in reaching high positions in employment and generally within society. The customary law reflects gendered divisions of labour. The civil law states, for example, that 'men are the bread winners'. This stems from the customary law which implies that women's employment is not essential. Therefore, women are marginalised, especially in high employment positions. Furthermore, according to the civil law women have to gain permission from their husband to work. Article 1117 of the civil law states that a husband is allowed to stop his wife from working in a position which may be interpreted as being against the interests of the family. This interpretation is based on the *Sharia* law which has become a customary law. It is these interpretations that limit women's access to leadership, judgement and other high positions. Thus there is a clear interrelationship between the customary law and the civil law which advocates that a man can object to his wife's employment, if the nature of the work is against the interest of the family (Nejadbahram, 2012, pp. 73–90).

In some cases, however, this law does not affect the employment of women, particularly where families are in favour of women's employment and also where poorer families are dependent on women's income. Many families believe that women's employment is not against the interests of the family but necessary for its well-being: it improves the relationship between members of the family and enhances the family's financial position. In other cases the family needs the earnings of women: in these cases men and women do not see this discriminatory law as a real obstacle for women's employment and treat it as a technical problem, and the husband automatically gives permission for his wife to go to work. Furthermore, the majority of women work in the informal sector of the economy which does not require the permission of the husband (Rostami-Povey, 2010a, pp. 113–114).

Despite families favouring the employment of women, it is the patriarchal regime, mingled with conservative traditions, which has created an irrational male-dominated system that constantly attempts to exclude women. Women's limited access to economic, political and cultural resources is an important obstacle to national productivity. The exclusion of women means that the economy and society are denied the benefit of women's contribution to economic, social, cultural and political developments. Nevertheless, women's economic activities are growing in the informal sector. Hence women as formal sector and informal sector workers together challenge patriarchal gender relations.

# CONCLUSION

Since the 1990s women's struggle for change and political reform has contributed to producing the phenomenon of the dramatic growth in women's presence in higher education. Higher education raised women's awareness and increased women's activism in social, cultural, economic and political spheres. As I have argued in this chapter, many limitations are imposed on young women's education by conservative traditions, culture, and religion. However, the massive presence of female students at universities reflects the contradictions of the patriarchal state and society.

While many opportunities are created for women by their participation in higher education, conservative traditions and perceptions still dominate their lives. Large segments of women's knowledge and capabilities, especially in formal employment and decision-making arenas are ignored, mainly due to unequal power relations, which are derived from strict gender divisions of labour. The barriers in the path of women's employment are to do with the way the economic structures, together with male-dominated structures, are reproduced and reconstructed. As discussed above, women in Iran have been challenging institutional power, especially gender-specific access and influence, and have achieved substantive goals in terms of education. They are recognised as a social group that shares common interests and legitimate claims on society. As a recognised social group these women have been struggling for gender equality and challenging conservative gender ideologies on women's formal employment and, as discussed above, in some cases the state and authorities have had no choice but to employ women in specialised positions. Thus, gender relations are not static and the dynamic nature of women's struggle is constantly changing the male-dominated state and society.

## NOTES

1. The Iranian secular feminists of the 1960s and 1970s viewed *sighe* as a degrading institution for women. However, since the 1980s, many secular and Muslim feminists have argued that under the social restriction imposed by the Islamic Republic, temporary marriage, which is religiously, socially and culturally acceptable, opens up opportunities for young women and men to live together without committing to a long-term relationship. In more recent years this institution has been used by many young women and men as a form of civil partnership *ezdevaje sefid* (white marriage). For this discussion see Zanan Magazine (2014).

2. The massive expansion of the Iranian NGO sector since the 1990s can be seen as a consequence of the New Policy Agenda, which regards markets as the most efficient mechanism for development, states as facilitators, and NGOs as service-providing agencies. In this context NGOs are seen as appropriate vehicles for democratisation and the strengthening of civil society.

3. The Iranian secular feminists of the 1960s and 1970s viewed *mahr* as a degrading institution for women. However, since the 1980s many secular and Muslim feminists have argued that the institution of *mahr* is positive for women, especially for poorer women, as they have the right to demand their *mahr* at any time, especially at the time of divorce. According to the reformed marriage and divorce law of the 1990s, if a man wishes to divorce his wife, he has to pay her *mahr* index linked and the equivalent of her contribution to the family throughout their married life, similar to wages for a housewife.

## REFERENCES

Aryan, K. (2012). The boom in women's education. In T. Povey & E. Rostami-Povey (Eds.), *Women, power and politics in 21stcentury Iran*. Farnham: Ashgate Publishing.

Beneria, L. (2003). *Gender, development, and globalisation, economics as if all people mattered*. New York, NY: Routledge.

Dehghan, S. K. (2015). Take it to the bridge: The Tehran architect striking the right chord in Iran and beyond. *The Guardian*, April 20.

Ebtekar, M. (2012). Women and the environment: A politico-environmental experience. In T. Povey & E. Rostami-Povey (Eds.), *Women, power and politics in 21st century Iran*. Farnham: Ashgate Publishing.

Farhadpour, L. (2012). Women, gender roles, media and journalism. In T. Povey & E. Rostami-Povey (Eds.), *Women, power and politics in 21st century Iran*. Farnham: Ashgate Publishing.

Honarbin-Holliday, M. (2012). Autonomous minds and bodies in theory and practice: Women constructing cultural identities and becoming visible through art. In T. Povey & E. Rostami-Povey (Eds.), *Women, power and politics in 21st century Iran*. Farnham: Ashgate Publishing.

Hoodfar, H. (2000). Iranian women at the intersection of citizenship and the family code, the perils of Islamic criteria. In S. Joseph (Ed.), *Gender and citizenship in the Middle East*. Syracuse, NY: Syracuse University Press.

Human Development Report in Middle East and North Africa (HDR in MENA). (2010). Research paper 2010/26, UNDP (United Nations Development Programme). Retrieved from http://hdr.undp.org/en/reports/global/hdr2010/papers/HDRP_2010_26.pdf

Iran Statistical Yearbook for 1977/1978; 1986/1987; 1996/1997; 2002/2003; 2008/2009, 2009, 2011, 2012 Statistical Center of Iran, Tehran. Retrieved from http://www.amar.org.ir/Default.aspx?tabid = 133.

Kadivar, J. (2012). Women and executive power. In T. Povey & E. Rostami-Povey (Eds.), *Women, power and politics in 21st century Iran*. Farnham: Ashgate Publishing.

Khosrokhavar, F. (2009). Iran's new scientific community. In A. Gheissari (Ed.), *Contemporary Iran: Economy, society, politics*. Oxford: Oxford University Press.

Koolaee, E. (2012). Women in the parliament. In T. Povey & E. Rostami-Povey (Eds.), *Women, power and politics in 21st century Iran*. Farnham: Ashgate Publishing.

Nejadbahram, Z. (2012). Women and employment. In T. Povey & E. Rostami-Povey (Eds.), *Women, power and politics in 21st century Iran*. Farnham: Ashgate Publishing.

Olmsted, J. C. (2011). Gender and globalisation, the Iranian experience. In R. Bahramitash & S. Esfahani (Eds.), *Veiled employment, Islamism and the political economy of women's employment in Iran*. Syracuse, NY: Syracuse University Press.

Pearson, R. (2004). Organising home-based workers in the global economy: An action research approach. *Development in Practice, 14*(1–2), 136–148.

Povey, T. (2015). *Social movements in Egypt and Iran*. London: Palgrave Macmillan.

Razavi, S., Pearson, R., & Danloy, C. (2004). *Globalisation, export-oriented employment and social policy, gendered connections*. Basingstoke: Palgrave Macmillan.

Ross, M. L. (2008). Oil, Islam, and women. *American Political Science Review, 102*(1), 107–123.

Rostami-Povey, E. (2001). Feminist contestations of institutional domains in Iran. *Feminist Review Collective 69*. London: Routledge.

Rostami-Povey, E. (2010a). *Women, work and Islamism, ideology and resistance in Iran* (2nd ed.). London: Zed Books.

Rostami-Povey, E. (2010b). *Iran's influence: A religious-political state and society in its region*. London: Zed Books.

Rostami-Povey, E. (2012). The women's movement in its historical context. In T. Povey & E. Rostami-Povey (Eds.), *Women, power and politics in 21st century Iran* (pp. 17–34). Farnham: Ashgate Publishing.

Rostami-Povey, E. (2013a). Women in the Middle Eastern and North African (MENA) countries workforce. In N. J. DeLong-Bas, A. Asafaruddin, H. Abugideiri, H. Ezzat, & J. L. Esposito (Eds.), *The Oxford Encyclopedia of Islam and women.* Oxford: Oxford University Press.

Rostami-Povey, E. (2013b). Women, borrowing and credit. In N. J. DeLong-Bas, A. Asafaruddin, H. Abugideiri, H. Ezzat, & J. L. Esposito (Eds.), *The Oxford Encyclopedia of Islam and women.* Oxford: Oxford University Press.

Zanan Journal. (2014). 1 and 5, Farsi Language.

# PART II
# SEXUALITY AND GENDER
# SECURITY: INDIA AND AFRICA

# GENDER AND CASTE INTERSECTIONALITY IN INDIA: AN ANALYSIS OF THE NIRBHAYA CASE, 16 DECEMBER 2012

Adrija Dey and Bev Orton

## ABSTRACT

Purpose — *This chapter deals with the concept of intersectionality with particular reference to the interconnectedness of gender, class and caste discrimination in India. Even though much of the work on intersectionality has been carried out by scholars from the United States with specific emphasis on gender and race, this framework can be applied universally to understand the multiple axes of power within a society that results in further marginalisation of certain groups of women. The 16th December 2012 Nirbhaya rape case forms the core of this chapter as it resulted in one of the biggest gender movements in India.*

Design/methodology/approach — *In order to develop a critical analysis a case study approach was adopted and data collected by analysing online news reports, videos, articles on blogs and posts on social media outlets such as Facebook and Twitter.*

Gender and Race Matter: Global Perspectives on Being a Woman
Advances in Gender Research, Volume 21, 87–105
ISSN: 1529-2126/doi:10.1108/S1529-212620160000021006

Findings — *The findings of the research showed interesting intersections of gender and class with relation to this case, which has not been deeply analysed in order to understand the reasons behind the public uprising which resulted in the government action.*

Originality/value — *It is important to look at gender violence in India through the lens of intersectionality since often it is the result of multiple levels of discrimination on the basis of class, caste, religion and geography. This is important to recognise in order to ensure that activism, education and changes in policy help to resolve problems related to extreme oppression and violence against women across the country.*

**Keywords:** Intersectionality; India; caste; class; gender activism; Nirbhaya rape case

# INTRODUCTION

This chapter deals with the concept of intersectionality with particular reference to the interconnectedness of gender, class and caste discrimination in India. India is significantly multilingual and multicultural, which has led to vastly different perspectives on gender, inequalities and power relations (Purkayastha, Subramaniam, Desai, & Bose, 2003). The concept of intersectionality, as advanced by Crenshaw (1989), draws attention to the fact that the experiences of women of colour are often a result of intersecting patterns of sexism and racism. The marginalisation, oppression and abuse faced by women of colour cannot be understood in full by considering feminist discourses and racism separately since race and gender intersect in shaping structural, political and representational aspects of violence against women (Crenshaw, 1991, p. 1244). The concept of intersectionality arose from the pioneering work done by black feminists in the United States and United Kingdom on the hierarchical nature of inequality and dominance (Bilge, 2010). Although this chapter deals with gender violence in an Indian context, intersectionality is used to explore the influence of intersecting factors such as class and caste.

Indian society being extremely multi-layered, with the existence of class, caste, urban and rural divides, means that the inequality and abuse faced by women differs as a result of the intersections of two or more of these categories. In India, gender violence is often not only gender-related crime but a combined effect of various other factors including caste, class and religion. A hierarchy based on caste, class and geographical location separates women across India and they experience varying degrees of abuse and marginalisation. Thus we concur with Crenshaw's statement that 'intersectional subordination need not be intentionally produced; in fact, it is frequently the consequence of the imposition of one burden that interacts with pre-existing vulnerabilities to create yet another dimension of disempowerment' (Crenshaw, 1991, p. 1250). Therefore it is vital to recognise structural intersectionality in cases where women from rural areas of India are more susceptible to violence than educated women from the urban areas. This is also true of women belonging to lower castes as compared to those of higher caste (Anne, Callahan, & Kang, 2013).

## METHODS

In order to develop a critical analysis a case study approach was considered to be most appropriate. The main focus of this research is the Nirbhaya case that took place on 16 December 2012. The importance of this case is that it resulted in one of the biggest gender movements in post-independence India. Yin (2014) defines a case study as, 'an empirical inquiry that investigates a contemporary phenomenon within its real-life context, especially when the boundaries between phenomenon and context are not clearly evident' (Yin, 2014, p. 16). The case study approach adopted here aids in the detailed analysis of events, environments and relationships through the use of multiple sources of evidence. Further, a single case study approach has been adopted. This case has also been chosen because it is an unusual case. India had not previously witnessed a gender movement of such scale and impact, and this case has given rise to several questions that warrant critical study and analysis.

By analysing the Nirbhaya case through the lens of intersectionality an understanding of the different factors involved in the case is facilitated, as is the rationale for the production of social media attention and resultant action. Further to discussing this high profile case, three other prominent cases of gender violence are referred to in order to provide an in-depth understanding of the nature of Indian society, gender norms and gender violence.

Data were collected from online news reports, videos, articles on blogs and posts on social media outlets such as Facebook and Twitter, and then

analysed. Indian news websites such as CNN-IBN and NDTV were followed regularly and important articles were archived so that they could be
used for the purpose of this research. Additionally Twitter and Facebook
posts of protest participants and blogs such as Youth Ki Awaaz and Kafila
were followed. Several Facebook groups and communities were formed
online after the incident, which involved discussions about the Delhi Rape
Case, but all of them had different agendas. Some groups spread information about the case and the protest marches, with others, such as 'Swift
Justice in Delhi Gang-Rape Case', being specifically formed to create general awareness about crimes against women. Other groups, such as 'Delhi
Rape case, penalty to death', were formed specifically to advocate the death
penalty for the rapists. Few of the groups are still active and most were
closed and become inactive within a few months of the incident.

# INTERSECTIONALITY: THE
# THEORETICAL FRAMEWORK

The intersectionality perspective emphasises that an individual's social
identity exerts particular influences on the individual's beliefs and experiences with respect to gender, making understanding gender within the
context of power relations an essential task. Shields (2008, p. 301) defines
intersectionality as 'the mutually constitutive relations among social identities' and argues that this has become central to feminist thinking and
contemporary studies on gender. McCall (2005) echoes this, stating that
intersectionality is one of the most important contributions to feminist
theory in relation to the contemporary understanding of gender. According
to Shields (2008) it is the 'individual's social identities [which] profoundly
influence one's beliefs about and experience of gender' (2008, p. 301) and
this will be shown to be especially true in India. If we consider violence
faced by women in India, it can be seen that the experiences of different
women are often shaped by other dimensions of their identity including
race, caste, and class. The intersection of race and sex has been considered
in feminist practices and anti-racist theories, and has even ascended to the
levels of policy and advocacy, yet this is in the context of the privileged
groups who marginalise those who are multiply burdened (Crenshaw,
1989). For many marginalised groups, identity-based politics has been a
source of strength, community, and intellectual development. In many

cases, however, the problem with identity politics is that it ignores intra-group differences.

Since Crenshaw proposed the concept of intersectionality it has been considered and approached in different ways and this has given rise to certain controversies regarding the theory itself. While some scholars have considered it as a theory, others have considered it as a heuristic process and a strategy for feminist analysis. This has given rise to questions regarding whether intersectionality should be applied only to understanding individual experiences and theorising identities or if it should be considered as a characteristic of social structures and cultural discourses (Davis, 2008). In the context of intersectionality, British feminists have talked about the concept of 'triple oppression', claiming that black women often suffer a combination of three different levels of oppression or discrimination. They suffer oppression because of their colour, gender and as members of the working class (Lynn, 2014). However, this concept has also been critiqued by Yuval-Davis (2006) who maintains that, 'any attempt to essentialise "Blackness" or "womanhood" or "working classness" as specific forms of concrete oppression in additive ways inevitably conflates narratives of identity politics with descriptions of positionality as well as constructing identities within the terms of specific political projects' (Yuval-Davis, 2006, p. 195). Such narratives can be harmful and further marginalise the experiences of women belonging to certain specific social categories.

Essentially, the importance of intersectionality as a concept cannot be ignored, as it is increasingly difficult to speak about gender without considering other social identities and structures of dominance. In this respect Knapp (2005, p. 253) suggests that, 'the political and moral need for feminism to be inclusive in order to be able to keep up its own foundational premises opened up the avenues for dispersion and acceleration of race/ethnicity, class, gender/sexuality etc.'. Intersectionality is a reflection of reality and in reality there is no single social identity category that can describe how individuals respond to their social environment and how others respond to them in the same environment *and* it is important to consider an interconnection of multiple identities in order to fully understand the complex nature of reality (Shields, 2008). Intersectionality may, as a theory, lack precision, but it is this very imprecision which makes it a dynamic and important device for critical feminist analysis. Thus on intersectionality, Davis (2008, p. 79) comments that, 'it encourages complexity, stimulates creativity, and avoids premature closure, tantalizing feminist scholars to raise new questions and explore uncharted territory'.

## THE NIRBHAYA CASE: 16 DECEMBER 2012

On 16 December 2012 a female psychotherapy student from Delhi was on her way home with a male friend after watching *Life of Pi* in a popular theatre in Saket, South Delhi. At about 9:30 pm they boarded a bus from Munirka, Dwarka (a popular area in south Delhi). They were summoned into the bus by a teenage boy stating that the bus was going in the same direction as their destination. There were only six people on the bus including the driver Ram Singh, his brother Mukesh, Vinay Sharma, an assistant gym instructor, and Pawan Singh, a fruit seller. The student and her friend became very suspicious when the bus was diverted from its usual route. The doors of the bus were shut and the men started taunting the couple about their relationship, asking what she was doing with a man so late at night and making lewd and offensive comments. Her male companion tried to protest but he was immediately beaten, gagged and hit with an iron rod. As he lay unconscious on the floor of the bus the six men attacked her with the same iron rod because she tried to protect her friend (Biswas & Malik, 2013). Then two of the accused men forced her to the back of the bus where she was raped, first by Ram, followed by the juvenile and then by the others. When she lost consciousness she was again raped by Ram Singh and the juvenile (Osborne, 2013). After raping her, the half-naked bodies of both victims were thrown into the street from the bus where they were discovered around 11 pm by a passer-by and taken immediately to the hospital.

After 13 days of struggle Nirbhaya died in the Mount Elizabeth hospital in Singapore. The Indian Penal Code (Section 228) states that the name of a rape victim cannot be publicly revealed. Hence, in compliance with Indian laws, the actual name of the victim was never released to the media and pseudonyms like 'Damini' (lighting), 'Jagruti' (awareness) and most commonly 'Nirbhaya' (the fearless one) were used to honour her courage and struggle. This particular case is important for two main reasons. Firstly, after this case of sexual violence, India witnessed one of its largest gender-based movements, which stimulated questions about gender not previously included in public discourse. Secondly, the case exposed the complex nature of intersectionality with respect to gender, class and caste in India.

Section 375 of the Indian Penal Code provides the definition of rape and section 376 provides the punishment for rape (Indian Law Cases, 2014). According to section 375, a man is said to have committed rape if he has sexual intercourse with a woman against her will or without her consent.

He is also said to have committed rape if the consent has been obtained by unlawful means such as fear of harm or death or under circumstances, such as intoxication, where the women is unable to understand the nature and consequences of such consent (Indian Law Cases, 2014). New Delhi is often referred to as the 'rape capital' of India (Singh Shah, Kapur, & Smith-Spark, 2013), with official data showing that overall rape cases rose almost 875 per cent over the past 40 years. There were 2,487 rape cases in 1971 and by 2011 the number had risen to 24,206. Only 572 rape cases were reported in New Delhi in 2011 and more than 600 in 2012. Human rights activists point out that due to under reporting, the real figure is likely to be much higher.

After the Nirbhaya Case a separate commission, headed by Supreme Court judge J. S. Verma, was set up on 23 December 2012 to identify what changes should be made to the criminal law in order to provide more severe punishment for those convicted of sexual assault. The committee was asked to complete its report as a matter of urgency and submit its findings within 30 days (Verma, Seth, & Subramanium, 2013). The Verma Commission handed over its reports to the government on 23 January 2013, exactly 30 days after the commission was set up by the government. The first few words of the report stated that 'the constitution of this Committee is in response to the country-wide peaceful public outcry of civil society, led by the youth, against the failure of governance to provide a safe and dignified environment for the women of India, who are constantly exposed to sexual violence [...] It is unfortunate that such a horrific gang rape (and the subsequent death of the victim) was required to trigger the response needed for the preservation of the rule of law − the bedrock of a republic' (Verma et al., 2013).

After much deliberation the recommendations of the Verma Commission became the Criminal Law (Amendment) Act that amended various sections of the Indian Penal Code, the Code of Criminal Procedure and the Indian Evidence Act (The Times of India, 2013). Even though many of the recommendations of the commission were incorporated into law, other recommendations such as criminalising marital rape and rape by military officials were not included in the new law, with major changes including harsher punishment for those accused of sexual assault. However, capital punishment was sanctioned for only two instances. Firstly, if it led to the death of the victim or if the accused left the victim in a 'persistent vegetative state', and secondly, if the accused were repeat offenders. People accused of rape could be subjected to rigorous punishment of no less than 20 years and this could be extended to life imprisonment and the payment of a considerable fine. Punishment for acid attacks, stalking and voyeurism were also included. The new law stated that an offender in an acid attack could attract jail terms of five to seven years, and if the attack caused harm to the victim the convicted would be subject to a jail term of a minimum of 10 years, which might again be extended to a life term. Stalking and voyeurism were also defined in the law for the first time as non-bailable offences if repeated a second time. The new law only recognised rape as a gender specific crime and only men could be punished for such offences (The Times of India, 2013).

## CASTE, CLASS AND GENDER VIOLENCE IN INDIA

It is important to contextualise the social, political and economic background in order to understand the impact of caste and class on gender violence in India, and particularly the intersectionality of caste and class in the Nirbhaya case. India has a long history of rape by authority and custodial rape, where women have been raped by landlords, police and other men in positions of authority. Women in lower caste tribal or rural areas have most commonly been the victims of custodial rape, thus establishing a belief that it is people belonging to higher and more powerful castes or authoritative positions who exploit these positions and take advantage of women. That the representation of rape in the eyes of the law has been associated with a patriarchal process has resulted in women being under constant scrutiny and questioned as to their chastity and purity. Gender-based stereotyping often assigns blame to women for being raped and they are judged on their clothes, attitude and past relationships. If a case gets to court, it is often suggested that the victim was not raped but was asking for sex, thereby breaking gendered (and acceptable) social norms (Naqvi, 2015).

It is important to look briefly at past cases of sexual violence and anti-rape activism and to examine the detail of the changes in rape law previous to the amendments after the Nirbhaya case. Her vicious rape underpins Hanmer and Maynard's (1987) contention that rape is one of the ultimate forms of violent expression of class and patriarchal oppression. According to Crenshaw, in cases of rape involving minority women (lower caste tribal or rural women in India), their interests often disappear into the void between concerns about women's issues and concerns about racism. However, 'when one discourse fails to acknowledge the significance of the other, the power relations that each attempts to challenge are strengthened' (Crenshaw, 1991, p. 1282). It is of interest to note that the 1970s witnessed a new wave in the Indian women's movement (Gandhi & Shah, 1992). In 1978, a large number of women's groups across the country started a conversation about violence against women. New feminist groups were just in the process of formation when the case of the rape of a women called Rameezabee was reported (Rao, Vaid, & Juneja, 1979). It was then that police rape was highlighted by several of the feminist organisations with the result that these issues received special attention.

In 1978 Rameezabee and her husband were returning from the cinema when she was arrested on charges of prostitution and then raped by a group of policemen. Her husband, a rickshaw puller, was brutally beaten up by the police when he tried to protest and died from his injuries. This incident sparked intense anger amongst the people of the city (Kannabiran, 1996). Though this case received substantial media attention, some of the core issues of this particular case became side-lined as the agitation grew. Gandhi and Shah (1992, p. 39) remarked that '[t]he Rameezabee case will be remembered as a particularly grotesque rape; for the fantastically arrogant and cunning police cover-up, for the sexism and blindness of the court's judgement and the spontaneity of public protest'. The Enquiry Commission declared that the policemen were guilty but later they were acquitted by the Session Court (Kannabiran, 1996). A few feminist groups came out and protested and went on to appeal against the verdict in the higher courts.

In June 1980 the rape of Maya Tyagi, a 23-year-old woman from a well-to-do farmer's family, was reported. When Maya was teased and taunted on the street by two policemen her husband and his friend retaliated in order to protect her. In response to this action the police fired at them, killing the husband. They then dragged Maya out of the car, brutally beat her up, robbed her of all her jewellery, stripped her naked and paraded her in the marketplace. She was then dragged to the police station and raped. In their defence the police claimed that they had shot three *dacoits*[1] (Sahai, 1981). After much pressure from the government a commission headed by P. N. Ray was set up to investigate the incident. The report presented by Ray accepted the fact that Maya's husband and friends were killed and framed as *dacoits*. The report also accepted that the police dragged Maya out of the car and stripped her. But the commission asserted that Maya was not raped by the police (Sahai, 1981). Women's groups across India took up the issue of police/landlord rape and many demonstrations and rallies were held.

Campaigns against incidents such as this remained isolated events until, in 1980, an open letter was published by four senior lawyers against a judgement that was passed in the case of a police rape in Maharashtra (Baxi, Kelkar, Sarkar, & Dhagamwar, 1978). This letter, protesting against a decision of the Supreme Court, was in connection with a rape case that had occurred in 1972, and initiated an intense campaign uniting feminist organisations across the country. A young tribal Dalit (untouchable) girl called Mathura, aged between 14 and 16, was gang raped in a police station. Under pressure from her family and other villagers a case was registered against the accused policemen. When taken to court the policemen were acquitted on the grounds that she had previous sexual intercourse with her boyfriend which made her non-virtuous (Basu, 2013). The case was later taken to the High Court where the accused were punished with one and five years of imprisonment. However, the verdict was later reversed by the Supreme Court on the grounds that she had a boyfriend and was thus loose and could not be raped (Keira, 2015). The court stated that there was no reasonable evidence that the policemen were guilty, as there were no visible marks of injury on her body and no signs on the men's body to show that she resisted rape (Basu, 2013).

As a protest against this incident, in January 1980, the Forum Against Rape (FAR), a women's organisation, was formed in Mumbai in order to fight against violence against women. This later came to be known as the Forum Against Oppression of Women (FAOW) (CEHAT, 2015). They decided to campaign for the reopening of the case and called on feminist organisations across India to join them in demonstrations across the country on 8 March, International Women's Day, to demand a retrial of the case, implementation of different sections of the Indian Penal Code (IPC) and changes to the law against rape. This was the first time feminist groups across the country had come together in a coordinated campaign. In major cities like Delhi and Mumbai joint action committees were formed, which comprised of mainly feminist groups, socialist and communist party fronts and students, to coordinate the campaign (Mondal, n.d.). This marked a new stage in the development of feminism in India.

Soon after the formation of FAR, protest marches against police rape were held all over the country, only some of which were actually organised by feminists. All of these protests received reasonable media coverage. As a result of substantial interest from the press, the issue of police rape was acknowledged in a new way in India. The kind of press coverage the incidents received made it an issue of political significance and various political parties allied themselves to the cause which was widely debated in the House of Parliament. In a short space of time the campaign was not only joined by centre-right political parties but controlled by them. Thus when a politician resigned from his party and went on hunger strike, the government decided to amend existing laws on rape. The Criminal Law (Second Amendment) Act 1983 was introduced based on the suggestions made by feminists. The major part of the amendment concentrated on defining the category of custodial rape and also added the categories of mass and gang rape to that of individual rape cases. The bill laid down a mandatory 10 years punishment for custodial rape with the onus of proof to be shifted to the accused. It also codified distinctions between different categories of rape (Wright, 2013).

There were several drawbacks to this campaign and it was weakened due to various factors, a major problem being the nature of the issue itself and the manner of social sanction accorded to rape. In India sophisticated medical technologies are available only in big cities, making the task of obtaining evidence and proving guilt increasingly difficult. This was the first time a joint action committee had been set up for a feminist cause bringing together women's organisations across the country, opening doors for future projects where rape was dragged out of the closet forcing people to try to understand the nature and extent of the crime (Gandhi & Shah, 1992). Most importantly it introduced custodial rape as a distinct category in the law (Wright, 2013).

All three cases mentioned above are examples of cases of rape that received considerable attention, both from the public and feminist groups across India. The common link between all these cases was the factor of power and authority related to the positions of the perpetrators. In two out of the three cases the victims were low caste and low class women and in all the above cases the perpetrators belonged to a higher class in terms of power and authority. Even though caste and class are recognised forms of discrimination in Indian society, people tend to ignore the importance of both these factors when addressing issues related to gender violence. In the Mathura case, for instance, there was very little attention focussed on the issues of class and caste violence. Even feminists of that era ignored the intersectionality of gender and class identity in this case.

Mrudula, Callahan, and Kang (2013) state that caste and gender are the two major forms of discrimination in Indian society, and people simultaneously belonging to both the minority groups experience the majority of suffering and sexual violence. Orchard (2004) supports this view, stating in her study that women from lower castes, especially Dalit women, are regularly raped by men belonging to upper castes in order to reinforce their power and authority. She adds that in many villages lower caste women are forced to have intercourse with high caste men in order to settle debts and disputes (Orchard, 2004). However, in the same village women belonging to the upper caste do not encounter the same level of violence and men belonging to the same lower caste do not face similar discrimination. It is those existing at the intersection of gender and caste who are the primary victims of violence and discrimination (Anne et al., 2013).

Gender violence is not constrained to rural India but is equally prevalent in the urban landscape (Koenig, Stephenson, Ahmed, Jejeebhoy, & Campbell, 2006). According to the UNIFEM report, 'one in three women around the world will be raped, beaten, coerced into sex or otherwise abused in her lifetime' (UNIFEM, 2003). However, the nature of the violence faced by women in the urban landscape can be quite different to that faced by women from the lower castes and lower class rural landscape. Patriarchal ideas of gender, power and honour hinder the recognition of intimate partner abuse and domestic violence, especially within the urban middle class. These experiences are similar to those faced by women of colour, as Indian women are often unwilling to report cases of domestic violence in an effort to protect themselves from public scrutiny. This silence is linked to the question of social respect and stigma and prevents women from reporting cases of intimate partner abuse and domestic violence. In addition, the lack of trust in authorities such as the police and the legal system increases women's vulnerability and maintains their silence. However, as evidenced above, there have been attempts to politicise the issue of violence against women and to challenge beliefs that violence occurs only in the homes of rural, deprived or uneducated families.

Patriarchy is a system that operates on both the ideological and material levels and interacts with the relation of production and transforms itself accordingly to benefit both men and the capitalist system. It reproduces itself in different ways, through different relations and institutions to maintain systemic inequality between the sexes. Whilst the majority of women share the prevalent understanding of male domination and patriarchy, their reactions differ relative to the intensity of the violence and their class origins. Research by Gandhi and Shah (1992, p. 63) has shown that 'working class or peasant women were more used to occasional slapping, kicking or thrashing and were not vehemently opposed to it [...] On the other hand, middle class women are shocked and become numb with terror'. Middle class women's reactions to domestic violence are often self-blaming. They are made to feel that it is not the man's problem but it is their failure as a wife which culminates in violence, and the humiliation of being beaten often silences these victims. The family as an institution has not been sufficiently analysed as a site of patriarchal dominance and oppression. Patriarchy, unlike its earlier usage as a father's right, is now understood more as a 'distinct system of control men have over women's labour, fertility, sexuality and mobility in the family, workplace and society in general' (Gandhi & Shah, 1992, p. 89). Thus, in order to understand the violence and discrimination faced by women in different parts of India, it is essential to consider other intersecting factors such as caste, class and geography.

## THE INTERSECTIONALITY OF GENDER, CLASS AND CASTE IN THE NIRBHAYA CASE

The Nirbhaya case demonstrated a very peculiar case of intersectionality. In all the cases discussed above the perpetrators belonged to a higher class or were in a position of authority with respect to the victims. However, in the Nirbhaya case this was reversed. In terms of class, the victim belonged to the middle class but the perpetrators were extremely disempowered and came from very poor backgrounds. They migrated from their villages and lived in the slums of New Delhi. Only one of the perpetrators had a school education (BBC, 2013). In this instance the dynamics of the sexual hierarchy, where some female bodies are superior to others, were reversed. In this context Kabeer (2015) comments that the Nirbhaya case has shown the world the effects of widening inequality in a modernising and globalising economy. She says, 'this was violence perpetrated by men from the underclass of Delhi, men who will never share in the benefits of "shining" India, against a woman who symbolised the country that India hopes to become' (Kabeer, 2015). It was the class and the background of the victim that struck a chord with people across the country.

Middle class people across the country could relate to Nirbhaya and her story, and she was perhaps the ideal victim to trigger a protest like this (Christie, 1986; Gilmartin-Zena, 1983). She was educated, belonged to the urban middle class, was accompanied by a male companion who would be expected to protect her, it was not late at night, and the incident happened in a very popular and populated area in one of the busiest cities in India. Everything about the circumstances was extraordinarily ordinary. Almost every urban middle class woman could relate to her background and circumstances and felt that if it could happen to her it could happen to anyone (Brown, 2013). Geography also played an important role as the case happened in the heart of the capital city of Delhi, which prompted the media to report the story very quickly. In the several cases of rape and sexual violence that have been reported since the Nirbhaya case some have caught public attention, some have disappeared, but none of them have resulted in a mass movement. The Nirbhaya case made gender violence a reality for the people of urban India. It was no longer something that they could ignore by saying it was a rural phenomenon, and it was this realisation that motivated people to take action.

Active participants in a movement are usually networks of groups and organisations who mobilise and protest to promote or resist social change, which is the ultimate goal of a social movement. When looking at new social movements, extensive participation by the middle class can be observed. This middle class 'participation revolution' was rooted in deep post-materialist values, emphasising direct participation and a moral concern for the plight of others. It is often said that new social movements are the movements of the educated middle class or the 'new middle class' or of the more educated and privileged sections of generally less privileged groups (Karatzogianni, 2006). Apart from organisations, the protests after the Delhi rape case saw a large number of individuals belonging to the urban middle class participating in protest activities and contributing resources without actually being attached to movement groups or organisations. To describe the mobilising structure of the protest Barn commented that, 'What has been striking about the Indian protests is that while they were led by both young men and women, who were educated, urban and middle class, they reached out and connected with others from a diverse range of backgrounds throughout Indian society' (Barn, 2013).

Another factor that resulted in the Nirbhaya case becoming one of the biggest gender movements in India was the media attention the case received. According to Patil and Purkayastha (2015) there are some myths, especially when it comes to the coverage of rape by the mainstream media. Within the mainstream media there are a core set of assumptions that distinguish 'real rape' or 'ideal rape' from 'not real' rape. In an 'ideal' or 'real' situation 'rape occurs in a non-domestic setting typically at night, in which the rapist is a monstrous (male) stranger who attacks a (female) victim with a weapon, where the victim's appearance, dress, behaviour are unimpeachable, and where the victim physically resists and sustains visible injuries' (Patil & Purkayastha, 2015, p. 600). In the case of Nirbhaya, she was not only the ideal victim but it was also the 'ideal rape', such that it was picked up by the media immediately, given publicity and sparked a mass public outcry.

Many scholars have suggested that the reason for devaluation of minority women is linked to questions about how they are represented in popular culture. According to Yuval-Davis (2006) social divisions are not only expressed in the way that minority people experience discrimination in their daily lives but also in the way that they are represented through images, texts, symbols, ideologies and even legislation. However, the much debated issue of representation rarely takes into account the question of intersectionality. In talking about representational intersectionality Crenshaw says that it is 'the ways in which these images are produced through a confluence of prevalent narratives of race and gender, as well as recognition of how contemporary critiques of racist and sexist representation marginalised women of colour' (Crenshaw, 1991, p. 1283).

Bilge, in her essay, says that 'intersectionality reflects a transdisciplinary theory aimed at apprehending the complexity of social identities and inequalities through an integrated approach. The intersectional approach goes beyond simple recognition of the multiplicity of the systems of oppression functioning out of these categories and postulates their interplay in the production and reproduction of social inequalities' (Bilge, 2010, p. 58). According to Crenshaw, with reference to the rape of minority women, their interests often fall in the void between concerns about women's issues and concerns about racism. However, 'when one discourse fails to acknowledge the significance of the other, the power relations that each attempts to challenge are strengthened' (Crenshaw, 1991, p. 1282). Intersectionality helps establish the fact that sexism and racism are mutually reinforcing. Minority women are not marginalised by the politics of race alone or gender alone and a political response to each form of subordination must also include a political response to both.

## CONCLUSION

India is extremely diverse and over the past decade it has undergone various changes socially, politically and economically. Over the years, it has been proven by various research that people who exist at the intersection of both gender and caste in India suffer the most discrimination (Anne et al., 2013). Mrudula et al. (2013) in their research maintain that most studies conducted with respect to intersectionality are based in the western context of gender, race and class. In India the case is much more complex, where various levels of discrimination where intersectionality requires more attention. In the case of India women not only have to deal with the abuse but they also have to deal with many other obstacles, including routinised forms of domination, poverty, childcare and lack of job skills. In many cases these women are completely dependent on their husbands and their lack of access to resources makes them less likely to have knowledge about available alternatives. Women who are from rural areas of India are more susceptible to violence than women of educated urban areas and those women belonging to lower castes have to contend with more abuse compared to women of higher castes. Therefore it is important to contextualise the type and nature of violence faced by women and to argue that it might differ according to class, caste and geography.

The sexual violence faced by the young middle class woman in Delhi (December 2012) gave rise to one of the biggest gender-related movements of recent times. It also gave rise to various conversations about gender and sexuality in public discourse. However, the case also displays the complex nature of class, caste and gender intersectionality that has not been much discussed. The social status of the victim and the geography of the incident played a vital role in the case, garnering both national and international attention. Hence, in order to understand the nature of gender violence in India and to find possible solutions it is important to take into consideration all other intersecting social and political discrimination. Even though caste and class are recognised forms of discrimination in Indian society, often people fail to recognise the importance of these factors when addressing issues related to gender violence. In this chapter class is not proposed as the only factor that led to the success of the Nirbhaya movement. However, the class aspect of the case necessitates further discussion in order to point out the hierarchies and contradictions that exist within the society, especially when looking at cases of gender violence. The intersection of factors including class, caste, geography and religion cannot be ignored because gender violence in India is often not separate but intrinsically linked with one or more of these factors. Such discussions are important not only at the level of activism, but they should also reach the level of policy making. According to Mrudula et al. (2013) '[a] strategical framework which is sound in its basic building blocks is needed to address the burning issue of gender and caste discrimination especially as this practice has been rooted historically into the Indian society'. Therefore it is of the utmost importance to educate and empower those women who fall within the intersections so as to actualise and resolve problems related to their extreme oppression and subjection to violence.

# NOTE

1. A *dacoit* is a robber or member of a gang.

# REFERENCES

Anne, M., Callahan, J. L., & Kang, H. (2013). Gender and caste intersectionality in the Indian context. *CEJSH: Human Resource Development, 6*(95), 31–48.

Barn, R. (2013). *Social media and protest – The Indian Spring?* Retrieved from http://www. huffingtonpost.co.uk/professor-ravinder-barn/india-social-media-and-protest_b_2430194. html?utm_hp_ref = uk. Accessed on May 2, 2015.

Basu, M. (2013). *The girl whose rape changed a country.* Retrieved from http://edition.cnn. com/interactive/2013/11/world/india-rape/. Accessed on November 7, 2015.

Baxi, U., Kelkar, R., Sarkar, L., & Dhagamwar, V. (1978). *An open letter to the Chief Justice of India.* Retrieved from http://pldindia.org/wp-content/uploads/2013/03/Open-Letter-to-CJI-in-the-Mathura-Rape-Case.pdf. Accessed on June 1, 2015.

BBC. (2013). *Profiles: Delhi gang rapists.* Retrieved from http://www.bbc.co.uk/news/world-asia-india-23434888. Accessed on October 16, 2015.

Bilge, S. (2010). Recent feminist outlooks on intersectionality. *Diogenes, 57*(1), 58–72.

Biswas, T., & Malik, S. (2013). *Juvenile raped 'Amanat' twice, once while she was unconscious: Police sources.* Retrieved from http://www.ndtv.com/article/india/juvenile-raped-amanat-twice-once-while-she-was-unconscious-police-sources-313129. Accessed on July 23, 2015.

Brown, S. (2013). *'She could have been me': Action urged after Delhi gang rape case.* Retrieved from http://www.cnn.com/2013/01/04/world/asia/irpt-new-delhi-gang-rape-ireport-reaction/. Accessed on October 16, 2015.

Center for Enquiry into Health and Allied Themes (CEHAT). (2015). *Violence against women: Collective struggles against gender violence.* Retrieved from http://violenceagainst-women.cehat.org/ong-mumbai-help-center.php?page = Womens + Movement + in + India. Accessed on May 31, 2015.

Christie, N. (1986). The ideal victim. In E. A. Fattah (Ed.), *From crime policy to victim policy* (pp. 17–30). Basingstoke: Macmillan.

Crenshaw, K. (1989). Demarginalizing the intersection of race and sex: A black feminist critique of antidiscrimination doctrine, feminist theory and antiracist politics. *University of Chicago Legal Forum*, 138–167. Retrieved from http://heinonline.org/HOL/Landing Page?handle = hein.journals/uchclf1989&div = 10&id = &page =

Crenshaw, K. (1991). Mapping the margins: Intersectionality, identity politics, and violence against women of color. *Stanford Law Review, 43*(6), 1241–1299.

Davis, K. (2008). Intersectionality as buzzword: A sociology of science perspective on what makes a feminist theory successful. *Feminist Theory, 9*(1), 67–85.

Gandhi, N., & Shah, N. (1992). *The issues at stake: Theory and practice in the contemporary women's movement in India* (1st ed.). New Delhi: Kali for Women.

Gilmartin-Zena, P. (1983). Attribution theory and rape victim responsibility. *Deviant Behavior, 4*(3–4), 357–374.

Hanmer, J., & Maynard, M. (1987). *Women, violence and social control* (Vol. 23). Basingstoke: Palgrave Macmillan.

Indian Law Cases. (2014). *Indian penal code, 1860, section 375 — rape*. Retrieved from http://www.indianlawcases.com/Act-Indian.Penal.Code,1860-1831. Accessed on May 21, 2015.

Kabeer, N. (2015). *Grief and rage in India: Making violence against women history?* Retrieved from https://www.opendemocracy.net/5050/naila-kabeer/grief-and-rage-in-india-making-violence-against-women-history. Accessed on June 9, 2015.

Kannabiran, K. (1996). Rape and the construction of communal identity. In K. Jayawardena & M. de Alwis (Eds.), *Embodied violence: Communalising women's sexuality in South Asia* (pp. 32–41). London: Zed Books.

Karatzogianni, A. (2006). *The politics of cyberconflict* (1st ed.). London: Routledge.

Keira. (2015). *From Mathura rape case to Delhi 2012: The pain of ineffective laws and dignity on trial*. Retrieved from http://feminisminindia.com/from-mathura-rape-case-to-delhi-2012/. Accessed on May 31, 2015.

Knapp, G. A. (2005). Race, class, gender reclaiming baggage in fast travelling theories. *European Journal of Women's Studies, 12*(3), 249–265.

Koenig, M. A., Stephenson, R., Ahmed, S., Jejeebhoy, S. J., & Campbell, J. (2006). Individual and contextual determinants of domestic violence in North India. *American Journal of Public Health, 96*(1), 132–138.

Lynn, D. (2014). Socialist feminism and triple oppression: Claudia Jones and African American women in American communism. *Journal for the Study of Radicalism, 8*(2), 1–20.

McCall, L. (2005). The complexity of intersectionality. *Signs, Journal of Women in Culture and Society, 30*(3), 1771–1800.

Mondal, P. (n.d.). *Rape: The movement against rape in India*. Retrieved from http://www.your articlelibrary.com/essay/rape-the-movement-against-rape-in-india/32972/. Accessed on May 31, 2015.

Mrudula, A., Callahan, J., & Kang, H. K. (2013). *Gender and caste intersectionality in the Indian context*. Conference Paper, University Forum for Human Resource Development (UFHRD).

Naqvi, M. (2015). *'A girl is more responsible for rape than a boy': The statement that shocked the world ... except India*. Retrieved from http://www.independent.co.uk/news/world/asia/a-girl-is-more-responsible-for-rape-than-a-boy-the-statement-that-shocked-the-world-except-india-10084409.html. Accessed on May 31, 2015.

Orchard, T. (2004). *A painful power: Coming of age, sexuality and relationships, social reform, and HIV/AIDS among Devadasi sex workers in rural Karnataka, India*. University of Manitoba. Retrieved from http://mspace.lib.umanitoba.ca/handle/1993/20127

Osborne, H. (2013). *Delhi gang rape: Youngest attacker 'ripped out victim's intestines with bare hands'*. Retrieved from http://m.ibtimes.co.uk/delhi-gang-rape-juvenile-attacker-brutal-raped-420247.html. Accessed on October 16, 2015.

Patil, V., & Purkayastha, B. (2015). Sexual violence, race and media (in) visibility: Intersectional complexities in a transnational frame. *Societies, 5*(3), 598–617.

Purkayastha, B., Subramaniam, M., Desai, M., & Bose, S. (2003). The study of gender in India: A partial review. *Gender & Society, 17*(4), 503–524.

Rao, A., Vaid, S., & Juneja, M. (1979). *Rape, society and state.* New Delhi: People's union of civil liberties and democratic rights. Retrieved from http://www.unipune.ac.in/snc/cssh/HumanRights/07%20STATE%20AND%20GENDER/01.pdf

Sahai, R. (1981). Baghpat report supports oppression. *Dinmaan*, February. Retrieved from http://www.pucl.org/from-archives/may81/baghpat.htm. Accessed on October 16, 2015.

Shields, S. A. (2008). Gender: An intersectionality perspective. *Sex Roles, 59*(5), 301−311.

Singh Shah, H., Kapur, M., & Smith-Spark, L. (2013). *New Delhi police fire water cannon at India rape protest.* Retrieved from http://edition.cnn.com/2012/12/22/world/asia/india-rape-protest. Accessed on July 27, 2015.

The Times of India. (2013). President gives his assent to anti-rape bill. Retrieved from http://timesofindia.indiatimes.com/india/President-gives-his-assent-to-anti-rape-bill/articleshow/19372967.cms. Accessed on August 12, 2015.

UNIFEM. (2003). *A learning programme in action: UNIFEM Gender Responsive Budgeting Programme Mid-term Review*, Summary Report, October.

Verma, J. S., Seth, J. L., & Subramanium, G. (2013). *Reports of the committee on amendments to criminal law.* New Delhi: Government of India. Retrieved from http://apneaap.org/wp-content/uploads/2012/10/Justice-Verma-Committee-Report.pdf.

Wright, T. (2013). *A short history of Indian rape-law reforms.* Retrieved from http://blogs.wsj.com/indiarealtime/2013/01/09/a-short-history-of-indian-rape-law-reforms/. Accessed on July 28, 2015.

Yin, R. K. (2014). *Case study research.* London: Sage.

Yuval-Davis, N. (2006). Intersectionality and feminist politics. *European Journal of Women's Studies, 13*(3), 193−220.

# NEGOTIATING GENDER SECURITY: THE TRANSNATIONALISATION OF LOCAL ACTIVIST DISCOURSES IN POST-CONFLICT BURUNDI AND LIBERIA

Maria Martin de Almagro

## ABSTRACT

Purpose — *The chapter seeks to examine how local women's groups in Burundi and Liberia have responded to the opportunities offered by UN Security Council Resolution 1325 on Women, Peace and Security and how transnational understandings of gender security have affected the way the locals advocate for gender policies at home.*

Design/methodology/approach — *Through discussion of data collected during extended fieldwork, the chapter illustrates the internal negotiation process between the international and the local elements of the transnational campaign for the implementation of Resolution 1325. The chapter first looks at the processes of identity creation and learning that enable*

Gender and Race Matter: Global Perspectives on Being a Woman
Advances in Gender Research, Volume 21, 107–125
ISSN: 1529-2126/doi:10.1108/S1529-212620160000021007

*local activists to adapt to transnational understandings of gender security. Second, it looks at the (re)production and adaptation of those understandings in local campaigns for gender security in post-conflict[1] Burundi and Liberia.*

Findings — *The chapter demonstrates how a very particular discourse on 'gender security' is used and reproduced through power relations between local and transnational activists, thereby enabling certain practices and policies to become natural and the best possible option.*

Social implications — *This implies that while transnational advocacy networks help grassroots social movements to be heard at international fora, these networks also impose certain discourses and practices, contributing to a depoliticisation of the grassroots activity.*

Originality/value — *Understanding how transnational advocacy networks negotiate and transform local women's rights discourses is all the more important since these transnational networks have been considered as moral authorities in the global political arena.*

**Keywords:** Gender security; transnational advocacy networks; civil society; women organisations; Burundi; Liberia

# INTRODUCTION

A growing number of scholars and policy-makers, particularly within the liberal-cosmopolitan approach (Archibugi, 2008; Held, 1995; Juris, 2008; Kaldor, 2003; Kaldor, Anheier, & Glasius, 2003), assert that international NGOs and transnational advocacy networks[2] (TANs) are emerging as a powerful new force in international politics and are transforming global norms and practices by giving a voice to individuals globally (Boli & Thomas, 1999; Keck & Sikkink, 1998; Reitan, 2012; Risse-Kappen, 1995; Smith, Chatfield, & Pagnucco, 1997). Nevertheless, the power dynamics between a TAN and their constituency of members, supporting organisations and beneficiaries has so far remained understudied. This chapter seeks to fill this gap by analysing how TANs and local activists — in this case women's organisations in post-conflict contexts — negotiate the discourse and the strategy they will use when advocating together for the implementation of international norms on gender security.

There is not a single definition, and therefore not a single discourse, on what constitutes 'gender security' (Detraz, 2012). Indeed, 'gender security' relies upon the intersection of two sets of logics: what constitutes 'gender' and what constitutes 'security' (Shepherd, 2008). However, generally, the term is used to point to instances of insecurity arising out of particular experiences of gender, where gender is a noun, verb and logic shaping our environment (Shepherd, 2010). Since the UN Security Council passed Resolution 1325 (UNSCR 1325) on 31 October 2000, urging for an increased consideration of gender in all post-conflict and reconstruction processes, deliberations about how to implement 'gender security' have been amplified across activist and institutional sites (Cohn, 2008).

The chapter seeks to examine how local women's groups in Burundi and Liberia have responded to the opportunities offered by this resolution and its transnational activists and institutional sites *and* how transnational understandings of gender security have affected the way the locals advocate for gender policies at home. The chapter first looks at the processes of identity creation and learning that enable local activists to adapt to transnational understandings of gender security. Second, it looks at the (re)production and adaptation of those understandings in local campaigns for gender security in post-conflict Burundi and Liberia. I seek to demonstrate how a very particular discourse on 'gender security' is used and reproduced through power relations between local and transnational activists, enabling certain practices and policies to become seen as the only option. That is, how discourses create boundaries and identities amongst actors, and how these actors use their agency to stretch those boundaries and identities in order to steer other activists towards certain behaviour. The starting point is therefore that *gender security* is a dynamic and contested concept whose meaning depends on spatiotemporal circumstances (McLeod, 2013). It travels through space and time, crossing national and institutional boundaries, and it is precisely through this process that its meaning is stretched, shrunk and bent (Lombardo, Meier, & Verloo, 2009). As such, it is open to interpretation and contestation by different actors and activists.

The analysis presented herein is based on data collected from 60 semi-structured interviews with activists, politicians and employees of international organisations in Burundi and Liberia in 2012 and 2013. Most of the contextual information was collected through participant observation in Bujumbura and Monrovia and analysis of documentation produced by NGOs and local women's organisations. The interviews helped me illustrate the internal negotiation process between the international and local elements of the transnational campaign for the implementation of UNSCR 1325. This internal negotiation has barely been documented because of the difficulties in accessing the field.

## COLLECTIVE FEMINISMS IN POST-CONFLICT CONTEXTS

The Secretary General of a women's collective in Liberia is well educated, speaks good English, has had plenty of opportunities for engaging with international activists from all over the world and has travelled extensively. In her discourse, she conceives feminist identity as a collective act. That is, by leaving aside differences and performing as a group, the group will be created and collective action will emerge as the best approach for achieving women's emancipation. Women's organisations had formed a cohesive group during the war in Liberia advocating for peace. They received support and resources from the international community to carry out their advocacy activities. However, this cohesion ended some time just after the war. In her discourse, she engaged with other feminist groups and tried to respond to the lack of cohesion and understanding amongst them by convincing them that as women they had common needs and dreams. Therefore, the common femininity should act as the glue reuniting them.

Feminist scholars have long understood that local political dynamics build cultural constructions of the female Other as having different and stagnant disparities (Nader, 1989). Building on this finding, I found that local women's involvement in transnational campaigning enabled them to construct and modify their identity and personal experiences through intersecting discourses. It also enabled them to participate in the negotiation of a common discourse for the political campaign for the implementation of the UNSCR 1325 in their respective countries.

In this section, I argue that more than enabling local activists to act politically, the creation and argumentation of a collective identity is already a political instrument per se since the creation of discourses leads to the development of collective identities. That is, activists themselves are transformed during the course of strategic interactions. Their identities are formed and changed by the different temporalities and a diversity of spatial sites. In our case study, the identities of the feminist activities and the Burundian and Liberian women's associations entail a certain type of gender security narrative that excludes or includes connections to conflict and post-conflict (McLeod, 2013). As Stern claims, 'who (we say) we are matters in how we conceive of, strive for, and practice security', since the way we describe security 'implies (and indeed informs) a particular expression of our identity' (2005, p. 7). The way in which these activists link, or not, war violence to gender violence determines the ideological content of their gender security narratives, as well as how insecurities should be solved.

This section deals with whether the idea of a common discourse on what constitutes 'gender security' can be put forward and if a solution to gender insecurities can be found. This is with particular reference to the campaign for the implementation of UNSCR 1325 in Burundi and Liberia. What follows is a discussion on how collective identities are produced and whether they can help to create common discourses.

*Collective Activism in the Everyday: Educating about and*
*Articulating Gender Security*

The majority of my interviewees started their activism journey in the last phases of the war period in Burundi and in Liberia. I argue that many scholarly accounts of collective identity construction pay inadequate attention to the importance of low key political education and community work during war and post-war times, focusing only on strategy, protest and action carried out by an elite group of activists. Nevertheless, collective identity building is a long-term process which impacts the vision of the world 'giving life to ideas about the way the world is − and could be − by acting on one's convictions in daily life' (Wakefield, 2007, p. 331). That is, ideas, identities and the subsequent common discourses are developed through practices in daily life, particularly in post-conflict contexts, where society is re-building and actors have a lot of opportunities for political transformation. These two case studies might be seen as an example of how transnational discourses are translated and transformed through local practices in order to be of use in local everyday lives. I argue that local women activists are therefore not simply strategically 'framing' their claims in order to secure political opportunities to engage with transnational activists and their campaigns, but are, at the same time, re-imagining their identities, subject-positions and roles in the new post-conflict society.

There is a general agreement that education and knowledge production are key aspects of feminist activism (Hercus, 2005; Kuumba, 2001; Sudbury, 1998). A repeated theme in interviews with local and national activists was the idea of being an educator to the community and to other women, of assisting others in knowing about the international resolutions and thinking about women's issues in new ways. Those local activists who have benefitted from interaction with international groups expressed the idea of pedagogy as part of their work:

> At that time, our organisation had looked at having the two parties in the war to meet. We had sessions of peaceful conflict resolution, sessions on bonding with people from other ethnicities. (Project manager of a Burundian women's organisation)

For this project manager, teaching people how to resolve conflicts, even when those conflicts are of a domestic nature or between neighbours, was one of the main activities of women's groups. They also expressed the need to be sensitive about how to go about educating the community in a post-conflict context. For instance, begging for money was a current practice by repatriates and refugees when coming back after war to Burundi. However, begging is frowned on in Burundi and contributes to strengthening discrimination. Several interviewees coming from grassroots groups indicated that exiting begging and starting small businesses helped them reconcile with themselves and become useful to the community. A grassroots leader in the province of Cibitoke told us:

> One of the things that we have got as an added value of associating with national women's organisations is that they have prevented us from going on begging for money. They have shown us how a woman can organise herself to be a woman of worth for her family and her community. (Grassroots leader, Cibitoke)

In turn, the national women's organisation representative who worked closely with this grassroots leader in Cibitoke indicated that:

> A woman begging is always the first source of family conflict, because if a woman is able to participate economically to the household, then she is part of the conflict resolution at home. (National women's organisation representative)

One example of the importance of economic participation was put forward by the main policy officer of an established women's association for reconciliation and peace in Burundi:

> Today, I would like to reinforce the grassroots, the women in the collines,[3] because those are the ones producing and working on agriculture. Because today they need to have this feeling of citizenship, they should know how to take part in decision-making in their communities. They need to speak as women, because they have a lot of problems within their households. (Policy officer, women's association, Burundi)

This leader was very conscious of the fact that it was thanks to the international organisations that brought UNSCR 1325 to Burundi that her association could survive and learn. She was therefore keen to pass that knowledge on to others and to empower those rural women who are the economic backbone of the country and the last people to be taken into account. In sum, she had to respond to the needs of two types of communities: the grassroots women and the international activists offering help. The dilemma of how to include the most marginalised actors while securing their very own interests is not recognised because of their behaviour:

> We have created this synergy because we must give back all the international NGOs have taught us. (Policy officer, women's association, Burundi)

However, it is not only the leaders of large national associations who feel the need to educate and empower. Grassroots women, who have been approached by national associations and who have started benefitting from reconciliation and economic empowerment programmes, also felt that educating the population on how to achieve peace was part of their job. One of these women in the rural province of Cibitoke told me:

> I go to the village and I show women how to start an economic activity, I tell them how to work in groups in order to find better ways of accessing resources. (Grassroots activist, rural province, Cibitoke)

Some only want their voice to be heard and feel that being part of a women's group helps them to have a say in the affairs of the community. One of the grassroots women explained that it is through the constant work of women's groups that women have rights and are valued in the community:

> It is not men who will come to serve us things in silver. If today local administration gives us any value, if our surroundings, neighbours give us value [...] it is because we have been working at the level of the organisation of the life in the commune, in the zone, in the province [...] That's how our voice can go far. (Grassroots activist)

Others tried to take the message to schools and were conscious about how their experiences as little girls during wartime, of suffering economic and sexual violence, had shaped their present. The founder of an organisation for girls' rights who also works at the Liberian Ministry of Gender explained:

> So, I had to sell, you know the water in the plastic bag? Sometimes the profit was only 10 Liberian dollars, which is nothing when you do that for the whole day. So even when you go out to sell, you find men who could be your father who want to sleep with you, I mean, it was just a lot. So all those challenges we had to stand up against, I think

kinda positioned me in a sense that I see there is a lot to be done. [...] So I felt there
were a lot of young women in those communities like myself that just found it so difficult to rise above and they had to remain there. So for me, my passion was to go back
to that community and help those girls. So that I could serve as an inspiration to them.
(Founder of girls' rights organisation and Liberian Ministry of Gender employee)

All these instances evoke an important element worth highlighting:
when studying local women activists in a post-conflict context we are facing
a wider community of women, not only activists in the strict sense of the
word. Education and self-education made women more open to participating in collective action and the opportunities offered by a post-conflict context, in which an outpouring of international resources and information
arrives in a short period of time and is taken up by women at all levels of
the socio-economic scale.

Apart from learning, educating and outreach, women activists use their
ideas in different sites where political debates and arguments take place.
Working with the international community helps them put their experiences into words in order to generate feminist ideas and arguments. By
adopting the programme provided by the international NGOs, these local
associations engage in working together to achieve a common goal − the
creation and implementation of UNSCR 1325 and a common understanding of security. This common goal also provides them with a sense of
belonging to a new international community. This is most clearly exemplified by one of the respondents, who is the manager of a women's national
association in Bujumbura (Burundi):

Very few state actors knew what the Resolution (UNSCR 1325) was. Therefore, since I
had taken part in several meetings organised by international NGOs advocating before
the Security Council, we created together with International Alert and UNIFEM a programme to systematically integrate UNSCR 1325 in all consultation programs for
peace. (Manager, women's national association, Bujumbura)

This Burundian activist explained how she was more educated than government officials on issues concerning the implementation of the resolution
because she had had privileged access to international programmes and
funds. Indeed, belonging to an international community of peacemakers, as
well as the internalisation of a master framework for collective action gives
these associations another powerful advantage: a sense of authority and
legitimacy to negotiate on behalf of Burundian and Liberian women at an
international level and to provide instructions back home. For instance,
one of my interviewees stated proudly that she had to remind the Ministry
of International Affairs of their international commitments:

And I said at the Ministry: 'when you sign an agreement you are responsible for it, you don't know what you are signing; when you ratify international standards, you have to know that you are liable'. (Manager, women's national association, Bujumbura)

### *Crafting Common Discourses with a Transnational Taste*

In this section I examine the creation of new claims and discourses by local women's groups through their links with transnational actors. I also show how transnationalisation enables local activists to connect ideas with political creativity, negotiation and conflict in order to articulate their political engagement. The phenomenon of articulation is hereby understood as a process: first, becoming conscious of one's own discursive power; secondly, producing a discourse; thirdly, putting that discourse into action (Rogstad & Vestel, 2011).

First, in both countries, women's grassroots groups became conscious of their own power during war times. They managed to bring together groups of women to improve the situation of their communities. For Burundian women who had to stay at home alone while their husbands went to war, the collaboration with women from the 'enemy' ethnic group helped them economically and physically through the organisation of food exchanges and even child care. One member of staff from a women's organisation in Burundi exemplified this with the following quote:

These women said to themselves that they could not stay like that [...] There were Tutsi and Hutu neighbourhoods in Bujumbura and you were not supposed to cross them. So women Hutus started leaving their neighbourhoods to join Tutsi women and exchange food. And at the same time, they exchanged information like that: 'don't go here, you have to take that road'. And we took care of each other's children. And then when the Secretary General of the United Nations came to Burundi, we found it was a wonderful initiative. So at the time we didn't have any notion of conflict resolution, it was just pure instinct. Therefore, the Secretary General said that 'we have to back these women to do something'. (Staff member, women's organisation, Burundi)

Similarly, the mobilisation capacities of Liberian women to overcome religious barriers in order to achieve peace in the country took their story to an international level. The leaders of the Mass Action to Stop War in Liberia realised that their mobilisation capacity was so big that they could reunite women from every background who had suffered from the war in a similar way *and* organise sit-ins every day. The manager of the women's programme of a religious association in Monrovia explained how she worked with Lemah Gbowee, winner of the Nobel Peace Prize in 2011, to carry out the Mass Action, and realised that women's groups had the potential to become important players in peace-building:

> Ok, the Mass Action gave [...] when Lemah and I talked, every village we went to, every community we went to, working with women it was almost always the same story. This woman got raped, her son was either forced into become a rebel, her husband was like [...] I mean, the story was just the same everywhere we went. And so that was one of the reasons and I said to Lemah: 'I think we can do something out of these women, we can have them turning their victimhood into a victory. They are surviving, so we can tap on that and move somewhere else'. (Manager, women's programme, religious association, Monrovia)

Participation in these activities helped local activists develop articulatory practices to produce and deploy new arguments in everyday life. They began to claim their rights to participate in public life by evoking laws and established practices. This is expressed by a project manager of a national women's association in Burundi:

> So there is this communal law that says that the population has the right to meet every six months with the leaders of the community so that they can exchange issues and problems. That way the leaders can say what they are going to do relating to that problem. However, in reality this dialogue does not exist. And women found that this was a priority because the community is of no use if people cannot start a dialogue. So for some meetings they said: 'We want to participate in meetings, but we won't participate if we cannot give our opinion. We are very poor, so all these communal projects have to be directed to people affected by conflict.' But the government didn't understand. (Project manager, national women's association, Burundi)

The women also began to organise their claims in order to make the link between the community and the local government so that the latter is held accountable to its policies. Furthermore, they carried out a gendered analysis of local policies in order to understand the implications of new policy for women. This is stated clearly by a president of a national women's association in Liberia:

> So what we do as civil society actors is that if the government calls XXX [name of the association] and say 'we have this policy', we take it and explain it in the women organisations, in churches, etc. We sit down, we look at what this means for women, how we can have access to it for women, and then you know [...] And then sometimes what we do is to ensure that government comes in a particular way and comes back and gives us feedback. (President of a national women's association in Liberia)

Secondly, when examining the production of discourses, it was observed that community participants responded to transnational discourses by drawing on localised concepts in order to adapt discourses to suit their particular priorities. In doing so, they change the discursive boundaries which determine what it is possible to advocate for in the campaign and what not. For instance, international donors, governments and NGOs disbursed enormous quantities of money and resources for the 2005 and 2010 general elections in Burundi. The objective was to comply with UNSCR 1325 and its article 2, which calls for an increase in the participation of women at decision-making levels in conflict resolution and peace processes. Burundian women leaders of female organisations understood very quickly that they needed to focus their priorities and work within the election campaign. Part of the resources was used to raise awareness amongst women about the importance of going to vote and also to raise awareness amongst politicians about how to win the votes of women. Pamphlets were produced and distributed by a coalition of Burundian local women's associations and international NGOs. They were directed at local and national politicians in the electoral race. Using very simple language, they described the priorities of women in every policy sector, from the political to the socio-economic, and proposed an electoral programme to be adopted by politicians wanting to win the elections and the support of 50% of the Burundian population. In a very skilful way, local activists used funding for elections in order to ask for socio-economic equality for women and men, something they considered vital to achieving gender security.

## EMPOWERMENT AND CO-OPTATION OF LOCAL WOMEN'S ASSOCIATIONS AND THEIR DISCOURSES

One of the main objectives of the Women, Peace and Security agenda has been to empower women in conflict and post-conflict settings (Article 8(b) of UNSCR 1325). In this section I argue that the process of implementing the Women, Peace and Security agenda in local settings has empowered sectors of the local civil society, particularly sectors of women's groups that now have much more political power and visibility in the public sphere. However, at the same time, the last phases of the campaign for the implementation of the UNSCR 1325 on Women, Peace and Security saw the eruption of conflict due to different understandings of gender security between the advocacy network represented by the UN NGO WG on Women, Peace and Security[4] and its local partners in Burundi and Liberia. Although all members of the campaign agree on the need to provide physical and political security for women in post-conflict contexts, the clash amongst actors rests upon the question of how to advocate for socio-economic security after conflict. Indeed, as reflected in the National Action Plans of both countries and the funding received by local advocacy organisations, the implementation campaign concentrated efforts to increase women's participation in electoral processes. This section of the chapter brings together earlier discussions of how certain gender security discourses are selected and others are marginalised in the transnational campaign for the implementation of UNSCR 1325 in Burundi and Liberia. It also shows how local articulations and representations of gender security are products of the transnationalisation of their local battles.

*Accepted Discourses and Identities: Securitising*
*Gender through Quotas*

In Burundi, the participation of women in governance at 30% is defined in the Constitution (2005), the Municipal Law (2010) and the Electoral Code (2009). This 30% is respected at Parliament and Council level, but it is neglected at the *colline* (local government) level. As explained above, UNSCR 1325 has been used by the transnational advocacy network on Women, Peace and Security to mobilise women to elect women and to get themselves elected at all levels of government. Indeed, when asked about which campaign related to 1325 has been the most successful, Burundian women's associations speak about the mobilisation for the participation of women in the election processes of 2005 and 2010. In this case, the Ministry of Gender, the international NGOs and the local women's movements created synergies and worked together. The Secretary General of a synergy of women's association indicated that:

> There were three things that made the campaign a success. First, women's groups stayed together. Second, there was good collaboration with the national authorities in charge of the question. Third, the international community accepted to support our strategic planning. For other programmes that we have, we have good ideas, but we do not have the international co-operation, so they don't work. (Secretary General of women's associations)

The alliance that made the campaign on women's participation in election a success worked together again after the electoral process in order to train elected female politicians on negotiation, communication and effective representation of women. A local staff member of an international NGO office in Burundi explained how they had trained elected women on how to advocate for women's rights while in office:

> We have trained elected women thanks to a project titled 'Yes, she also can.' The project has the objective to raise awareness for having women elected at the colline level. And now we have this specific project to work with women that are able to effectively represent women at the level of the colline. Because, for instance, even if there is a 30% of women elected, there are still holes [...] So that's why we are reinforcing their capacities, leadership and their advocacy techniques. (Staff, international NGO, Burundi)

The local members of the campaign feel successful because women, as previously excluded political actors, are now part of governmental structures. Nevertheless, in their success stories there is no place for gender security, understood as freedom which would allow them to pursue a professional career and to take decisions independently from other family members. This is what they conceived as essential in order to transform post-conflict societies. The pursuit of economic independence and business opportunities for women is not reflected in the type of advocacy activities they carry out with the help of international partners. Hence, empowerment dynamics come about hand in hand with co-optation and depoliticisation. A quote by a president of a national synergy of women's organisations is symptomatic of this fact:

> And now for the moment we have collected data on the issues where we got some resources. And it was for the electoral processes of 2005 and 2010 and women's participation in elections. We normally have funding for that. We work on five thematic lines, but we have been funded twice for the same thematic line because our partners had an interest in it. But that doesn't mean that we do not work on other issues as well. (President, national synergy of women's organisations)

As she explains, although the synergy works on five thematic lines, only the thematic line on elections and political participation has been funded twice, because the international partners prioritise it. Liberia constitutes a similar, but not totally equal, case. The poster child of women rights in post-conflict countries has been unable to pass a law on compulsory quotas for women in government. The Parity Bill (also known as the Equity Bill) has been on the negotiating table since 2005, and an influx of funds and human resources coming from international activists has not helped to move this on. Local activists complain that the international activists do not take their advice seriously and have spent monetary resources without taking the local situation into consideration:

> You know, it is such a pity. Because the international organisations that come and give money to issues do not do investigation. That Equity bill has been wrapped and unwrapped, washed and washed [...] The first time the Equity bill was discussed it was around 2005–6. But the situation was not taking in the context, so one day they were running in circles. [...] Three of the senators agreed to sponsor the bill. On the day of

the sponsorship, there were three women that went to the legislator to tell the men not
to pass the bill, so as a result, the issue did not come to the agenda. Even if it died from
a natural death, the bill was left in a committee room when the legislature went to
recess in September 2011. 2012 January we went to the legislature. The President was
there and a few others, and they told us that when they elect their core officers they
would tell us to come back. But guess what? While we were strategising what we would
do, a new group of women were elected in the Women Legislative Caucus. And they
said that whatever we had done they were not interested in it. And that is the thing, we
keep on going into cycles. (Local activist, Liberia)

Two issues are particularly interesting in this testimony. Firstly, international activists have a clear set of priorities and passing quotas for female
politicians is one of them. They have received extraordinary amounts of
money from donors to carry out advocacy campaigns in the country and
they need to make the Equity Bill a success. Secondly, female politicians
were amongst those voting against the Equity Bill project. The question is,
therefore, why would the international activists believe having more women
in Parliament is a means to empower women when those same women in
Parliament vote against women's interests?

Other women activists do not even see the point in having this law
passed. To the question 'would you run for election?' a grassroots leader
indicated that she didn't have the money and that:

It is the educated women that are running. We [rural women] don't have money. And
then they are not even supporting women when they are in office. (Grassroots leader)

They would prefer to concentrate efforts in the passing of a Local
Government Act that is currently under discussion in Parliament. This Act
would change appointed positions in local government to elected positions.
According to the president of a national women's association in Liberia,
local women would have many more possibilities of being elected and
make women's rights one of their main priorities in office. In addition, this
would close the gap between women in high positions in government and
grassroots women:

So if you start at the local level, and this is where you have a bulk of the women, at the
national level you have very few of us, and very few of us who in most instances turn
out to be gatekeepers to the other women. You know? Most of the fellow women don't
help other women to actually excel so why don't you start building a constituency at
the lower level and then come up! (President, national women's association, Liberia)

After several years with no results and a negative reaction from the government, the UN and its donors still go on giving funds to the campaign to
achieve a 30% quota. This is a clear example that advocacy priorities are

established by international organisations and donors, and local activists who fight for causes related to those priorities get help from international activists who, at the same time, receive funds from donors for this.

### *Keeping Identity and Discursive Boundaries Closed: De-securitising the Economy*

In other cases, however, the negative response from the government has been used as the excuse for stopping women's rights campaigns. The transnational advocacy network on Women, Peace and Security has claimed that difficulties with the national government in Burundi made them decide to stop campaigning on inheritance rights based on UNSCR 1325. As one member of a national women's association in Bujumbura explained, Burundian women's organisations used UNSCR 1325 and the Burundian National Action Plan for the implementation of the Resolution. It proclaimed the need for women's economic independence in order to lobby for the passing of a law on inheritance giving equal rights to brothers and sisters to inherit their parents' land. For Burundian women a lack of access to land meant the return to a pre-war situation where women were subjected to the will of their husbands or male family members. Gender security in post-war Burundi could not be guaranteed unless socio-economic protection for both genders was enacted by law. One research participant explained that their campaign attracted international attention and that they managed to get some international funding and human resources. However, she complained about the fact that those resources ended when the President of the Burundian Republic expressed his refusal to pass the law while he was in power. Furthermore, she indicated that although several NGOs were critical in their reports and several governments at the Conference of Burundi development partners in Geneva in October 2012 pushed the Burundian government to improve the social, economic and political situation of women in the country, they failed to spend more resources in what became a more controversial issue than previously expected.

Although UNSCR 1325 does not make any reference to inheritance laws, the national associations argued that without economic security, no other security for women is possible, and therefore the implementation of UNSCR 1325 required the drafting of inheritance laws. They argued that without allowing women to own, it did not make any sense to make them public political figures through quotas. It would mean that power inequalities in society remained untouched, and women would still be victims and not agents of development. Some leaders of advocacy organisations complained about this issue and indicated that these types of gender security discourses have brought about more insecurities. The president of a Liberian women's organisation commented:

> So after 2003, we have people from international organisations telling the women: 'Don't go for him, you don't have to fetch his water, you don't have to do this or that'. And a lot of women started to do this and guess what? A lot of women got raped by their husbands. It is a rights issue, but this rights issue is not something that we practiced before, so it is something that has to do with a continuous advocacy and awareness around. We have committed ourselves to being victimised because we have copied what somebody else said. It is not going to happen that we look at it and value it in order to decide whether it is good or not for us. (President, Liberian women's organisation)

This testimony explains how although local activists believe issues brought by the international organisations are good causes and are worth fighting for the fight needs to be contextualised. Indeed, a certain discourse on gender security has been adopted as a global governance tool. That is, local feminist interpretations of insecurity and violence are merged with a liberal peace paradigm of quotas and gender equality proposed by the Security Council resolution. Empowerment has occurred, but within a political context that remains characterised by the weakness of democratic institutions in Burundi and in Liberia and the control of the state's resources by economic elites. In such a context, the concept of empowerment must be qualified. In the case of Liberian and Burundian women's organisations political empowerment means, among other things, establishing a position of being legitimate interlocutors in the eyes of the state, thus improving organisations' capacity to obtain and disseminate information on public policy. It also includes blocking government proposals that go against gender equality and women's empowerment, and, most importantly, obtaining direct access to financial resources.

In both cases, the complexity of the security situation in Burundi or Liberia is reduced or framed through concepts that resonate with global audiences and donors. The situation on the ground is reconstructed through the selection of events and key problems in order to create solidarity across boundaries and pass the message to those with the power to allocate resources and attention. A certain level of 'gender security' is required given the extent of violence against women during wartime in these countries and the need for quotas acts as a reference point for women's solidarity. Nevertheless, for the local activists it is not clear whether these reference points are aligned with their experiences and claims.

# CONCLUSION

Expanding upon identities and discourses, as this chapter has, enables the researcher to reveal data about the diverse ways in which local activists respond to transnationalisation and how transnational actors in turn respond to local contextualisation. Two issues need to be highlighted: First, new contextualised discourses do not float freely within the TANs. Who puts those discourses on the table matters as much as the discourse itself. That is, UNSCR 1325 represents a particular understanding of gender security (Shepherd, 2008) that is based on international practices and institutions that suggest that if women are formal political actors they will be secure. UNSCR 1325 is politically translated by international activists as a document designed to reinforce a notion of gender security promoted by the Security Council. Local discourses of gender security put forward by local activists that do not correspond to this notion are not considered valid.

The second related issue is that TANs and international NGOs are often referred to in the literature as 'moral authorities' due to their professed neutrality and the principled beliefs by which they are supposed to abide (Avant, Finnemore, & Sell, 2010, p. 13). By virtue of this role, I would anticipate that these organisations would resist or contest the meaning of gender security proposed by the Security Council, for which extensive funding is provided. While they do, they also contribute to its legitimacy and acceptance, contributing to a form of *depoliticisation*, which separates gender security from more critical feminist perspectives such as those that elucidate how gender inequalities function within post-conflict societies. Moreover, local experiential knowledge and expertise is being eclipsed and ruled out. That is, the discourse proposed by international advocates promotes an easy effective action (quotas), but also entails significant costs for effectively understanding local meanings of gender security. Additionally, the discourse that will constitute the master framework for the implementation of the Women, Peace and Security agenda is based on the notion of a global sisterhood that highlights women's shared and innate skills while forgetting about divisions of ethnicity, class and religion that serve to grant certain groups of women privileged status and relationships with transnational activists.

# NOTES

1. For 14 years (1989–2003) Liberia experienced two civil wars that devastated the country economically and politically. The 2003 Accra Comprehensive Peace Agreement marked the end of the conflict through the establishment of a National Transitional Government led by interim President Gyude Bryant. Ellen Johnson Sirleaf won the 2005 general election and became the first democratically-elected female Head of State in the country. The conflict developed an extraordinary level of female activism through strikes, sit-ins, rallies and protests enacted in order to end violence in the country (Fuest, 2008). Soon after Burundi won independence from Belgium in 1962, the Hutu majority suffered from oppression and discrimination from the Tutsi leaders. A Hutu candidate, Melchior Ndadaye, won the first democratic elections in the country in 1993 (Weissman, 1998, p. 6); however, Tutsi military factions assassinated him (CIGI, 2011, p. 1). This triggered a civil war that ended but officially in 2000 with the signing of the Arusha Accords. Although women were excluded from participation in the Accords, an All-Party Burundian Women's Peace Conference took place parallel to the peace talks and proposed a number of gender-sensitive recommendations to be included in the Accord (Barltrop, 2008, p. 22).

2. I use the term transnational to refer to interactions across national boundaries where at least one actor is a non-state agent (Risse-Kappen, 1995, p. 3). Transnational civil society is then a set of interactions among an imagined community to shape collective life that are not confined to the territorial and institutional spaces of states (Lipschutz & Mayer, 1996).

3. Local government level.

4. United Nations NGO Working Group on Women, Peace and Security. http://www.womenpeacesecurity.org/about/

# REFERENCES

Archibugi, D. (2008). *The global commonwealth of citizens: Toward cosmopolitan democracy.* Princeton, NJ: Princeton University Press.

Avant, D., Finnemore, M., & Sell, S. (Eds.). (2010). *Who governs the globe?* Cambridge: Cambridge University Press.

Barltrop, R. (2008). *The negotiation of security issues in the Burundi peace talks.* Geneva: Centre for Humanitarian Dialogue.

Boli, J., & Thomas, G. M. (Eds.). (1999). *Constructing world culture: International nongovernmental organisations since 1875.* Stanford, CA: Stanford University Press.

Burundi's Constitution of 2005. (2005). English Translation by William S. Hein & Co., Constitute Project.org, 2012.

Centre for International Governance Innovation [CIGI]. (2011). *Country Profile Burundi.* Available at: www.ssrresourcecentre.org/wp.../Country-Profile-Burundi-May-11.pdf. Accessed on January 23, 2016.

Cohn, C. (2008). Mainstreaming gender in UN security policy: A path to political transformation. In S. Rai & G. Waylen (Eds.), *Global governance: Feminist perspectives* (pp. 185–206). Basingstoke: Palgrave Macmillan.

Detraz, N. (2012). *International security and gender*. New York, NY: John Wiley & Sons.

Fuest, V. (2008). This is the time to get in front: Changing roles and opportunities for women in Liberia. *African Affairs, 107*(427), 201–224.

Held, D. (1995). *Democracy and the global order*. Stanford, CA: Stanford University Press.

Hercus, C. (2005). *Stepping out of line: Becoming and being feminist*. London: Routledge.

Juris, J. S. (2008). *Networking futures: The movements against corporate globalization*. Durham, NC: Duke University Press.

Kaldor, M. (2003). The idea of global civil society. *International Affairs, 79*(3), 583–593.

Kaldor, M., Anheier, H., & Glasius, M. (2003). *Global civil society*. Cambridge: Polity Press.

Keck, M. E., & Sikkink, K. (1998). *Activists beyond borders: Advocacy networks in international politics*. Ithaca, NY: Cornell University Press.

Kuumba, B. M. (2001). *Gender and social movements*. Oxford: AltaMira Press.

Lipschutz, R. D., & Mayer, J. (1996). *Global civil society and global environmental governance: The politics of nature from place to planet*. Albany, NY: SUNY Press.

Lombardo, E., Meier, P., & Verloo, M. (Eds.). (2009). *The discursive politics of gender equality: Stretching, bending and policy-making*. London: Routledge.

McLeod, L. (2013). Back to the future: Temporality and gender security narratives in Serbia. *Security Dialogue, 44*(2), 165–181.

Nader, L. (1989). Orientalism, occidentalism and the control of women. *Cultural Dynamics, 2*, 323–355.

Reitan, R. (2012). *Global activism*. London: Routledge.

Risse-Kappen, T. (1995). *Bringing transnational relations back in: Non-state actors, domestic structures and international institutions*. Cambridge: Cambridge Studies in International Relations.

Rogstad, J., & Vestel, V. (2011). The art of articulation: Political engagement and social movements in the making among young adults in multicultural settings in Norway. *Social Movement Studies: Journal of Social, Cultural and Political Protest, 10*(3), 243–264.

Shepherd, L. (2008). *Gender, violence and security: Discourse as practice*. London: Zed Books.

Shepherd, L. (2010). Sex or gender? Bodies in world politics and why gender matters. In L. J. Shepherd (Ed.), *Gender matters in global politics: A feminist introduction to international relations* (pp. 3–16). London: Routledge.

Smith, J., Chatfield, C., & Pagnucco, R. (1997). Social movements and world politics. In C. Chatfield, R. Pagnucco, & J. Smith (Eds.), *Transnational social movements and global politics: Solidarity beyond the state* (pp. 59–77). Syracuse, NY: Syracuse University Press.

Stern, M. (2005). *Naming security — Constructing identity: 'Mayan-women' in Guatemala on the eve of 'peace'*. Manchester: Manchester University Press.

Sudbury, J. (1998). *'Other kinds of dreams': Black women's organisations and the politics of transformation*. London: Routledge.

Wakefield, S. (2007). Reflective action in the academy: Exploring praxis in critical geography using a 'food movement' case study. *Antipode, 39*, 331–354.

Weissman, S. R. (1998). *Preventing genocide in Burundi: Lessons from international diplomacy*. Peaceworks, 22. Washington, DC: United States Institute of Peace.

# GENDER SECURITY/SEXUALITY IN SOUTH AFRICA: 'I AM HIV-POSITIVE. HOW COULD YOU DO THIS TO ME?'

Bev Orton

## ABSTRACT

Purpose — *This chapter focuses on gender, sexuality and security in post-Apartheid South Africa.*

Design/methodology/approach — *The methodology includes secondary analysis of policy and research with the aim of highlighting and assessing the position of gender, sex and security in post-Apartheid South Africa. Feminist theory and intersectionality are used to discuss issues of sexuality, security, construction of gender relationships and experiences of being a woman in South Africa. The normalisation of violence against women is challenged.*

Social implications — *The social implications of this research are that it challenges normalisation of gendered violence, questions gendercide and produces knowledge of a gendered social reality of living in South Africa. Women who consider assault a regular feature of their sexual*

Gender and Race Matter: Global Perspectives on Being a Woman
Advances in Gender Research, Volume 21, 127–147
ISSN: 1529-2126/doi:10.1108/S1529-212620160000021008

*relationships have been brought into a discourse which includes the liberalisation of sexual expression, claims to new sexual rights and aspirations to power and status through sexual relationships (Posel, 2005a).*

Practical implications − *Throughout the chapter the* achievement of gender equality is *problematised and questioned. However, gender and the relationship between power and sex remain at the centre of the inquiry, particularly with reference to the increasing culture of violence and men as the perpetrators of violence against women.*

Originality/value − *According to Posel 'one of the most striking features of the post-apartheid era has been the politicization of sexuality' (2005a, p. 125) and this chapter demonstrates that a response to the violation of the Women's Charter of Effective Equality, passed in 2000, is a priority as women and families are disproportionately affected by violence in multiple ways.*

**Keywords:** Corrective rape; gender; post-apartheid South Africa; security; sexuality; violence

# INTRODUCTION

This chapter focuses on how sexuality in South Africa has created intense anxiety, controversy and confrontation. Posel (2005a, 2005b) argues that the liberalisation of sexual expression, and claims to new sexual rights and conditions of citizenship contribute to a struggle for power and status. This is especially true for women in the context of gender security because it simultaneously highlights difficult questions about the family, generational differences, social class and masculinity. These issues are directly linked to the meaning of 'freedom, the moral fibre of the new order and the manner of the national subject' (Posel, 2005a, p. 150). The concerns of the chapter are sexuality and gender security, and as such feminist theory and intersectionality will be drawn upon as analytical concepts. I argue that women's participation in policy making and in security issues plays an instrumental role in the 'achievement of human security' (Manchanda, 2001, p. 4100). Their experiences of conflict and security are different from those of men, and women tend to be more pacifist in their approach to conflict situations and negotiations. However, women's exclusion and isolation from security issues needs to be challenged as women tend to have more experience of and knowledge about discrimination and inequality (Manchanda, 2001, p. 4102). This was highlighted by Thandi Modise, MP, at a conference on Women and Violence[1] when she stated that 'at night I cannot walk down a street in Johannesburg. What does economic security mean when I cannot be sure what will happen to my home when I am away at work?' (Manchanda, 2001, p. 4102). Statistics show that South Africa has the highest rate of reported rape and sexual violence internationally. This country attempts to enforce a constitution of women's rights; however I am concerned as to whether men are responding to this enforcement through violence. In order to answer my concern this chapter positions women's, and other marginalised people's, lives at the centre of the research. As I read women's testimonies and narratives of struggles against oppressive patriarchal practices, I acknowledge the burden of inequalities whilst challenging assumptions about women, and then go on to interrogate the normalising of gendered violence that prevails in post-apartheid South Africa. My research shows that it is through the normalising and trivialising of violence against those considered to be 'legitimate targets of violence' (Collins, 2013, p. 35) that the continuance of violence and sustained abuse of those oppressed by inequalities of gender, sexuality, power and privilege is justified.

## GENDER, HISTORY AND APARTHEID

During apartheid when women were interrogated by the Security Branch they were called prostitutes and made to strip naked in front of policemen who made derogatory comments about their bodies, their fallopian tubes were filled with water and rats were inserted into their vaginas. A man who did not break under torture gained the respect of the police, but a woman's refusal to break under torture angered the torturers because 'a black meid,[2] kaffermeid at that, had no right to have the strength to withstand them' (Krog, 1999, p. 272). Moffett's contention that sexual violence is seen as a means of 'social stabilisation' (Moffett, 2006, p. 132) is evidenced in Krog's narrative of the treatment of women by the Security Branch. It was therefore appropriate that, in his Freedom Speech, Nelson Mandela paid tribute to the women who fought against apartheid, acknowledging that they were 'the rock-hard foundation of our struggle. Apartheid has inflicted more pain on you than on anyone else' (Mandela, 1990). The truth of this statement is reflected in the performance of sexually racialised lives during apartheid, which is still evident in sexual relations and sexual intimacy in post-apartheid South Africa where HIV/AIDS poses a human security threat. Sipho Mthathi has expressed the urgency of the situation by stating that 'in South Africa 600 people die as the result of HIV/AIDS every day. And those are not statistics, they are real lives of people that have been lost [...] Most of them are women, the majority of them black women, and the vast majority of them poor black women' (Sipho Mthathi,[3] cited in Jungar & Oinas, 2010, p. 182).

Although there has been a decline in political violence since the transition, violence against women is extraordinarily high in South Africa, resulting in '[The] Government host[ing] an on-going campaign to voice our anger against violence against women and children. We have to find ways of making our homes and communities safe for all, especially for women and children' (South Africa Government: www.gov.za). Feminist analysis of violence against women maintains that the high level of violence is an indication of a general devaluation and objectification of women (Vogelman & Eagle, 1991) and in South Africa this has become an increasingly visible and destabilising sign of South Africa's violent past (Britton, 2006).[4] The Human Rights Watch in 1995 highlighted the fact that although South Africa had progressive domestic violence legislation this was largely ineffective as women had minimal knowledge about it and that the judicial system was responsible for subjecting women to secondary victimisation (Matthews & Abrahams, 2001). Section 12 of the Constitution (post-apartheid) states that '[f]reedom and security of the person, which includes the right to be free from all forms of violence, either from public or private sources, and the right to bodily and psychological integrity, which includes the right to make decisions concerning reproduction' (Palmary, 2001, p. 4). The National Women's Coalition, formed in 1992, was instrumental in drawing up the Women's Charter for Effective Equality. Principles of the Charter pertinent to this chapter are two sections: family life, and partnerships and violence against women (Palmary, 2001). Ending women's oppression was high on the agenda of the democratically elected government in 1994 with women's groups lobbying to ensure that gender equality was a priority in an attempt to ensure women's political and civil citizenship in post-apartheid South Africa was guaranteed by the South African Constitution. However, this is not so. According to Lewis, Kuzawayo, and Ramphele (1999, p. 38) an ethos of equal rights for women is undercut by sexism, especially when combined with the ever present threat of rape, developing a society that is oriented towards 'male service' (Card, 1996, p. 7). In 2013 South Africa's President Jacob Zuma, in his State of the Nation Address (SONA), emphasised that there was an urgent need to improve the status of women in the country, adding that this was a priority for the government. In his speech he referred to the Women Empowerment and Gender Equality Bill (passed in 2014) which criminalised practices adversely affecting women and girls, calling for women to be equally represented in decision-making structures (Mofane, 2015).

The history of South Africa is one of violence and military conquests, which impacted severely on notions of identity and citizenship (De Klerk, 2010). The resultant colonial policies regarding Africa sexuality denied the gendered personhood and citizenship of indigenous Africans (Salo & Qgola, 2006). This is evident in the scientific and legal discourse which encouraged and supported the colonial discourses of binaries: white/black, male/female (Salo & Qgola, 2006). White men in the nineteenth century became voyeurs of black women's bodies which were displayed and exhibited at slave auctions and treated as pornography. White male fascination with the sexual parts of the Hottentot[5] female anatomy ghettoised Hottentot women and represented them as being objects of illicit sexual desire. Saartjie Baartman, who was paraded around Europe 'as a human curiosity under the appellation "The Hottentot Venus" until her death in 1816' (Warner, 2008, p. 181) is reminiscent of this treatment. Her dehumanisation as a sexual object, beast and monstrosity with extraordinary buttocks and genitalia titillated her audience, presenting her as 'a collection of sexual parts' (Gilman, 2010, p. 18) with an essentialised black sexuality (Magubane, 2010). Thabo Mbeki, former South African president, said in his speech at her funeral in South Africa in 2002[6] that her story is one of how an ancient freedom was lost, of how Africans had been reduced to objects which were owned, used and disposed of. Indeed, the inhumane treatment of Africans has a long history which represents intersecting oppressions, of pornography, sexuality, race and gender (Hill-Collins, 2000).

The apartheid era was characterised by violently enforced population movements, violent conflicts and insecurity. In 1910 the South African state was established with the Centre for African Affairs residing securely in the 'white controlled departmental bureaucracies at the Centre' (Glaser, 2001, p. 75). Parliament was being pressurised into acting on the 'native question' (Feinberg, 1993, p. 93). The result of this pressure was that J.W. Sauer introduced the Natives Land Bill into Parliament on 25 April 1913 which was rushed through Parliament (Feinberg, 1993) and General J.B. Herzog instigated The Black (or Natives) Land Act No. 27 of 1913 which represented 'the first key piece of territorial segregationist legislation' (Feinberg, 1993, p. 93). This repressive law was 'one of the most important segregation laws of the century' (Feinberg, 1993, p. 65) as it was the first time that territorial segregation was introduced into legislation since the Union in 1910. The Act had devastating consequences for Africans, severely restricting their right to ownership of land and movement into urban areas. The apartheid government used The Natives Urban Act of 1923, which was amended in 1930 to include new provisions that severely restricted African women's access to urban areas, to calm white fears about the white population being overrun by the African population and to control the fertility of African women (Posel, 2004). Section 10 of the Blacks (Urban Areas) Consolidation Act (No. 25 of 1945) stipulated that no Black person could remain for 'more than 72 hours in a [white] prescribed area unless he had obtained permission from the local labour bureau' (Hindson, 1985, p. 403).

The Reservation of Separate Amenities Act, Act No. 49 of 1953 which enforced the segregation of races, was introduced to quell the colonialist and Afrikaner anxieties around potential mixed race relationships. The primary aim of this Act was the prevention of contact between white and other race[7] groups, for example by posting signs on buildings stipulating different entrances for Black and White people. Sex and sexuality was subjected to severe censorship and policing. The Immorality Act of 1927 which prohibited sexual relations between a white and black person was amended in 1957 to include sexual relations between white and non-white persons (www.Justice.gov.za/legislation/acts/1957-023.pdf). To achieve the fundamental objective of the apartheid system, the preservation of 'white supremacy, purity' and the prevention of 'the sullying of the white body' (Posel, 2004, p. 54) led to fanatical policing and repression of black sexuality, making it imperative to police and regulate intimate sexual practices. There was a tendency for sexual anxiety and fear of sexual violence to be seen as essentially the enclave of white women (Shefer & Ratele, 2011), a fear that was exacerbated by leitmotif about the size of the black man's penis as being of extraordinary proportions, thereby reducing the black man to an object of threat both physically and politically (Shefer & Ratele, 2011). Apartheid's racialised power was especially gendered as it extended policing of intimate relations over black lives. Any sexual violation of a white woman by a black man was thought to be a violation not only of the white woman but also of the white nation − thereby reinforcing the concept of ownership of women (Shefer & Ratele, 2011). The policing of sexuality was draconian and extensive, criminalising homosexuality, using legislation to prohibit media from displaying images of sexuality and nudity, and banning pornography (Posel, 2005a, 2005b).

# SEX AND SEXUALITY IN THE
# POST-APARTHEID ERA

Post-apartheid, post-1994, a dramatic change has taken place. Sex and sexuality have found a new visibility and politicisation (Posel, 2005a, 2005b). The new Constitution of 1996 and the new Bill of Rights opened the way for radically revising the censorship laws and for sexual preference becoming a matter of right (Posel, 2005a, 2005b). Whereas once there was silence, now there was a new public discourse about sexual practice, sexual identity and violence. However, the status of women within post-apartheid society is questionable. Moffett (2006) states that the effects of racial hierarchies enforced during apartheid have significant consequences for women's experiences of gender-based and sexual violence regardless of the dismantling of apartheid's policies. Gender-based violence against women and girls has become both normative and excessively prevalent within a culture of violence that resists challenging as it is seen as one of the few ways in which men can assert their masculinity and resolve problems (Abrahams, Jewkes, Hoffman, & Laubsher, 2004; Abrahams, Martin, Mathews, Lombard, & Vetten, 2009). The lack of women challenging the culture of violence because of fear of rape and assault has serious consequences, for example the resultant reduction of female autonomy and personal safety combined with condoning men's violence impacts negatively on women's quality of life.

Mudhovozi, Ramarumo, and Sodi's (2012) study found that there was a high rate of teenage pregnancy. Abrahams et al. (2004) have argued that coercion and violence are used to force teenage girls into sexual submission. They are intimidated by the men and remain silent about their enforced sexual submission, which cannot be classified as rape because it is based on a form of 'consent'. Discussions about sexual intimacy are considered taboo and parents find it difficult to talk to their children about sex. This is in sharp contrast to what has always been practiced in African society, that is, adolescents are educated about sexuality. For example, Pedie children, through sharing the same room as their parents, become aware of the sexual activities of their parents and amongst the Zulu, puberty is marked by a rite of passage (Mudhovozi et al., 2012). The breakdown of extended families, accompanied by the decline of traditional sources of authority and a loss of significant rituals, has resulted in silence regarding sex education. This results in a lack of preparation for adult life, especially for women. Research shows that mothers found it difficult to talk to their teenage daughters about sexuality as they feared making them aware of sexual ideas would encourage sexual activity (Mudhovozi et al., 2012). Due to the taboo surrounding sex and sexuality, parents tend to deny the possibility of youth sexuality or even that their own children (particularly girls) are sexually active. This results in a lack of knowledge about protection against sexually transmitted diseases and pregnancy. The refusal to discuss issues related to sexual health can be interpreted as a failure on the part of the parents 'to respect the rights of the child and to protect their sexual health' (Campbell, Nair, & Maimane, 2006). Indeed, Leclerc-Madlala's study showed that women were '"demonised" in the context of HIV/AIDS' (2002, p. 2) by being thought of as 'dirty' and 'out of control' (similar to the treatment of the 'Hottentot Venus'). The negative moralistic attitude towards women is linked to the perceived weakness of women sexually, in that they are unable to resist, and therefore promiscuous, which makes them responsible for the HIV/AIDS epidemic. The gendered dimension of HIV/AIDS is evident in the statistics. Young African women between the ages of 15 and 19 are four to six times more likely to be HIV-positive than young men of the same age. Indeed women tend to be more easily infected with HIV and this has a devastating impact in their lives (O'Sullivan, 2000). Their vulnerability to violence and HIV infection increases when they are married to polygamous and often older men, that is, they are rendered powerless (Abrahams et al., 2004).

Research exploring the negotiation of heterosex showed that 'a central discourse framing male sexuality [...] is central to the construction of male and female sexuality' (Shefer & Foster, 2001, p. 377). The discourse emphasises that sex is inherently masculine and dominated by uncontrollable biological urges, which rationalises male infidelity (Cily, 2010, p. 21; Shefer & Foster, 2001). Sexuality plays an important role in the social construction of masculine behaviours demanding sexual debut at an early age (14 years), which is a significant determinant of HIV infection[8] (Khangelani et al., 2010). For women, the discourse emphasised control of their physical desires and that in order to explore their sexuality they needed the safety of a committed relationship (Shefer & Foster, 2001). This discourse constructs men as being active and women passive in heterosex. Implicit in this discourse is the assumption that women can make independent decisions, thereby ignoring the power dynamics that structure heterosexual relations (Wood & Jewkes, 1997).

Sexuality and gender power relations reveal how men socially and culturally understand themselves and their relations to women. Research has shown that both men and women endorsed gender attitudes which represent women as submissive and passive. Nearly all men and women interviewed were of the opinion that women should be obedient to their husbands (Kalichman et al., 2005). Lacking structural employment and not having social standing means that many men tend to favour a masculine identity which is often based on violence and criminality. According to the Centre for the Study of Violence and Reconciliation (CSVR, 2009), this is associated with ideas of ownership and objectification of women which 'legitimises' sexual violence. One way to reaffirm male sexuality is through multiple sexual relationships with women. The result is positive for a man because he can then be referred to as a 'real man' (*ingagara*) in comparison to *being* called '*isithipa*', a man without many girlfriends (Juma & Klot, 2011). Varga's study in Durban reinforces the discourse that for men sex was a means of establishing power within a relationship, that is, 'to show that you control the relationship, you must be able to show your friends that you have slept with her' (Varga, 1997, p. 55). In this study most young women corroborated the necessity of having sexual intercourse to demonstrate love and commitment. It can be seen that powerful discourses place women in subordinate roles, resulting in loss of personal control in sexual relationships (Kalichman et al., 2005).

## MASCULINITY, VIOLENCE AND HIV STATUS

Lorna Mlosana and Nonvava, both HIV activists, decided not to go home after an end of year party but to visit a shebeen.[9] As she was leaving, Lorna was cornered and gang-raped by eight men. After being raped Lorna asked the men, 'I am HIV-positive. How could you do this to me?' (Orford, 2006, p. 72). The rapists were angered when they realised that they might now be infected with the virus and took their revenge on Nomvava, whom they physically assaulted by striking her head against the bonnet of a car. Nomvava was saved only by being rushed to hospital, however Lorna died. The silence surrounding this atrocity is due to intimidation of witnesses and is similar to the silencing of women such as Nomvava by community members (Orford, 2006). The blame culture used by men against women for infecting them with HIV/AIDS can be seen as a narrative for many relationships. It usually results in the man leaving the house into which HIV/AIDS has been introduced: the saying, '*le ndoda thalekile*' (this man, he ran away) sums up the behaviour of men (Brummer, 2012a, p. 27). There is also another complexity involved in sexual relationships – the acceptance of polygamy and refusal to use condoms which has contributed to the increasing high rates of HIV infection in South Africa.[10]

Mankayi's study (2008) demonstrates that the ruling masculinity in South Africa has embodied assertive heterosexuality, control of economic decisions both inside and outside the home, political authority, cultural dominance and support for male promiscuity (Ratele, 2006). With reference to promiscuity, the men in this study used animalistic terms to describe their sex drive.[11] A consequence of male promiscuity, which includes unprotected sex, is usually discovered by the woman on her first visit to the antenatal clinic after she has taken the HIV test. If she is HIV-positive she is enroled on the Prevention of Mother-to-child Transmission (PMTCT) programme to prevent the virus infecting the foetus. Despite the severity of the situation, the fear of abandonment and being left with sole responsibility for her children results in her not telling her partner about her HIV status. According to research by Mfecane (2012) in Bushbruckridge, Mpumalanga, men tended to test for HIV only when they were very ill and had physical symptoms because they felt that 'real men' sorted out their own problems. Due to the stigma attached to HIV-positive status, even when they were diagnosed men kept silent and continued having sexual relations with women. Infecting women with HIV can be regarded as a form of sexual violence which relies on women's fear of abandonment and an understanding of femininity which includes tolerance of male promiscuity and unprotected sex (Brummer, 2012b, p. 38).

## SEXUAL VIOLENCE

Sexual violence is defined by the World Health Organisation as being 'any sexual act, attempt to obtain a sexual act, unwanted sexual comments or advances, or acts to traffic, or otherwise directed, against a person's sexuality using coercion, by any person regardless of their relationship to the victim, in any setting, including but not limited to home and work' (Krug, Dahlberg, Mercy, Zwi, & Lozano, 2002, p. 149). Sexual violence and assault takes place in private, workplace and public spheres. Workplace and public spheres are becoming more dangerous and insecure for women and girls because few organisations and institutions have clear guidelines or policies that deal with sexual harassment and sexual violence (Tiemoko, 2004, p. 3). The home, once a place of safety, has become a place where 'burglary is accompanied by rape of women and girls' (Okumu, 2004, p. 8). The Sexual Offences Act passed in December 2007 provides a new definition of rape in section 3, which specifies that '[a]ny person ('A') who unlawfully and intentionally commits an act of sexual penetration with a complainant ('B') without the consent of B, is guilty of the offence of rape'.[12]

Rape is one the most under-reported of the serious violent crimes and the Commission on Gender Equality Annual Report (2000) questions whether enough effort has been expended in making rights on paper a reality for women. There are also many taboos surrounding rape, such as self-blame and fear of threats and reprisals against the woman, her family and secondary victimisation experienced in the criminal justice system. Therefore, 'many women will only try to report to the police incidents which fall within popular notions of "rape" because of fear of not being believed' (Jewkes & Abrahams, 2002, p. 1232). An example of secondary victimisation was when Judge Foxcroft awarded a lighter sentence to a father because his rape victim was his daughter and he had 'kept the rape in the family' (*State v. A SS.9/99C PD* in Samuel, 2001, p. 21). Women who have been raped or physically attacked in shebeens in urban South African townships are generally denied aid, with the reasoning being that women who accept drinks from men owe them sexual favours. About 8 per cent of rapes result in murder and one-third of the rape cases reported to the police in the Western Cape are committed by more than one perpetrator. According to Sam Waterhouse, Advocacy Co-ordinator for Rape Crisis, 'rape and especially gang rape is an extreme expression of male sexual entitlement over women and is used to control women either directly or indirectly' (cited in Orford, 2006, p. 78). The threat of gang rape perpetuates fear which gives rapists control over women in the community and allows them to punish those who do not conform to expectations. Gang rape is a trend particularly associated with groups of young men jackrolling[13] in order to put women, who were thought of as being snobbish, in their place (Wood, 2005). A convicted rapist, Dumisani Rebombo, admitted that he committed the rape of a young woman living in his village when he was 15 because of a need to be accepted and to prove that he was a boy. This indicates that boys are socialised to think that they are able to do whatever they wish to women (Jecks, 2009).

Kaufman (1997, p. 40) argues that men's violence towards women 'is probably the clearest, most straightforward expression of relative male and female power.' The othering and objectification of women results in violence which is used by men to reaffirm their masculinity, that is, to cope with their feelings of powerlessness and negative self-image (Kaufman, 1997). Walker's research (with the organisation Men for Change) with young men in Alexandra, a township in Johannesburg, revealed that men felt anxious and were threatened by 'women's improved status and their perception that woman have attained equality' (Walker, 2005, p. 168). Women were, therefore, regarded as the enemy, able to provide for themselves, confident and taking over roles previously viewed as men's roles. Furthermore, by making a link between rape and the history of apartheid, Moffett (2006) argues that discourses tend to sound like excuses. In a study conducted in 2005 on sexual violence in Cape Town, it was reported that over 40 per cent of women had experienced at least one sexual assault, and that 'more than one in five men openly admitted to having perpetrated sexual assault against women' (Kalichman et al., 2005, pp. 299–305).

Within the framework of gendered violence intimate partner violence is the most common form, which in the most extreme circumstances results in death, accounting for 57 per cent of female homicides in 2009, five times higher than the global average (Vetten, 2014). Intimate partner violence is included in the broad term domestic, which includes child abuse, elder abuse and violence between siblings. The term takes into account physical, economic, emotional, verbal and psychological abuse, and any other controlling behaviour such as intimidation, harassment, stalking, damage to property and entering the victim's home without permission (Vetten, 2014). In 1993 the Prevention of Family Violence Act was introduced to deal with domestic violence and was followed by the Domestic Violence Act of 1998, 'which is widely considered one of the more progressive examples of such legislation internationally' (Vetten, 2014, p. 1). Since the introduction of this Act women have been the major applicants for protection orders. However, victims are also as dependent on protection by the courts as they are on the police. The low number of protection orders made final is attributed to the women's failure to return to court due to them dropping charges against abusive partners. A variety of reasons have been cited regarding the charges being dropped, which include that the respondent had promised to stop the abuse, male partners had begged them not to go back and finalise the order, and family members persuaded the women to drop charges. Some women stated that they faced further violence if they returned to court and some commented that the abuse worsened (Vetten, 2014).

## HOMOSEXUALITY AND VIOLENCE

In spite of the terms of the Constitution, which explicitly includes sexual orientation as a prohibited ground for discrimination, lesbian, gay, bisexual and transgender (LGBT) people are targets of general violence and crime. They are stigmatised for being perceived as sexual and/or gender deviants and frequently discriminated against through misunderstandings of their sexual orientation and/or gender identity. According to a 13-year-old girl, a victim of corrective rape in Pretoria, her assailant told her he was 'curing' her of lesbianism (Brown, 2012). In South Africa the rate of sexual violence is high, which has impacted negatively on the lives of women and men. The highest rates of rape are of male rape of women; however there is a significant rate of male rape of males which brings the discussion around to homosexuality and lesbianism in South Africa (Jewkes et al., 2006).

Sigamoney and Epprecht's research highlights the prejudice associated with the phrase 'homosexuality is un-African' (2013, p. 83) or that 'it is just a fashion to be gay or lesbian' (2013, p. 83), a comment which relates to a view expressed by an ANC spokesperson who dismissed the rights-based claims of lesbians and gays as homosexuality being a trend which was fashionable in the West. When the participants in Sigamoney and Epprecht's research were asked about the term 'homosexual' their replies were: 'It is the first time I am hearing this word' or 'people whose hormones make them "horny" and who like a lot of sex', 'I think a homosexual person is a person who has two private parts' (2013, pp. 88–89). The responses suggest the promiscuous behaviour amongst heterosexual men is projected onto homosexuals and lesbians. As a result LGBT people are often discriminated against; however, violence is not experienced equally within this 'group'. The LGBT 'group' is fractured along lines of class, race and gender, with women from low socio-economic backgrounds being more susceptible to rape, domestic violence and child abuse (Nel & Judge, 2008).

Further to this, the politics surrounding lesbian sexuality and poverty intersect with masculine behaviour. Similar to heterosexual men, Sowetan lesbians, according to Swarr and Nagar (2003), tend to use masculinity strategically in order to assert their agency, to claim masculine privileges and to declare that they desire relationships with women. Butchness may enable some Sowetan lesbians to achieve social power despite living in impoverished conditions, being subjected to violence, and experiencing the racism of apartheid and colonialism. Furthermore Swarr (2012) states that this visibility through their embodied masculinity may result in their vulnerability to violence, which affects how lesbians negotiate their environments specifically to maintain their safety (Swarr & Nagar, 2003). They need to be constantly aware of their environments and, through the negotiation of their identities, try to balance being known as a lesbian or maintaining their secrecy (Swarr, 2012; Swarr & Nagar, 2003). Despite exhibiting agency, there have been cases of 'corrective rape' to teach lesbians how to be 'real women'. 'Corrective rape' is used by men to 'correct' undesirable alternative forms of sexuality and to force people to conform to gender stereotypes perpetuated by patriarchal male domination (Mwambene & Wheal, 2015, p. 58). Communities are ambivalent and will not condemn the rapist's actions outright. A report by Actionaid (2009) highlights the fact that crimes against lesbians are unrecognised by the state and unpunished by the legal system. Eudy Simelane, a former member of the South African national football squad Banyana Banyana, was openly gay. She was viciously attacked, gang-raped, brutally beaten and stabbed 25 times in her chest, legs and face. Her partially clothed body was found in a creek in a park in Kwa Themba on the outskirts of Johannesburg. Her death provoked public outrage and disgust. Harrison (2009), writing for Reuters, says that the murder of Eudy Simelane 'brought homophobic violence, especially towards women, to the fore.' Her mother said that she feared for her daughter's life but 'never imagined her life would be taken in such a way' (Kelly, 2009). In February 2009, one man pleaded guilty to rape and murder and was sentenced to 32 years in jail while three other men pleaded not guilty. The judge said that the accused had shown no remorse and had maintained he was not to blame for the death of Eudy Simelane. The judge made a statement saying that Eudy's sexual orientation played no significant part in her death, thereby reinforcing the government's evasion of dealing with 'corrective' rape (Martin, Kelly, Turquet, & Ross, 2009, p. 6).

In addition to being subjected to 'corrective' rape, lesbians are ostracised and disowned by their families, resulting in dislocation, depression and non-belonging. They are subjected to everyday abuse that tells them that they deserve to be raped, and that if they are they will become straight (Martin et al., 2009, p. 7). Furthermore, communities ignore the plight of lesbians and have been shown to condone sexual violence because 'any deviation from the traditional constructions of masculinity and femininity aligned with African patriarchy is not acceptable' (Reddy, 2001, p. 83). Same-sex relationships are seen to contradict the model of an African family as being heteronormative. Indeed African womanhood is measured by having children. However, there is an anomaly because if a woman has a husband or boyfriend and children, yet keeps her same-sex relationship secret then that woman could still be considered an 'African woman' (Sigamoney & Epprecht, 2013, p. 101).

Lesbians in South Africa are further victimised by homophobic police officers who are lax in their investigations of sexual violence (Bucher, 2010). 'Corrective' rape therefore is legitimised through a discourse that demonises lesbians and sees them as powerful and dangerous and therefore needing to be subjugated to the dominant heterosexual norm by men (Moffett, 2006, p. 137). There tends to be an assumption that same-sex sexuality is a criminal offence which is punishable by both the formal and informal justice systems: 'The more severe the punishment, the more of a deterrent it was thought to be' (Sigamoney & Epprecht, 2013, p. 97). Despite the Constitution protecting both lesbians and gays and promoting the legalisation of same-sex marriage, there is widespread support for same-sex relations to be *umholo* (forbidden) (Sigamoney & Epprecht, 2013, p. 99).

The first case of homophobic violence to gain prominence was the murder of 19 year old Zoliswa Nkonyana who was walking down a street in a Cape Flats township with her partner. She was surrounded by a mob of 20 youths, clubbed, stoned and beaten to death on 4 February 2006 (Marks, 2006). It took at least two weeks for the media to report her murder. Nine men were accused of her murder and to date none of them have been sentenced, with the trial delayed 32 times (Middleton, 2011). This occurred in spite of South Africa's constitutional protection against discrimination. Human rights are a fundamental right of every human being, regardless of culture or societal norms. Corrective Rape is not being covered by editors in South Africa because the level of crime is so high that there is not much public interest in a lesbian who has been raped in the township (McCabe, 2010). There is a movement by activists and organisations such as Lulekisiwze against corrective rape, demanding that the government classify lesbian rape as a hate crime. Lulekisiwze started a petition which was signed by 150,000 people, however Justice Minister Jeffrey Thamsanqa Radebe responded by saying that motive crimes such as lesbian rape are irrelevant (Robertson, 2011).

# CONCLUSION

This chapter has shown that gender security is something that needs to be fought for in South Africa. With alarmingly high rates of reported rape and sexual violence, the government is facing a very difficult dilemma of how to achieve gender equality in a country that has experienced years of oppression, discrimination and racism. During the years of the struggle for liberation the fight for gender equality was marginalised. President Mandela acknowledged this in his speech when he opened the first democratically elected government in April 1994. He clearly stated that freedom can only be achieved once women have been freed from all oppression (Manjoo, 2005, p. 2). Regardless of the Women's Charter, one of the most progressive Constitutions prohibiting discrimination based on sexual orientation, and the Equality Act passed in 2000 (including hate crimes), gay and lesbian people in post-apartheid South Africa are still extremely vulnerable to violent attacks and are generally unprotected by society's justice system. Women are being actively denied their rights as members of a democratic country and the failure of police to prosecute perpetrators of 'corrective rape' demonstrates that they are not interested in solving hate crimes of a sexual nature. The issues of homosexuality and security raise important and difficult questions about the family, gender, masculinity and femininity which have to be contextualised in a situation where HIV/AIDS rates are high. Sexual violence against lesbians has been shown to be normalised and trivialised − they are considered 'legitimate' targets (Collins, 2013, p. 35). The high levels of violence and abuse of women have stark implications for social responsibility and policy making in South Africa. In the past, apartheid wounded many people yet men are now turning to deliberately wounding women in a silent cycle of hate. The evidence above highlights how far women in South Africa are from achieving Mandela's goal of being freed from all oppression.

# NOTES

1. Conference on 'Women and Violence: Global Perspectives' International Alert, London April 1999.
2. Meid is a derogatory term for woman.
3. Activist and the Treatment Action Campaign's (TAC) General Secretary.
4. Over three quarters (77%) of women in Limpopo; 51% of women in Gauteng; 45% of women in the Western Cape and 36% of women in KwaZulu Natal report experiencing some form of violence (emotional, economic, physical or sexual) at least once in their lifetime both within and outside their intimate relationships (http://www.genderlinks.org.za/article/the-warhome-findings-of-the-gbv-prevalence-study-in-south-africa-2012-11-25).

5. Hottentot is a pejorative term and used by the Europeans when referring to the Khoisan People.

6. In 1994 President Nelson Mandela met with French President Mitterrand and requested that Baartman's remains be repatriated. In 2002 her remains were returned to South Africa (Warner, 2008, pp. 185–186) where a formal funeral was held.

7. The Population Registration Act of 1950 provided the basic framework for apartheid by classifying all South Africans by race, including Bantu (black Africans), Coloured (mixed race) and white. A fourth category, Asian (meaning Indian and Pakistani) was later added (http://www.history.com/topics/apartheid).

8. This early sexual debut is 'associated with increased likelihood of risky sexual behaviour later in life' (Khangelani et al., 2010, p. 48).

9. A shebeen is an unlicensed drinking place, providing beer, music and dance. They are usually found in the townships, such as Soweto, in South Africa. Initially most shebeens were run by women known as Shebeen Queens.

10. According to research by Brummer (2012b, p. 35) 'Xhosa people don't like it if girls tell them they have HIV'.

11. This view is reflected in Daniel's (one of the respondent's) response that men want a lot of sex and that 'If we had our own way, we'd just like to have sex with a woman. Then two or more nights later [...] have sex with another woman' (Ratele, 2006, p. 51).

12. The Criminal Law (Sexual Offences and Related Matters) Act, 32 of 2007 was signed into law by President Thabo Mbeki on 16 December 2007.

13. Jackrolling is a form of gang rape.

# REFERENCES

Abrahams, N., Jewkes, R., Hoffman, M., & Laubsher, R. (2004). Sexual violence against intimate partners in Cape Town: Prevalence and risk factors reported by men. *Bulletin of the World Health Organization*, *82*(5), 330–337.

Abrahams, N., Martin, R., Mathews, L. J., Lombard, C., & Vetten, L. (2009). Mortality of women from intimate partner violence in South Africa: A national epidemiological study. *Journal of Violence and Victims*, *24*, 546–556.

Actionaid. (2009). *Hate crimes: The rise of 'corrective' rape in South Africa*. Retrieved from http://www.actionaid.org.uk/101756/hate_crimes_the_rise_of_corrective_rape_in_south_africa.html. Accessed on October 27, 2010.

Britton, H. (2006). Organising against gender violence in South Africa. *Journal of Southern African Studies*, *32*(1), 145–163.

Brown, R. (2012). Corrective rape in South Africa: A continuing plight despite an international human rights response. *Annual Survey of International and Comparative Law*, *18*(1), 45–66.

Brummer, W. (2012a). Where have all the fathers gone? In M. Meyer & H. Struthers (Eds.), *(Un)covering men: Rewriting masculinity and health in South Africa* (pp. 27–28). Auckland Park: Jacana (Pty) Ltd.

Brummer, W. (2012b). Hush brother there goes a real man. In M. Meyer & H. Struthers (Eds.), *(Un)covering men: Rewriting masculinity and health in South Africa* (pp. 34–40). Auckland Park: Jacana (Pty) Ltd.

Bucher, N. (2010). *Law failing lesbians on 'corrective rape'*. Retrieved from http://ipsnews.net/ africa/nota.asp?idnews=48279. Accessed on October 27, 2010.

Campbell, C., Nair, Y., & Maimane, S. (2006). AIDS stigma, sexual moralities and the policing of women and youth in South Africa. *Feminist Review (Special Edition on Sexual Moralities), 83*, 132–138.

Card, C. (1996). Rape as a weapon of war. Hypatia (Women and Violence), *11*(4), 5–18.

Centre for the Study of Violence and Reconciliation [CSVR]. (2009). *Why does South Africa have such high rates of violent crime?* Johannesburg: CSVR. Retrieved from http://www. csvr.org.za/docs/study/7.unique_about_SA.pdf. Accessed on October 27, 2010.

Cily, T. (2010). *Cultural practices (e.g. polygamy) prevent the spread of HIV and AIDS among the Botswana people of Botswana*. Pretoria: Human Science Research Council. Retrieved from http://www.hsrc.ac.za/research/output/outputDocuments/6356. Accessed on October 27, 2010.

Collins, L. A. (2013). Realisation or oversight of a constitutional mandate? Corrective rape of black African lesbians in South Africa. *SA Crime Quarterly, 43*(1), 29–37.

Commission on Gender Equality [CGE]. (2000). *Commission on gender equality: A framework for transforming gender relations in South Africa: Annual Report*. Retrieved from http:// www.gov.za/sites/www.gov.za/files/transformation_0.pdf. Accessed October 27, 2010.

De Klerk, L. M. (2010). *Democracy and the people: Gender and security in post conflict South Africa*. Retrieved from http://www.moot.org.uk/pdf/conference-democracy-23062010-De-Klerk.pdf. Accessed on January 14, 2016.

Feinberg, H. (1993). The 1913 natives land act in South Africa: Politics, race, and segregation in the early 20th century. *International Journal of African Historical Studies, 26*(1), 65–109.

Gilman, S. (2010). The Hottentot and the prostitute: Towards an iconography of female sexuality. In D. Willis (Ed.), *Black venus 2010: They called her 'hottentot'* (pp. 15–31). Philadelphia, PA: New Temple.

Glaser, D. (2001). *Politics and society in South Africa: A critical introduction*. London: Sage.

Harrison, R. (2009). *South African gangs use rape to 'cure' lesbians*. Retrieved from http:// www.reuters.com/article/2009/03/13/us-safrica-rape-lesbian-idUSTRE52C3MN20090313. Accessed on February 10, 2015.

Hill-Collins, P. (2000). *Black feminist thought: Knowledge, consciousness, and the politics of empowerment* (2nd ed.). Boston, MA: Unwin Hyman.

Hindson, D. C. (1985). Orderly urbanisation and influx control. *Cahiers d'Etudes Africaines, 25*(99), 401–432.

Jecks, N. (2009). *Tackling South Africa's rape epidemic*. Retrieved from http://news.bbc.co.uk/ 1/hi/world/africa/8171874.stm. Accessed on February 2, 2010.

Jewkes, R. I., & Abrahams, N. (2002). The epidemiology of rape and sexual coercion in South Africa: An overview. *Social Science and Medicine, 55*(7), 1231–1244.

Jewkes, R. I., Dunkle, K., Koss, M. P., Levin, J. B., Nduna, M., Nwabisa, J., & Sikweyiya, Y. (2006). Rape perpetration by young, rural South African men: Prevalence, patterns and risk factors. *Social Science and Medicine, 63*(11), 2949–2961. Retrieved from http:// www.sciencedirect.com/science/article/pii/S0277953606003832. Accessed on April4, 2014.

Juma, M., & Klot, J. (Eds.). (2011). *HIV/AIDS, gender, human security, and violence in Southern Africa*. Pretoria: Africa Institute of South Africa.

Jungar, K., & Oinas, E. (2010). A feminist struggle? South African HIV activism as feminist politics. *Journal of International Women's Studies, 11*(4), 177–191.

Kalichman, S. C., Simbayi, L. C., Kaufman, M., Cain, D., Cherry, C., Jooste, S., & Mathiti, V. (2005). Gender attitudes, sexual violence, and HIV/AIDS risks among men and women in Cape Town, South Africa. *The Journal of Sex Research, 42*(4), 299–305.

Kaufman, M. (1997). The construction of men's masculinity and the triad of men's violence. In L. O'Toole & R. Schiffman (Eds.), *Gender violence: Interdisciplinary perspectives* (pp. 30–51). New York, NY: New York University Press.

Kelly, A. (2009). *Raped and killed for being a lesbian: South Africa ignores 'corrective' attacks.* Retrieved from http://www.guardian.co.uk/world/2009/mar/12/eudy-simelane-corrective-rape-south-africa. Accessed on October 12, 2010.

Khangelani, Z., Setswe, G., Ketye, T., Mzolo, T., Rehle, T., & Mbelle, N. (2010). Age at sexual debut: A determinant of multiple partnership among South African youth. *African Journal of Reproductive Health, 14*(2), 46–54.

Krog, A. (1999). *Country of my skull.* London: Vintage.

Krug, E. G., Dahlberg, L. L., Mercy, J. A., Zwi, A. B., & Lozano, R. (Eds.). (2002). *World report on violence and health.* Geneva: World Health Organization.

Leclerc-Madlala, S. (2002). On the virgin cleansing myth: Gendered bodies. AIDS and Ethnomedicine. *African Journal of AIDS Research, 1*, 87–95.

Lewis, D., Kuzawayo, E., & Ramphele, M. (1999). Myths and citizenship in two autobiographies by South African women. *Agenda, 15*(40), 38–44.

Magubane, Z. (2010). Which bodies matter? Feminism, post-structuralism, race and the curious odyssey of the 'Hottentot Venus'. In D. Willis (Ed.), *Black venus 2010: They called her 'Hottentot'* (pp. 47–61). Pennsylvania, PA: Temple University Press.

Manchanda, R. (Ed.). (2001). *Women, war and peace in South Asia: Beyond victimhood to agency.* New Delhi: Sage.

Mandela, N. (1990). *Nelson Mandela's address to a rally in Cape Town on his release from prison.* Retrieved from http://www.anc.org.za/show.php?id = 4520. Accessed on May 20, 2015.

Mandela, N. (1994). *Statement of Nelson Mandela at his inauguration as president.* Retrieved from http://www.anc.org.za/show.php?id = 3132. Accessed on October 28, 2015.

Manjoo, R. (2005). Case study: The commission for gender equality South Africa. *Griffith Law Review, 14*(2), 263–279.

Mankayi, N. (2008). Morality and sexual rights: Constructions of masculinity. *Culture, Health and Sexuality, 10*(6), 625–634.

Marks, S. M. (2006). Global recognition of human rights for lesbian, gay, bisexual, and transgender people. *Health and Human Rights, 9*(1), 33–42.

Martin, A., Kelly, A., Turquet, L., & Ross, S. (2009). *The rise of corrective rape in South Africa.* Retrieved from http://www.actionaid.org.uk/doc_lib/correctiveraperep_final.pdf. Accessed on September 17, 2010.

Matthews, S., & Abrahams, N. (2001). *Combining stories and numbers: An analysis of the Domestic Violence Act (no 116 of 1998) on women.* Pretoria: Gender Advocacy Project and Medical Research Council.

McCabe, J. (2010). *Samira Ahmed, behind the scenes with C4 News.* Retrieved from http://www.thefword.org.uk/blog/2010/03/samira_ahmed_be. Accessed on October 10, 2010.

Mfecane, S. (2012). Narratives of HIV disclosure and masculinity in a South African village. *Culture, Health & Sexuality: An International Journal for Research, Intervention and Care.* 14(Suppl. 1), doi:10.1080/13691058.2011.647081

Middleton, L. (2011). 'Corrective rape': Fighting a South African scourge. Retrieved from http://www.time.com/time/world/article/0,8599,2057744,00.html. Accessed on March 10, 2011.

Mofane, R. (2015). Preventing violence against women: All talk and no action. Retrieved from http://vc.bridgew.edu/jiws/vol11/iss4/13. Accessed on May 15, 2015.

Moffett, H. (2006). 'These women, they force us to rape them': Rape as a narrative of social control in post-apartheid South Africa. Journal of Southern African Studies. Women and the Politics of Gender in Southern Africa, 32(1), 129–142.

Mudhovozi, P., Ramarumo, M., & Sodi, T. (2012). Adolescent sexuality and culture: South African mothers' perspective. Adolescent Sexuality and Culture, 16(2), 119–138.

Mwambene, L., & Wheal, M. (2015). Realisation or oversight of a constitutional mandate? Corrective rape of black African lesbians in South Africa. African Human Rights Law Journal, 15(1), 59–88.

Nel, J. A., & Judge, M. (2008). Exploring homophobic victimisation in Gauteng, South Africa: Issues, impacts and responses. Acta Criminologica, 21(3), 19–36.

O'Sullivan, S. (2000). Uniting across global boundaries – HIV-positive women in global perspective. Agenda, 44, 25–31.

Okumu, M. (2004). The critical issues: Gender based violence in Africa. Sexuality in Africa Magazine, 1(3), 7–8.

Orford, M. (2006). The deadly cost of breaking the silence: A tribute to Lorna Mlasana. Feminist Africa, 6, 77–82.

Palmary, I. (2001). Social crime prevention in South Africa's major cities. Johannesburg: Centre for the Study of Violence and Reconciliation. Retrieved from http://www.csvr.org.za/wits/papers/papalm2.htm. Accessed on May 26, 2015.

Posel, D. (2004). Sex, death and embodiment: Reflections on the stigma of AIDS in Agincourt, South Africa, Conference Paper, WISER Symposium, Johannesburg, 14–16 October.

Posel, D. (2005a). Sex, death and the fate of the nation: Reflections on the politicization of sexuality in post-apartheid South Africa. Africa: Journal of the International African Institute, 75(2), 125–153.

Posel, D. (2005b). 'Baby rape': Unmaking secrets of sexual violence in post-apartheid South Africa. In G. Reid & L. Walker (Eds.), Men behaving differently. South African men since 1994. Wetton: Double-Story Books.

Ratele, K. (2006). Ruling masculinity and sexuality. Feminist Africa, 6(6), 48–64.

Reddy, V. (2001). Homophobia, human rights and gay and lesbian equality in Africa. Agenda, African Feminisms One, 50, 3–86.

Robertson, D. (2011, January 24). South African lesbians targeted for rape and violence. Retrieved from http://www.voanews.com/english/news/africa/South-African-Lesbians-Targeted-for-Rape-and-Violence-114495619.html. Accessed on March 9, 2011.

Salo, E., & Qgola, P. D. (2006). Editorial: Subaltern sexualities. Feminist Africa, 6, 1–6.

Samuel, S. (2001). Achieving equality: How far have women come? Agenda, 47, 21–33.

Shefer, T., & Foster, D. (2001). Discourses on women's (hetero)sexuality and desire in a South African local context. Culture, Health and Sexuality, 3(4), 375–390.

Shefer, T., & Ratele, K. (2011). Racist sexualisation and sexualised racism in narratives on apartheid. Psychoanalysis, Culture and Society, 16(1), 27–48.

Sigamoney, V., & Epprecht, M. (2013). Meanings of homosexuality, same-sex sexuality, and Africanness in two South African townships: An evidence-based approach for rethinking same-sex prejudice. African Studies Review, 56(2), 83–107.

Strudwick, P. (2015, May 31st). *Crisis in South Africa: The shocking practice of 'corrective rape' — aimed at 'curing' lesbians.* Retrieved from http://www.independent.co.uk/news/ world/africa/crisis-in-south-africa-the-shocking-practice-of-corrective-rape–aimed-at-curing-lesbians-9033224.html. Accessed on May 29, 2015.

Swarr, A. L. (2012). Paradoxes of butchness: Lesbian masculinities and sexual violence in contemporary South Africa. *Signs: Journal of Women in Culture and Society, 37*, 961—988.

Swarr, A. L., & Nagar, R. (2003). Dismantling assumptions: Interrogating 'lesbian' struggles for identity and survival in India and South Africa. *Signs: Journal of Women in Culture and Society, 29*, 491—516.

Tiemoko, R. (2004). Belief, culture and sexual pleasure in Africa. *Sexuality in Africa, 3*(3), 3.

Varga, C. A. (1997). Sexual decision-making and negotiation in the midst of AIDS: Youth in KwaZulu/Natal, South Africa. *Health Transition Review, 7*(Suppl. 3), 45—67.

Vetten, L. (2014). Rape and other forms of sexual violence in South Africa. *Institute for Security Studies. Policy Brief, 72*, 1—8.

Vogelman, L., & Eagle, G. (1991). Overcoming endemic violence against women in South Africa. *Social Justice, 8*(1—2), 209—229.

Walker, L. (2005). Negotiating the boundaries of masculinity in post-apartheid South Africa. In G. Reid & L. Walker (Eds.), *Men behaving differently. South African men since 1994*. Wetton. Double-Story Books.

Warner, S. L. (2008). Suzan-Lori Parks's drama of disinterment: A transnational exploration of venus. *Theatre Journal, 60*(2), 181—199.

Wood, K. (2005). Contextualizing group rape in post-Apartheid South Africa. *Culture, Health & Sexuality, 7*(4), 303—317.

Wood, K., & Jewkes, R. (1997). Violence, rape and sexual coercion: Everyday love in South Africa. *Gender and Development, 5*(2), 41—46.

# PART III
# WOMEN'S BODIES, NATION AND PERFORMANCE

# AGENCY, RESISTANCE AND SUBVERSION: VOICES IN THE FIELD

Jaya Gajparia

## ABSTRACT

Purpose — *Historically, as a result of complex intersections of marginalisation, women and girls in India are known to have had less access to economic and social capital than men and boys. Progress on poverty alleviation and the advancement of women's and girls' development continues to be slow and has even been described as 'regressive' (UN Women, 2015). This chapter provides a microanalysis of experiences and perceptions of gender and poverty in Mumbai, India. It puts forward new insights into everyday forms of agency, resistance and subversion while confronting western centric ideas around development and colonialist notions of victimhood.*

Design/methodology/approach — *Based upon research conducted in 2012–2013, the qualitative study adopting a multi-methods approach draws on participatory action research, participant observation and ethnography. This chapter draws on a small number of interviews from the original sample of 40 participants.*

Gender and Race Matter: Global Perspectives on Being a Woman
Advances in Gender Research, Volume 21, 151–170
ISSN: 1529-2126/doi:10.1108/S1529-212620160000021009

Research implications/limitations — *This chapter is based on findings from a small research sample.*

Findings — *The study finds evidence that confirms experiences of gendered poverty permeate across class divides, suggesting that access to economic capital does not necessarily result in equitable gender relations. The findings also uncover the diverse ways in which women and adolescent girls strategise and negotiate to acquire agency, through acts of resistance and/or subversion.*

Originality/value — *There are two key aspects of this research that can be considered original: the use of a multi-methods approach and by bringing together of a combination of different voices. The theoretical and sociological contribution of this research lies in showcasing the value of expanding the definition of poverty and gender beyond a purely economic analysis.*

**Keywords:** Gender; poverty; agency; neoliberalism; development; Mumbai

# INTRODUCTION

In 1995 at the Fourth World Conference held in Beijing, after two weeks of debate, arguably one of the most progressive blueprints for women's advancement was produced, a report called The Beijing Declaration and Platform for Action (BPfA). Consequently, on the twentieth anniversary, UN Women revisited the original concerns about the advancement of women's status highlighted in 1995. Captured in a publication titled 'The Beijing Declaration and Platform for Action Turns 20' (2015) the report claims that although some gains have been made since 1995 there is a lot more work that needs to be done. The report states:

> [t]he overall picture is of slow and uneven implementation, with serious stagnation and even regression in several areas. Progress has been particularly slow for the most marginalized women and girls who experience multiple and intersecting forms of discrimination. (UN Women, 2015, p. 6)

Over the last three decades much has been written about the oppression of black and third-world women. Indeed western feminist discourse has been the subject of much criticism by black, third-world and lesbian women (Lorde, 1984; Mohanty & Russo, 1991). More recently, in the context of poverty, development and human rights, Purewal (2015) has offered a non-western feminist critique of BPfA and Education for All. She argues that the declaration has been used to further neoliberal economic policies and neocolonial intervention in developing countries, thereby affecting women's ability to mobilise, thus suggesting that the reports published by the UN are used strategically as an ideological weapon to proliferate a free market ideology. Purewal argues that the World Bank has used girls' education in countries such as Afghanistan as a 'development investment' to rationalise the assertion of moral and ideological authority. Furthermore, she argues that the liberal discourse on rights by those who sit outside the periphery of western power, in fact local women who mobilise in countries like Afghanistan are resisting against the oppression of both the occupiers and the fundamentalists. With this in mind, my research aims to contribute different ways of knowing (which often means challenging dominant discourses) by exploring the disjuncture between macro-level framings and micro-level everyday lived experiences and perceptions of gender and poverty.

Drawing on original empirical research this chapter aims to explore the reasons why women and girls in countries such as India continue to experience high levels of gendered poverty. This qualitative research, based on a multi-methods approach, is used to critically evaluate its potential to inform development practice. This approach to gendered poverty includes drawing on participatory action research, participant observation and ethnography in order to understand, '[t]he everyday, fluid, fundamentally historical and dynamic nature of the lives of third world women' (Mohanty & Russo, 1991, p. 6). The research also aims to show the value inherent in broadening the concept of poverty to include deprivation, discrimination, prejudice and inequalities, thus moving beyond a limited economic analysis. The usefulness of this approach is supported by Perrons (2015, p. 208), who argues that '[…] it is critical to devise policy that is founded on recognition of how inequality is simultaneously gendered, racialised, and marked by other dimensions of social disadvantage if more equitable and economically and socially sustainable development is to be achieved'. This chapter therefore presents a nuanced understanding of the lived experiences and perceptions of gender and poverty in Mumbai, India, by uncovering the complexity of intergenerational oppression, resistance and subversion.

India is a particularly interesting place to study as it is the second most populous country in the world. The last census carried out in 2011 estimated the population at 1.2 billion with a sex ratio of 940 females per 1000 males (Census India, 2011). India's largest city, Mumbai (formerly

Bombay), the capital of Maharashtra, is known as the commercial capital of India and is home to over 19 million people, making it the fourth most populous city in the world (World Population Review, 2014). The levels of inequality in Mumbai are reflected by the vast majority of the population (64 per cent) living in slum settlements (World Population Review, 2014). In light of recent international interest in rape and violence against women and girls, arising from the horrific 2012 rape and murder of Jyoti Singh Pandey, questions have resurfaced about the status of women and girls.

## THE RESEARCH

The methodology for the research was partly inspired by an ambitious study led by Narayan (2000) for the World Bank titled 'Voices of the Poor'[1]. Consulting the poor is not a novel approach, and in fact Participatory Poverty Assessments (PPAs) have been used by international development agencies to explore experiences of poverty, with focus groups favoured over other qualitative methods (Kabeer, 2003). Where participatory methods have been used they have helped to develop a deeper understanding of poverty. Understanding poverty as multi-dimensional, including for example, vulnerability, provides insight into the needs of poor people beyond consideration of food and nutrition. It highlights the creative and resilient ways the poor achieve their goals through reliance by human, social and material resources and labour (Kabeer, 2003). Although participatory approaches have been thought to have great potential to capture the complex and diverse aspects of poverty, it has been argued that they have been used 'unevenly' and 'incidentally' with a lack of reference to gender (Kabeer, 2003, p. 101). For my research, using a mixed methodology including participatory action research, the participants were given the opportunity to have their voices heard without the researcher leading the enquiry with a list of predetermined questions. The rationale was based on the argument that 'our understanding of the problems of "real" women cannot lie outside the "imagined" constructs in and through which women emerge as subjects' (Sunder Rajan, 1993, p. 10). All of the women and adolescent girls (groups 1 and 2 respectively) were considered to be economically poor because they were living in, or had previously lived in, slum communities or in precarious housing in and around Mumbai.

A second dimension of the research was inspired by Reis and Moore's (2005) edited collection, *Elite Perceptions of Poverty and Inequality*, which explores the elite's perception of poverty. Similarly, I explore the perceptions held by upper and middle class women in Mumbai. By challenging the idea that the growth of the middle classes reduces levels of poverty, Wietzke and Sumner (2014) make an important contribution and argue that there is a more complex and conflictual relationship between the middle and lower income classes than theories suggest. I selected women from upper and middle class backgrounds (group 3) by mapping income earning localities in Mumbai. I use the term 'the middle classes' to describe women who live in apartment buildings that are family owned. I differentiate the middle classes from the socio-economic category 'upper class', with the latter describing women who live and own property in the more affluent areas of Mumbai. In sociology, social class and social stratification are used to define groups of people into hierarchies of social categories, commonly described as upper, middle and lower class. As Dorling (2013) reminds us, class categorisation relies on comparisons between groups, without which it would be difficult to conceptualise. Although I understand the complexities and limitations of using class categorisations beyond upper, middle and lower income classes, due to the small sample size of my empirical research I believe mapping class based on differences in housing and spatial localities (see Dorling, 2014) serves the purpose of this study. The final dimension of the research investigated the role of local, grassroots, national and international NGOs, exploring the impact they have on women and adolescent girls from low socio-economic backgrounds primarily resident in slum communities.

The subjects of the research were 40 participants divided into four groups. It consisted of eleven women and eleven adolescent girls from low socio-economic backgrounds; nine women from upper and middle class backgrounds; nine practitioners working in local, grassroots, national and international non-government organisations and one social science researcher. Drawing on participatory methods, ethnography and participant observation, the participants in the first two groups chose from a range of methods such as photography, writing and drawing which was then followed by an unstructured conversational-style interview. During this 'conversation' they described how their photographs, drawings and writings illustrated their experiences (or perceptions) of gender and poverty in Mumbai. Using semi-structured interviewing, the participants in the third group were asked questions about their perceptions of poverty from a higher class positioning. Lastly, the participants in the fourth group were asked about the impact of their organisation's intervention strategies. The analysis of the data was shaped through a coding strategy informed by my theoretical framework, with a focus on the 'everyday' since I was concerned with capturing experiences of poverty rather than reinforcing pre-conceived notions. For the purpose of this chapter, I will draw upon the commonalities and differences between women and adolescent girls (groups 1 and 2) living in poverty and upper and middle class women (group 3) (Table 1).

# MORE THAN VICTIMS OF POVERTY: AGENCY, RESISTANCE AND EMPOWERMENT

Women and adolescent girls from the first two groups (1 and 2) offered an alternative reading of oppression and agency to that found in colonial discourses of women in India as victims. The participants in the research challenged the persistent discourse of victimhood by uncovering acts of resistance evidenced through their agency. Agency is about understanding the 'capacity of different groups to exercise choice and pursue their goals [and provides an insight into] less empowered groups and their struggles to challenge structures and negotiate change' (Kabeer, 2010, p. 107). There are three ways to categorise the ability to exercise choice, which is through resources, agency and achievements (Kabeer, 1999). It is also argued that to acquire agency there needs to be an agent who is defined as being active

*Table 1.* Research Participants[a].

| Group 1 Poor Women | Group 2 Poor Adolescent Girls | Group 3 Upper and Middle Class Women | Group 4 Local, National and International NGOs |
| --- | --- | --- | --- |
| Bhavna | Usma | Kanbai | Manjeet from NGO 1 |
| Valbai | Sonali | Priya | Assam from NGO 2 |
| Rambai | Alina | Premila | Neema from NGO 3 |
| Saja | Radha | Panaa | Marie from INGO 4 |
| Kalavanti | Rubeena | Ragani | Seema from NGO 5 |
| Neha | Sona | Parini | Premila from NGO 6 |
| Sheela | Lina | Neesha | Meera Researcher 7 |
| Farah | Anna | Anita | Vaneeta from INGO 8 |
| Champa | Saila | Muskaan | Sumita from NGO 9 |
| Deeya | Presha | | Ruby from NGO 10 |
| Rambai | Poonam | | |

*Note*: [a]Pseudonyms are being used in this list of participants.

(Takhar, 2013). Agency is therefore a process where one has 'the power within' (Kabeer, 1999, p. 438).

Furthermore, agency is not only acquired through decision-making, but can be acquired through bargaining and negotiation, deception, manipulation, subversion and resistance (Kabeer, 1999). Therefore, if we are to understand how individual women and girls acquire agency, a more nuanced approach is required. For instance, agency describes people's ability to act for themselves, but if obstructed from doing so they are considered to have been denied their agency, or oppressed. This research is concerned with gaining a critical understanding of the complexity of agency for individual women and adolescent girls from low socio-economic backgrounds in relation to structural oppression. It is also useful to remind ourselves that the relationship between agency and structure has been debated in social theory.[2] The developments in social theory and feminist theory around the concepts have been increasingly used in development discourse on gender and poverty. Indeed the work of black feminists has been well documented and, by drawing on poststructuralist work on subjectivity and identity, a more complex understanding of oppression, resistance and empowerment has been put forward. Although the concept of empowerment is contested (Karlekar, 2004) it could be argued that it is precisely the 'fuzziness' of the concept that adds to its value (Butalia, 1993; Kabeer, 1999). This is supported by Patricia Hill-Collins:

> Empowerment remains an elusive construct and developing a Black feminist politics of empowerment requires specifying the domains of power that constrain Black women, as well as how such domination can be resisted. (Hill-Collins, 2000, p. 19)

Understanding empowerment as a 'process of change' (Kabeer, 1999), where one acquires power in order to make choices, suggests that agency is not static and that empowerment enables individuals to (re)claim their agency. In the context of my research on women in poverty there are various methods that NGOs use to empower women, and this is particularly evident in poverty alleviation strategies. Although NGOs in India play an important role in empowering women, it is worthwhile to note that outside of NGO intervention women are constantly negotiating and (re)constituting their positions in society through forms of resistance and subversion. Even though it has been established that agency is fluid, women in India, and particularly poor women, continue to be assigned the status of victim. This is due to a number of factors related to the othering of poor women: firstly by powerful colonial and postcolonial discourses (Said, 1978); secondly, through the historical 'cultural' practice of sati (widow immolation); and thirdly, privileged spaces reserved for privileged bodies, resulting in educated upper and middle class women speaking for poor women, as evident in the contemporary Indian women's movement. Crimes against women are experienced across socio-economic classes, yet it is those who occupy spaces of privilege who get to be heard. It could be argued that women from low socio-economic backgrounds then become multiply marginalised. The fluidity of agency is supported by Sunder Rajan, who contends:

Women's 'agency' (like their 'empowerment') can neither be viewed as an abstraction, nor celebrated as an unqualified good. Agency is never to be found in some pure state of volition or action, but is complexly imbricated in the contradictory structures of patriarchy (Sunder Rajan, 1998, p. 10)

Agency is fluid and dependent on context (race, class, gender, caste, time, location), and therefore needs to be theorised and understood in relation to multiple dimensions: resistance, oppression, power and empowerment. This is particularly important in the field of development as development programmes can be restrictive in nature. For instance the interplay between agency and structure becomes more evident in programmes of empowerment for women as they operate within strict systemic and structural parameters of power. Therefore, '[w]omen are either recipients of development, or instruments, never agents of development as they understand and conceptualise it' (Chakravarti, 2008, p. 12).[3] Madhok (2007, 2013) takes up this complexity further by questioning whether there is a sufficient theoretical framework that considers the context, and particularly the constraints imposed on women.

Despite the constraints that women experience they are involved in subtle forms of everyday resistance. These acts of resistance could arguably be read as passive compliance, but Scott (1985) argues that these are self-interested acts of survival and that there is awareness of action within local parameters, which makes everyday resistance covert and undercover. The nuances and subtlety of resistance amongst women in poverty can be captured using this approach, although multiple subjectivities are important in my research — an aspect that is overlooked in Scott's work. Interestingly, Agarwal's (1995) gendered analysis of women's land rights in India locates everyday resistance in resources and how struggles are defined. She pays particular attention to women's consciousness and perceptions, arguing that women's everyday resistance could include acts such as foot-dragging, withholding sex from husbands and practicing silence. Rather than being actions of false consciousness, she argues they could be acts of self-awareness. As I maintain, research on poverty has often failed to capture such nuances. The next section, therefore, offers examples that challenge understandings of women and girls from low socio-economic backgrounds as lacking agency.

## EVERYDAY 'MOMENTS' OF AGENCY

Farah, in her twenties, lives in a women's NGO in Mumbai after many years of violence and abuse from their father. Farah is incredibly passionate about social justice and gender equality and shared her plans to work in the social sector by including boys and men in intervention programmes. She displayed eagerness to learn and had an inquisitive spirit. For the research, Farah produced a drawing to describe women's agency and structural oppression. Using the metaphor of a tree and its strength to weather any storm, she described women as strong survivors (Fig. 1):

*Fig. 1.*   Farah's Drawing.

[This] means [referring to the picture] how a lady is and what things are within her. What happens to her and what she wants. How much of what she wants, she is able to get and the things she is not able to get. I have drawn the woman as the tree, how she grows and how she progresses and how women's welfare should be and what do people do with her. So I have depicted a woman through the tree, she will become strong but there are questions on whether she will get all the things such as education, security, rights, welfare, independence, and her own identity. (Farah, Group 1, lives in an NGO)

By using this metaphor to describe women's strength and resilience, Farah suggests that it is 'society' that decides what women have access to, even though women have dreams and ambitions for their future. Farah distinguishes between an individual agent and society as structural, demonstrating that she understands ideas of agency, structure and oppression. Although Farah has never been married she appears to draw on her personal experiences of violence. For instance, she told me that a husband only beats up his wife because of his need for power. She displays a multifaceted account of gender and poverty through her drawing, where she demonstrates the strength of a woman yet also shows she understands that society, traditions, and the power of patriarchy stifle and subjugate women. During the interview, Farah covered an array of topics by peppering our conversation with many questions, mostly starting or ending with 'why?' She reminded me that, 'in our constitution it is enshrined that we have a right to live, right to live everywhere, right to equality'.

Referring back to her picture, she continued to question what she sees as unchallenged customs and traditions that continue to push women into poverty:

So, like the question is that, why do girls always have to go to her husband's home [after marriage]? Why she has to leave her own family? Why doesn't a boy come [to the bride's home to live]? Why does she have to change her surname? Like her roots, she will grow strong as I told you before. There are questions in her mind, which don't come out and stay in her mind like a big question on why this is happening to me? Why people are like this for me? Why I am not getting these things? Why this thing is going to my husband? Why only men are getting these things? Why am I not getting these things? The question of what is my identity, and MY identity alone and what is my identity. Until I don't get my identity how will the society know about me? That's why these questions in some way or the other will dry out and eventually disappear and come to an end. (Farah, Group 1, lives in an NGO)

Farah's ability to identify the social problems related to gender discrimination, along with her questions, disrupts normative customs. Farah questions why it is an accepted norm for married women to leave their families and live with their husband's family, that is, questioning the status quo. Similar to black feminist epistemology, Farah rejects discourses that disempower her, and through her engagement with the NGO finds alternative ways to create social change (Hill-Collins, 2000). Kabeer (2010) argues that one's sense of agency and self-worth is critical for change to happen, which is evident in Farah's narrative where she states that her identity is her own. Farah's narrative must be situated in the context of the NGO she lives in which works to 'empower' its beneficiaries. Kabeer (2010, pp. 107−108) refers to this as a 'critical relational dimension to empowerment: *the power with* [as] changes in individual women are unlikely to go very far in changing structures but women coming together to reflect, to question and to act on their subordinate status can be a powerful force for change.'

This suggests that NGOs and/or political movements are essential for any social change or significant impact to take effect, without denying the potential and power of individual agency. Looking at the interviewees in the first two groups, I am able to identify (by comparing interviews) which women have engaged with NGO feminist praxis and which have not. For instance, Valbai, Rambai and Bhavna living in Dharavi (Asia's largest slum community), and Deeya and Champa from neighbouring smaller slum communities, have never accessed an NGO and their responses are very different.

As a result of drawing on participatory research methods with no structured interview questions the participants revealed different means and experiences of accessing agency without being directed or led by me, the researcher. Even though the research did not exclusively aim to find out how poor women locate and access everyday agency, many participants made reference to agency. For instance, Radha explained how she felt after their NGO organised a day outing to the beach on India's national holiday.

> For the first time I felt that I was really out and I was enjoying and I can enjoy, I didn't get a chance at home to really enjoy. I enjoyed singing and I started feeling that I should have friends that I should go out, out of the home, I felt absolutely good that I could do this. (Radha, Group 2, lives in an NGO)

Radha left her family to marry a young man without her parents' blessing. She moved from her place of birth to the city. When she became pregnant her marriage broke down and she ended up running away from her husband. She was not able to support herself or her baby so, with the help of the NGO, she gave up her child for adoption. She is currently living with a women's NGO receiving counselling, shelter and guidance. Even in her position, living in an NGO, having given up her daughter for adoption and having lost contact with her family, she has located symbiotic moments of individual and collective agency by accessing a public space, the beach. The interview captures Radha's revelation that she can feel good, have fun and access public spaces where perhaps previously she felt this was not possible. Understanding these moments of agency allows us to build a fluid and complex idea of gendered experiences of poverty that is usually lost in statistics. Locating Radha's subjectivity allows us to understand how domination and resistance impact individual agency (Hill-Collins, 2000). As Mohanty (2003, p. 83) states, agency is 'thus figured in small, day to day practices and struggles of Third World women'. In other words, in the context of women accessing NGOs, small acts of empowerment and consciousness-raising about women's position in society can lead to rethinking definitions of local and individual action.

The next example draws on an interview with Bhavna, the youngest of three women interviewed in a family living in Dharavi. Initially Bhavna was hostile but then settled into the conversation. In her late twenties, she has two children, a son and a daughter. During the interview, while she was preparing dinner for her family before she started her last working 'shift' of the day cooking for a middle class Jain family, she came across as quite assertive. She spoke openly in front of her mother-in-law and grandmother-in-law when recalling the challenges she experienced living in a joint family with her in-laws when she got married. When talking about whether she felt happy living in her own sectioned-off room, which is part of the family home, she replied, 'yes, I am happy'. I asked her, 'How long has it been since you made this room [a partition to create a separate room from the main and only room]?'

Bhavna replied:

> I lived here [referring to the main room] for 5 years with my in laws then I've been here [referring to her family room] for five years. There were disagreements with my mother-in-law so we separated. (Bhavna, Group 1, lives in a large slum community)

What Bhavna means by 'separating' is building a partition wall on one side of a narrow room, which is used interchangeably as an open plan kitchen, living room and bedroom for three adults, measuring approximately $3 \times 2$ square metres (some of this space is also taken up by a narrow stairwell). The second room (Bhavna's family room) that is sectioned off, measuring approximately $2 \times 2$ square metres contains a compact second kitchen and a small God shrine hanging on the wall. By night the room becomes a sleeping area for her family (two children and husband). The agency that is particularly interesting is Bhavna's transparency and honesty with a stranger in the presence of her in-laws, sharing information about why she has a separate home to that of her mother-in-law. This differs from the interview given by Priya, an upper class woman, who, despite having grievances about the management of her finances with her husband and his parents, fails to be open in the presence of her mother-in-law or to take any action to make changes. On the one hand Bhavna, living in a slum community, would appear to have more agency as she creates change that she equates to her idea of self-worth (Kabeer, 2010). On the other, Priya is careful not to divulge these feelings of resentment in the presence of her mother-in-law during the interview, and in fact shared this information with me when walking me out of the apartment onto the main road. This comparison challenges an understanding of poor Indian women as docile, powerless, and with little agency to create change. Although this comparison challenges (to a certain extent) ideas of agency, power and poverty, it however forms part of a collection of experiences that cannot be generalised.

## UPPER AND MIDDLE CLASS WOMEN'S PERCEPTIONS OF THE POOR AND THEIR AGENCY

This last section of the chapter explores upper and middle class women's agency, and locates the imagined agency they attribute to women and girls from lower socio-economic backgrounds. One of the dimensions of my research on poverty and gender was to explore upper and middle class women's perceptions of poverty in Mumbai. Without my probing some of the women willingly shared their own experiences of gendered poverty. Here, the aim is to demonstrate there are no class boundaries when it comes to how gendered poverty is experienced. Women and girls living in the rich neighbourhoods of Mumbai are heavily policed and a great deal of emphasis is put on the preservation of their reputations (Phadke, Khan, & Ranade, 2011). For upper class women, access to public space is limited to a chauffer driven car. It can be seen that economic power is often used to purchase an escape from the city entirely, to a form of privacy away from the gaze of the community and gendered public spaces. Here there is minimum pressure to perform class identity. Although wealth gives access to material products and expensive luxurious experiences, access to choice outside of this seems limited. This raises questions about whether upper class women can fully exercise, or have similar levels of access to, agency as compared to poor women.

Reminiscent of the findings in Phadke et al.'s (2011) study, Parini, an upper class woman from group 3, offered an account of her perception of agency from an elite upper class perspective. When talking about marriage and divorce, Parini comments:

> I think women are definitely becoming more educated they are beginning to give it back to the guys. I know a lot of women who are getting divorced because they're not putting up with it absolutely not putting up with the string of bad treatment by their husbands, they would rather be single and have a life rather than pander around and be stuck with a marriage that is not doing anything so which I applaud. (Parini, upper class woman, Group 3)

Parini's perception is that women are responding differently to bad marriage experiences, where historically women have stayed due to family pressure and responsibilities to perform class and gender. Furthermore, she equates this to an increase in education, which allows women to make an alternative choice. In order to challenge oppressive practices, or in Parini's words the 'string of bad treatment', empowerment needs to be deployed which could be in the form of 'self-confidence, education and economic development' (Sudbury, 1998, p. 61). However, another participant, Ragani from group 3, suggests that education can only help women to a certain degree, stating:

> For them [the poor] it's even worse, at least in our [upper and middle classes] case people are educated so the girls can be rebellious about it and can get their way sometimes. (Ragani, middle class woman, Group 3)

This quote leads me to question whether 'getting away with it sometimes' suggests an expression of agency. Agency and poverty were also conveyed by another participant, Priya, who retold the story of her friend who left her marital family home because her husband's family rejected her unborn female foetus, demanding that she terminate the pregnancy because of their preference for a boy child. Priya shared this anecdote as an example of the structural oppression that women from upper and middle class families experience. It offers insight into first- and second-hand experiences and perceptions of agency and structural oppression. My interest in upper and middle class women's agency is to question whether economic 'poverty increases the likelihood of agency deprivation' (Klugman et al., 2014, p. 5), and to explore whether gendered poverty extends to all women across class divides. Therefore, it could be argued that women from rich, upper or middle class families who are unable to exercise choice are in fact experiencing poverty due to gendered oppression. The poverty I refer to does not have to be exclusively economic and/or material deprivation (although for some they may well also experience this), but could include other forms of structural deprivation, such as unequal access to decision-making and resources within the home. Drawing on perceptions that upper and middle class women have of women from low socio-economic backgrounds, the research findings showed that some of the women in group 3 perceived poor women to have agency that would allow them to exit poverty. I use the term 'imagined agency' to describe the construction of the belief that the poor have the ability to exit deprivation, that is, if they choose to. For example, when I asked Priya from group 3 to share her thoughts on what she believed poor women could do to lift themselves out of poverty, she replied with great conviction:

> There are a lot of self-help groups that can be formed by women, sometimes you need a lot of support in terms of sponsoring your initiatives except that at the end of the day if you have any skill and you really want to make something out of it and everybody gets together anything is possible. Secondly, they all need to get educated and this is the biggest problem. (Priya, upper class woman, Group 3)

Priya has put forward an imagined idea of agency that she believes women and girls from lower socio-economic backgrounds have access to in order to lift themselves out of poverty. She gives little consideration or thought to the structural oppression that women experience. Although very complex and fluid, the participants across the four groups pointed to various forms of structural oppression as the cause of gendered poverty, and these formed three distinct groups of governance. I have attempted to capture this in the model I have termed the 'tri-dynamic system of oppression'. The term aims to foreground the dynamism, fluidity and changeability of those structural forces which are the three sources of oppression the participants alluded to in their interviews. They include State governance, that is, failure to protect women and girls; strong orthodox norms, values and beliefs which are based on morality and woven into culture and religion; and neoliberal economic policies (Fig. 2). The triangular area at the centre of the diagram shows the interconnected relationships between the three sources of oppression which collectively impact the lived experiences of women and adolescent girls.

In group 3, the group of upper and middle class women, Priya's response was very similar to Muskaan's and Anita's perceptions of poverty. Although many of the women in the upper and middle class group understood poverty as an economic issue there was some understanding that culture had an impact on women's quality of life. However, this was not made very explicit in relation to their ideas about how women could escape

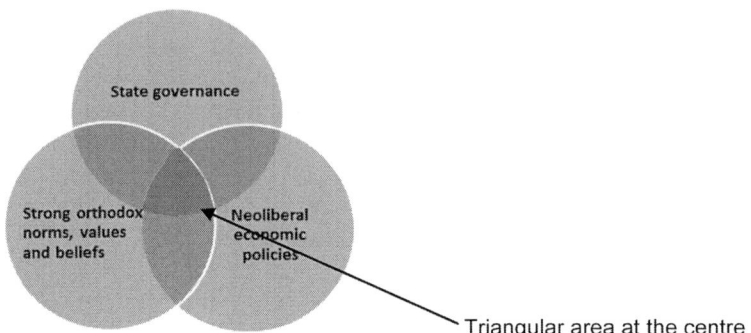

State governance

Strong orthodox
norms, values
and beliefs

Neoliberal
economic
policies

Triangular area at the centre

*Fig. 2.*   Tri-Dynamic System of Oppression.

their poverty. In fact, the responsibility of continuing to live in poverty was placed on the women themselves. This meritocratic attitude to gender and poverty is evidenced in the following statement:

> You see poverty is not your choice but coming out of it is definitely your choice, so if you want to come out of it definitely you have many choices. You can be a housemaid, you do anything, and you can just earn your own money and come out of it you definitely do not have to stay in it. (Muskaan, middle class woman, Group 3)

Not only is Muskaan's quote an example of understanding poverty as solely economic but she believes that women and girls experiencing gendered poverty somehow have access to choices, although this is not clarified how. Neoliberalism impacts on how individuals are seen and how meritocracy 'naturally' rewards those who strive to be better. Education featured in all of the interviews with upper and middle class women as the magic formula to exit poverty. However, none of the interviewees in group 3 made any reference to what 'education' actually meant to them and how an education could be transferred into a livelihood. In fact, Anita's quote was interesting as she said:

> See education to the females first, especially the adolescent girls before they get married, educate them so they can fend for themselves so they don't need to have to depend on the government so much. (Anita, upper class woman, Group 3)

This quote suggests that she believes gaining an education is empowering, but more than that, she reveals perhaps a normalised attitude to matrimony. Gendered heteronormativity is a discourse relating to how we think about sexuality and how identity is categorised. The programmed expectation of attaining a heterosexual marital union offers an insight into heteronormative discursive practice, a system that is carried on and normalised through religious practices and across the different classes studied within the research. This demonstrates commonality of experience by all the participants in the groups, through the State's incompetency to provide gender security, norms and values that dictate gendered behaviour and neoliberalism that promotes individualism and competition.


## CONCLUSION

To conclude, this chapter has attempted to offer new perspectives on how gendered poverty is examined through micro site research conducted in Mumbai, India. The empirical data has enabled me to generate a nuanced understanding of gender and poverty by describing the fluidity, synergy and complexity of the lives of poor women and adolescent girls. As a result, this has offered some insight into the persistence of gendered poverty despite ground-breaking work by feminists and activists over the years. While the economic analysis of poverty serves an important purpose it is nonetheless limited in its usefulness for understanding the complex relationship between poverty and gender. A multi-method research approach has enabled me to display some of the complexity around agency and oppression by allowing the women and adolescent girls in the research to contribute their own experiences and insights about how they experience, negotiate and perceive gender and poverty in Mumbai. As a result, the contributions serve as important examples and reminders of how much is missed out from economic analysis and poverty alleviation strategies. Indeed the accounts demonstrate how participants access their agency despite living under a myriad of systemic and structural oppression. As a result, the accounts challenge development discourses that have historically presented third-world women only as victims of the economic climate and/or cultural practices. This is not to say that this is not so, and in fact the research argues for a more complete complex articulation of gender and poverty, rather than one that overburdens poor women and girls with expectations of saving communities and the planet or one that underestimates their abilities.

With that said, partly inspired by the dynamism of the city, where the intimacy between the rich and poor is overtly evident, I integrated upper and middle class women's perceptions of gendered poverty in the design of the study, as explored in the latter part of this chapter. Although the initial aim was to juxtapose their perceptions of poverty with marginalised women in group 2, I quickly found that in fact there was a blurring of perceptions and experiences of gender and poverty among the upper and middle class women in group 3. Some of the findings that I highlight here include how upper and middle class women's perceptions of poverty underestimate real experiences of poverty, while many describe similar experiences of gendered oppression among affluent households to that of poorer women. As a result, the inclusion of perceptions and experiences of gender and poverty from different class positions has enabled me to contribute to the on-going investigation to understand gendered poverty.

# NOTES

1. 'Voices of the Poor' consists of three books which bring together the experiences of over 60,000 poor women and men. The first book, *Can Anyone Hear Us?*, gathers the voices of over 40,000 poor women and men in 50 countries using participatory poverty assessments; the second book, *Crying Out for Change*, draws material from a new 23 country comparative study. Lastly, the final book, *From Many Lands*, offers regional patterns and country case studies. www.web.worldbank.org/WBSITE/EXTERNAL/TOPICS/EXTPOVERTY/0,,contentMDK:20613045~menuPK:336998~pagePK:148956~piPK:216618~theSitePK:336992,00.html

2. For example, Giddens' (1984) structuration theory and Pierre Bourdieu's habitus, field and capital (1977) position agency and structure as interdependent and recognise them as equally important concepts for understanding society.

3. Drawing on the collaborative project between women activists and the state to develop a Women's Development Programme (WDP), also known as the 'Sathin' programme in Rajasthan, Chakravarti (2008) complicates the conceptualisation of agency and power. The women beneficiaries in the study identify two central concerns: land rights and access to health. However, unfortunately, in relation to the issue of land rights, the WDP fail to challenge the issue due to its political nature. Although evidently, there were some gains made by the WDP, unfortunately as a response to the long period of drought, the state integrated the food-for-work-programme with female sterilisation, to push through the family planning agenda while ensuring government targets were met. Although the women beneficiaries of the programme mobilised and protested, unfortunately this led to government officials terminating the entire WDP.

# REFERENCES

Agarwal, B. (1995). Women's legal rights in agricultural land in India. *Economic and Political Weekly*, (Bombay), *25*, 39–56.
Bourdieu, P. (1977). *Outline of a theory of practice*. Cambridge: Cambridge University Press.

Butalia, U. (1993). Community, state, and gender: On women's agency during partition. *Economic and Political Weekly, 28*(17), 12−24.

Census India. (2011). *Census 2011.* Retrieved from http://www.census2011.co.in. Accessed on January 13, 2014.

Chakravarti, U. (2008). Beyond the mantra of empowerment: Time to return to poverty, violence and struggle. *Institute of Development Studies Bulletin, 39*(6), 10−17.

Dorling, D. (2013). What class are you? Statistics Views Feature, Retrieved from http://www.statisticsviews.com/details/feature/4582421/What-Class-Are-You.html. Accessed on January 13, 2014.

Dorling, D. (2014). Thinking about class. *Sociology, 48*(3), 452−462.

Giddens, A. (1984). *The constitution of society: Outline of the theory of structuration.* Berkeley, CA: University of California Press.

Hill-Collins, P. (2000). *Black feminist thought: Knowledge, consciousness, and the politics of empowerment* (2nd ed.). Boston, MA: Unwin Hyman.

Kabeer, N. (1999). Resources, agency, achievements: Reflections on the measurement of women's empowerment. *Development and Change, 30*, 435−464.

Kabeer, N. (2003). *Gender main-streaming in poverty eradication and the millennium development goals: A handbook for policy-makers and other stakeholders.* Ottawa: Commonwealth Secretariat, CIDA, International Development Research Centre.

Kabeer, N. (2010). Women's empowerment, development interventions and the management of information flows. *Institute of Development Studies, 41*(6), 105−113.

Karlekar, M. (2004). A note on the empowerment of women. *Indian Journal of Gender Studies, 11*(2), 145−155.

Klugman, J., Hanmer, L., Twigg, S., Hassan, T., McClearly-Sills, J., & Santamaria, J. (2014). *Voice and agency.* Washington, DC: International Bank for Reconstruction and Development/The World Bank.

Lorde, A. (1984). Age, race, class and sex: Women redefining difference. In *Sister outsider: Essays and speeches* (pp. 114−123). Freedom, CA: Crossing Press.

Madhok, S. (2007). Autonomy, gendered subordination and transcultural dialogue. *Journal of Global Ethics, 3*(3), 335−357.

Madhok, S. (2013). *Rethinking agency: Developmentalism, gender and rights.* New Delhi: Routledge.

Mohanty, C. T. (2003). *Feminism without borders: Decolonizing theory practicing solidarity.* New York, NY: Duke University Press.

Mohanty, C. T., & Russo, A. (1991). *Third world women and the politics of feminism.* Bloomington, IN: Indiana University Press.

Narayan, D., Patel, R., Schaff, K., Rademacher, A., & Koch-Schulte, S. (2000). *Voices of the Poor. Vol. I: Can anyone hear us? Voices from 47 countries.* New Delhi: Oxford University Press.

Perrons, D. (2015). Gendering the inequality debate. *Gender & Development, 23*(2), 207−222.

Phadke, S., Khan, S., & Ranade, S. (2011). *Why loiter? Women and risk on Mumbai streets.* New Delhi: Penguin Books.

Purewal, N. K. (2015). Interrogating the rights discourse on girls' education: Neocolonialism, neoliberalism, and the Post-Beijing platform for action. *IDS Bulletin, 46*, 47−53.

Reis, E. P., & Moore, M. (2005). *Elite perceptions of poverty and inequality.* London: Zed Books.

Said, E. (1978). *Orientalism.* New York, NY: Pantheon.

Scott, J. C. (1985). *Weapons of the weak: Everyday forms of peasant resistance.* New Haven, CT: Yale University Press.

Sudbury, J. (1998). *Other kinds of dreams.* London: Routledge.

Sunder Rajan, R. (1993). *Real and imagined women: Gender, culture and post colonialism.* London: Routledge.

Sunder Rajan, R. (1998). Is the Hindu goddess a feminist? Jura Gentium Rivista di filosofia del diritto internazionale e della politica globale. *Economic and Political Weekly, 33*(44). October 31, 1998.

Takhar, S. (2013). *Gender, ethnicity, and political agency: South Asian women organizing.* New York, NY: Routledge.

UN Women. (2015). *The Beijing Declaration and Platform for Action turns 20.* Retrieved from http://www.unwomen.org/~/media/headquarters/attachments/sections/library/publications/2015/sg%20report_synthesis-en_web.pdf. Accessed on April 1, 2015.

Wietzke, F. B., & Sumner, A. (2014). *What are the political and social implications of the 'new middle classes' in developing countries?* International Development Institute Working Paper, Volume EADI Policy Paper Series 1.

World Population Review. (2014). Retrieved from worldpopulationreview.com/world-cities/mumbai-population/. Accessed on November 1, 2013.

# RE-MAPPING WOMEN'S TESTIMONIES INTO NETWORKED SUBJECTIVITIES: THE *QUIPU PROJECT*

Donatella Maraschin and Suzanne Scafe

## ABSTRACT

Purpose — *This chapter analyses a range of media outputs produced to raise awareness of the campaign of forced sterilisation conducted in Peru during the period 1993–1998. Focusing in detail on the* Quipu Project *the authors investigate the ways in which different media configure differently witness subjects, audiences and listeners. The chapter also analyses the effectiveness of these media outputs within the contexts of human rights discourses.*

Design/methodology/approach — *The chapter is framed by narrative theories of documentary video production, new media technology and intermediality. The authors also draw on theories of witnessing that have emerged in critical studies of witness testimony in video and new media. It uses secondary data, that is, the testimonies of women already collected, selected and, in most cases, edited by documentary makers and campaigners.*

Gender and Race Matter: Global Perspectives on Being a Woman
Advances in Gender Research, Volume 21, 171–192
ISSN: 1529-2126/doi:10.1108/S1529-212620160000021010

Findings — *The case studies compare the ways in which conventional video documentary and techniques of digital storytelling transform the content of women's testimony.*

Research implications/limitations — *Funding limitations have meant that progress on the site was, at the time of writing, temporarily suspended. We therefore analysed the pilot, or prototype, of the* Quipu Project, *which should be viewed as a work in progress. However, a more developed site for the* Quipu Project *went live after the chapter was completed.*

Originality/value — *This chapter represents the first attempt to analyse the effectiveness of an experimental project such as the* Quipu Project. *The authors were given access by the curators of the project to the site at various stages of its construction. The chapter provides insights into the potential of digital technology to create opportunities for media outputs to internationalise interventions into campaigns for justice and reparation.*

**Keywords:** Forced sterilisation; digital storytelling; intermediality; witness testimonies; women's agency; human rights

## BACKGROUND

In Peru between 1996 and 1998, 217,446 people, the majority of whom were women, were surgically sterilised. This was the result of a campaign launched by President Alberto Fujimori within a year of gaining office in a democratic re-election landslide (Carrión, 2006; Ewig, 2010). Peru is one of the poorest Latin American countries with 37% of its 26 million inhabitants living below the poverty line. Fujimori's government's sterilisation campaign was launched ostensibly to address the high rate of maternal mortality, the result of poverty and poor health care. It is estimated, for example, that in 1997, there were 265 maternal deaths for every 100,000 live births (Shepard, 2006, p. 100). Through the manipulation of international feminist discourses on reproductive rights and by creating alliances with feminist organisations in Peru, this popular and populist president undertook what would turn out to be a programme of population control (Ewig, 2006; Shepard, 2006). Fujimori's first presidency was characterised by what had been perceived as a successful intervention into a bloody internal war with the brutal Maoist guerrilla organisation, Shining Path

(Gorriti, 1999; Starn, 1995). Poverty, entrenched inequalities and racism enabled the violent, retributive ideology of Shining Path and paved the way for the increased militarisation of the Fujimori regime and the explicit, or thinly disguised, forms of coercion it used in its social campaigns (Burmiller, 2014). The Truth and Reconciliation Commission (TRC), set up in 2001 to investigate crimes committed during the civil war, found that rape committed by the military was perpetrated against women from communities that were 'overwhelmingly indigenous, with rural roots' (Amnesty International, 2004, p. 21, note 82; Henriquez & Ewig, 2014, p. 269).

The women targeted by Fujimori's sterilisation campaign were from precisely the same rural Andean, non-Spanish speaking, indigenous communities as those targeted for sexual abuse and political coercion by Shining Path. In both cases, racism and the fact that these communities were marginalised geographically as well as economically and socially meant that their suffering did not register, or was easily ignored by the more powerful urban, white or mestizo communities. Poverty and poor health care disproportionately affect women in indigenous Andean communities, who are over-represented in statistics that evidence Peru's poor development record (Henriquez & Ewig, 2014). Rebecca Rivas' documentary *At Highest Risk* (2006) illustrates this disproportionality: it includes the testimonies of women who were forcibly sterilised during the 1990s and identifies maternal mortality among indigenous women as a continuing problem in Peru. From these women's testimonies it is clear both that the spectre of sterilisation still haunts these communities and that attempts to address the lack of maternal health care provision continue to include elements of coercion. The narrator explains that in recent years 'maternal waiting houses' have been introduced, ostensibly to address the issue of high maternal and infant mortality. Women who are eight months pregnant are 'forced', according to one pregnant mother, to stay in maternal waiting houses before giving birth in a health clinic, and women interviewed for the documentary report that the authorities fine women for giving birth at home. In addition, if a baby is stillborn, a mother will bury her rather than face punishment for not giving birth at a health clinic.

Rivas' video documentary is one of several that have been produced in the last two decades as part of a campaign for justice for the women who have been forcibly sterilised. It is funded by the North American organisation DER (Documentary Educational Resources), which advertises itself as committed to 'promoting thought provoking documentary film and media for learning about people and cultures of the world' (www.der.org). Thus it can be argued that, in the same way that Fujimori's sterilisation agenda was partially influenced by the priorities of international aid donors, with their emphasis on permanent or semi-permanent methods of contraception, past campaigns initiated to expose those abuses have also been sponsored and often initiated by agencies operating outside Peru. In this way, as we demonstrate in this chapter, campaign rhetoric and campaign products, including the use of video documentary, are already determined and possibly limited by their political contexts (Szörényi, 2009, pp. 174–175). A unique feature of the *Quipu Project*,[1] one that is not of course without limitations, is its attempt at independence: after initial funding by the UK Arts and Humanities Research Council, its continuation has been dependent on independently raised funds.

## WOMEN'S VOICES AND THE CAMPAIGN FOR REPARATION

From the earliest stages of the programme itself, documentary videos such as Rivas' have been central to the reparation campaign for the women affected by the sterilisation programme. Some of the outputs were produced by women who were themselves activists before and during the height of the programme. It was in 1997, a year after the programme had begun, that Giulia Tamayo (1959–2014), feminist human rights lawyer with CLADEM (Latin American and Caribbean Committee for the Defense of Women's Rights), exposed the extent to which the sterilisation programme violated the human rights of Peruvian citizens. Tamayo's report documents 243 cases of sterilisation in nineteen regional departments, in response to which Peru's *Defensoria del Pueblo* (Independent Ombudsman) launched a public inquiry. As the women in Tamayo's report attest, the worst care was received by the poorest, rural, indigenous women, who were often herded into overcrowded and inadequate medical facilities. Posters advertising the sterilisation campaign featured rural Andean women with large families of unkempt children: sterilisation as family planning was advertised as a route to social mobility – depicted in these posters as a route to 'whiteness' (Ewig, 2006, p. 646, 2010). The campaign posters thus imply that by having smaller, planned families women 'become white and lose indigenous cultural traditions' (p. 646). In addition to the coercive measures used on the women who are forcibly sterilised, health care workers in Tamayo's report speak of being under pressure to meet targets for sterilisation at the expense of attending to their patients' reproductive rights.

    To accompany her report Tamayo produced, with Carlos Cardenas, the documentary *Nada Personal: Implementación de la Anticoncepción*

*Quirúrgica en el Perú* (Nothing Personal: Implementation of the Surgical Contraception in Peru) (1999) aimed at raising awareness of these issues. The video, which we address in the following section, documents the voices of health workers, activists and women who have been forcibly sterilised. Other videos produced to document the cases of women's abuse include *Secret Sterilization* (1999) and *Cicatrices del Engaño* (Scars of Deception) (2014) which used 15 stories of women from Ayacucho, Cusco and Huancavelia y Piuru who had been forcibly sterilised. We situate our analysis of the web platform the *Quipu Project* in the context of these earlier outputs, all of which explicitly campaign for reparation for the physical and emotional consequences of what amounts to State-sponsored acts of gender violence against rural Andean women during the sterilisation campaign. Our analysis demonstrates that despite the regular production of media campaigns organised to raise awareness of this issue, women's voices are still not being heard and their case for compensation has not been addressed. This is in part because there has been, historically, a lack of organisation on the part of poor, indigenous women and a lack of indigenous organisation among Peruvian highland communities (Ewig, 2006). The lack of progress of the political campaigns is also in part to do with the complex discourse of rights within which these violations are situated (Pieper-Mooney, 2010; Vasquez del Aguila, 2006). In this chapter we draw attention to the extent to which women's representation in traditional campaigning video outputs and their depiction as passive victims of a process outside of their control both reflect and contribute to the absence of a coherent political outcome and response to the campaign for compensation. The women's passivity is evident in the victim position they occupy in these media outputs, where they bear witness to their experience but are not the voice of the campaign: they are spoken for, rather than speaking for themselves. In contrast to this trend, we identify a shift in the ideological engagement of the women in the *Quipu Project* and we discuss the political surplus that generates from the possibility of women speaking in their own voices as a form of agency.

# METHODOLOGY

The analyses of media outputs produced to raise awareness of the campaign of forced sterilisation in Peru that follows draw on documentary theory, intermediality and new media technology studies, as well as critical work that theorises the role of the witness in both traditional and new media contexts. The examination of conventional linear video documentaries, selected as examples of material used in the campaign against human rights violations in Peru, employs established video documentary theorisations (Bruzzi, 2000; Nichols, 1981) to test both the form and the content of the women's testimony in these contexts. The investigation reveals the extent to which the media context shapes the person bearing witness, the experience being communicated and the role of the audience or listener of that testimony. Our findings demonstrate that in these traditional documentaries the women are represented as passive, ignorant victims, through a reliance on the rhetoric of compassion.

Theories of digital aesthetics, medial synthesis and intermediality (Elleström, 2010; Ljungberg, 2010) allow for a discussion of the extent to which the women in the *Quipu Project* website are repositioned as agents in the campaign for justice and reconfigured from digitally marginalised to globally networked subjects. This case study reveals that the interactive nature of the narrative promotes a re-definition of the women survivors as collaborators, offering the women an opportunity to speak in their own voices and for their agency to be recognised and engaged with by the audience.

These findings are further supported by recent critical work that theorises the role of the witness in video and new media contexts. The proliferation of video testimony necessitates a rethinking of how the witness position is defined, and what new relations are constructed between audiences and witnesses. This chapter's analysis of media outputs distinguishes between the witness in the video who is the primary witness or victim of the injustices being documented; the secondary witness, or interviewer/activist who interacts with the person bearing witness, and the tertiary witness, or the audience of the video (Wake, 2013). This distinction between different witness positions allows for a focus on the layers of mediation that distance the subject, who testifies to her own suffering, from the audiences of that testimony (Feldman, 2004; Lenart-Cheng & Walker, 2011; Wake, 2013; Yaeger, 2006).

## SPEAKING, LISTENING, VOICE AND RECOGNITION: DOCUMENTARY CONVENTIONS AND THE POLITICS OF PERSONAL TESTIMONY

In addition to international campaigns, many attempts have been made by the local media to regain and ascribe visibility to these women in the public sphere. Newspapers and television news programmes in Peru have covered this story and the video-sharing website YouTube has provided a platform for the archiving of video content on this issue. In many cases, different producers use the same women to take part in different documentaries. In these documentaries and media outputs women's testimonies are mediated by formal, generic conventions, which shape and limit both the stories that can be told and the complex identities of the women who tell these stories. Traditional documentary films constitute a genre regulated by strict conventions, which stem from their three-act linear narrative. As in fictional storytelling, documentary films tell a story, have engaging characters, a narrative arc and a coherent point of view. Documentary's discourse of sobriety (Nichols, 1991) is organised around the demonstration of cause and effect and advocates agency on the part of the viewer by mobilising a range of strong feelings. In most documentaries the argument is built through showing the audience how the issues addressed in the film affect the conditions of an individual's life (Rabiger, 2004). Therefore, the use of human subjects as living evidence of the plight of the human condition is an embedded rhetoric of documentary discourse. In the analyses that follow we focus on a number of documentary films that address Fujimori's forced sterilisation programme and we unpack some of their strategies of representation and character building.

The artefacts we select for analysis include *Cicatrices del Engaño* (2014) (Scars of Deception), *Nada Personal. Implementación de la Anticoncepción Quirúrgica en el Perú* (1999) (Nothing Personal: Implementation of the Surgical Contraception in Peru), *Justicia Pendiente. Esterilizaciones forzadas Perú* (2011) (Pending Justice. Forced Sterilization in Peru) and *Secret Sterilization* (1999). The chapter concludes with an analysis of the non-linear documentary, which is found on the above-mentioned *Quipu Project's* pilot website. The focus is on the ways in which female subjects within the narrative are assigned the status of both witness and victim. Responses to their testimonies are determined by the ethical frameworks that witnessing constructs, both through the video's exploitation of their emotional surplus and the discursive contexts of the witness statements.

As with all expository documentaries theorised by Nichols (1981), *Secret Sterilization* (1999) and *Cicatrices del Engano* (Scars of Deception) (2014) rely on voice over commentary to guide the audience through a heterogeneous collection of facts and material. This includes statistical data, testimonies, expert opinion, information acquired from other media and the exposure of legal documents, all of which are organised in the narrative structure of the film according to the conventions of the documentary mode. The voice over commentary plays an important role in the way in which the witnesses' voices are placed within the narrative of these films. Thus the voice over is both the structuring route of inquiry, which provides a sense of the variety and complexity of the facts exposed in the films, and the narrative device which positions the women as both witnesses and victims within their narratives. The voice over commentary is deployed as an explanatory and persuasive tool: to persuade the audience of the injustices these women have suffered and to win the audience round to the validity of their perspective. One clear example of this can be found in the documentary *Cicatrices del Engaño* (Scars of Deception), in the interview with Consuelo Elsa Salvaterra, the health care worker who was part of the team that carried out the procedure on Celia Ramos, who died in the following 38 hours. As Salvaterra provides her version of the fact (that Ramos died of causes unrelated to the procedure) the voice over commentary challenges her statement without providing Salvaterra with the opportunity to address the points raised in the narration.

However, as Bruzzi (2000) has argued, although narration-led documentaries are the most explicit example of how documentaries can only represent truth through interpretation, the voice over is not necessarily the only formal device to inscribe a point of view within the narrative. Other very powerful formal strategies are in fact deployed in these documentaries, the most effective of which is the use of the witness statement as testimony by the women who forcibly underwent the procedure. From the opening sequences, the films present the 'case studies', the human stories used as an emotional catalytic narrative device aimed at establishing empathic understanding. In many of the scenes in which the women provide their testimonies, the subjects are shot either in close-up or extreme close-up, presenting them as emotionally embodied, or in medium close up shots that emphasise their poor living conditions. In most of these scenes extra-diegetic music is added to intensify the impact of their stories. These scenes therefore rely on the emotional bodies of the subjects as a form of evidence of the truthfulness of the argument developed and as a tool of persuasion. Notably, the persuasive effect of these formal strategies is proportional to the emotional tone of the representation. They therefore insert in the film modes of emotional persuasion that act on a different register to the reasoning of the voice over commentary.

The problem raised by the video documentaries relates to issues of representation — not so much what the women say but how what they say is configured and reconfigured to elicit a particular response. These documentaries rely on modes of performativity or what Feldman refers to as the 'dramaturgy of witnessing' (2004, p. 169). All conventional video testimony relies on a degree of preparation and rehearsal before-hand in order to produce an emotionally charged intervention. In their brief appearance in the video the women interviewed speak only about the subject of the documentary – their sterilisation. No attempt is made to address who these women are outside of that experience. Although scenes of women bearing witness are repeated throughout and intertwined with other forms of evidence, their representation is de-contextualised from their everyday lives in such a radical way that they emerge as one-dimensional entities, whose indexical relation to their referent in the real is compromised by the extremely narrow selection of their plotlines. The effect of this is evident for example throughout *Secret Sterilization* (1999) and in the closing scene of the documentary *Cicatrices del Engaño* (2014) (Scars of Deception), in which the women's suffering bodies are closely scrutinised by the camera with extreme close up shots of watering eyes and fidgeting hands holding their violated stomachs. These shots are edited over the voice over narration and extra-diegetic dramatic music, while the women's voices are no longer heard. The women are fully dissociated from their real life identities and their bodies have become fetishised objects of a victim's pain.

Traditional linear video documentaries such as the ones discussed above situate the viewer or spectator in a relationship of compassion. They situate the victim in the 'elsewheres brought home and made inti-mate' in the forms of media that reconstruct their suffering (Berlant, 2004, p. 5). The packaging of suffering and the requirement to respond compassionately constructs compassion 'as a particular kind of social relation' (p. 7). In their insistence on provoking feeling, these documen-taries do not address the structural factors that have contributed to the women's suffering and that continue to construct them as victims. If, as Kennedy and Wilson (2003) urge, we take into account the mode of address of the witness statements, then it is clear that even though they are seen to be speaking, they are not speaking for themselves, but for the documentary makers. The layers of mediation constitute a further viola-tion of an experience that requires testimony. As Yaeger (2006, p. 418) argues, these moments of bodily inscribed suffering that intend to create intimacy often function, paradoxically, to distance the viewer and 'mark our non-entry into the place of intimacy'.

# THE *QUIPU PROJECT*

The *Quipu Project* is a web platform produced by a team of digital storytellers and visual anthropologists based in London. As the website at the time of writing is not yet live, the analysis that follows is based on the pilot website. The *Quipu Project* marks a radical shift in its use of witness subjects, its representation of testimony and in its self-conscious focus on issues of distance, compassion and responsibility. In one of the pages of the site the viewer can click on an interactive box (titled 'The *Quipu Project*') that explains the nature of this project:

> The *Quipu Project* is a living, interactive documentary connecting people who were sterilized without consent in Peru with people willing to listen. We bridge the digital divide by enabling contributors to record themselves and respond to each other over the telephone, then present the testimonies to a global audience online. With a growing archive of testimonies from people affected by sterilization without consent, the *Quipu Project* is a record of individual experiences that must be acknowledged. It also tells a larger story – of a country and people and of the need we share as humans to speak and to be heard.
>
> (*Quipu Project*)

Significantly, this information is not provided on the home page, but can be found on another page (where the testimonies are also presented) and it is not overtly signposted: it is visually represented only with a dot. To have access to the aforementioned information the viewer has to find and click on the dot, which is one of the many dots that launch (when clicked) the witnesses' voice recordings. The way in which this information is presented on this web page shifts the attention of the viewer away from the project and its creators, who thus assign to themselves a secondary role in the overall narrative. The focus is redirected to the witnesses. The pilot's home page contains a linear documentary that introduces the subject matter and the female witnesses involved in the project. Overall, the platform features a high level of interactivity, and on the home page the audience has the choice either to skip the documentary or play it. The option to skip the linear documentary, which is consistent with the digital interactive long-form storytelling mode (and is featured in many examples of this genre, for example, *Firestorm* [The Guardian, 2013]) is indicative of the ideological stand of the authors.

A summative, pre-constructed narrative of the events is not the necessary point of entry for an understanding of the facts involved: it is presented as optional. As a result, the witness testimonies, which can be found on the web platform in the pages that follow, are not framed and interpreted within a tight narrative structure. There is an attempt here to disentangle the witness testimonies from the storyteller's perspective and to assign them a role that transcends the passive testimony of a painful violation.

The 'Quipu' of the title is another mark of the difference of this project. In the documentary *Secret Sterilization* (1999) the women interviewed refer repeatedly to the 'thread' — used as a metaphor for the sterilisation process. For the creators of the *Quipu Project*, the 'quipu' is also a word for string or 'thread', but the meanings attached to the word in earlier outputs are subverted: in this project the threads are the knotted strings used in Inca civilisations to keep records. The 'brightly coloured cords have also been used to tell stories through generations', reads one text on a black screen in the opening of the linear documentary included on the *Quipu Project* home page (*Quipu Project*). In this documentary there are shots of women spinning the thread, taking control of the process of storytelling and reconfiguring their relationship both to the thread as sterilisation and to the production of their testimonies. The early scenes are scenes of community, of women working — selling by the roadside — and of children shouting and playing. This is a dramatic revision of the still, helpless bodies of women in other video outputs, as described above. Silent, dirty, sad-faced children are replaced by noisy, active children, representative of a new generation, and of the possibility that their community will be restored. The injunction in the commentary is to 'listen' and 'to connect to others in a global dialogue' (*Quipu Project*). This is an address both to the viewer and to other primary witnesses (the women giving the testimony) who will listen to the testimonies of other women, not only in Peru but, once the online platform is complete, to other women in other parts of the world with similar stories to tell.

The visual images and narrative commentary of the *Quipu Project*'s linear documentary lasts for just over three minutes. Once it is finished the viewer is directed to a new page that features an interactive box entitled 'Welcome to the Quipu Archive', which invites the audience to listen to the testimonies of three women (the women are named in the pilot site, but the authors opted for anonymity in the final site) reads: 'Now you can listen to Evangelina, Ferdinanda or Tamaya tell their stories' (*Quipu Project*).[2] These testimonies are edited to guide a listening experience. Viewers can then access the full, unedited archive of voices. By clicking on 'Continue' the box disappears and a blue thread slowly drops from the top of the page and unravels as it connects with the arrow of the viewer's mouse on screen. This thread is the 'quipu', and the listener is from this moment connected to it and to the other strings (each of a different colour) that signify the testimonies of other women. Whereas the conventional documentaries referred to above rely on an embodied subject, who function to provide a 'talking head testimony' (Avci & Spence, 2013, pp. 298–300), here the strings stand in metonymic relation to the women: they are signs both of their abuse and of their reconstituted roles as agents. The listener is prevented from engaging voyeuristically in sounds that come from the face, and instead, as the producers insist, she is forced to listen. Paradoxically too, although the intermediaries – the interviewers and video producers – are not physically present in the documentary as voices of narration, the interactivity of the form and metaphorical replacement of the women means that we are acutely aware of the technology used. As listeners, we are both emotionally present in the activity of listening and reminded of our socio-economic and geographic distance. We occupy a position twice removed from the primary witness, in a role theorised as that of 'tertiary witness' (Wake, 2013, p. 138). In the space that this distance creates we are forced to reflect on our relationship to the victim's words.

Amongst the testimonies collected by the project makers, so far only three have been edited and uploaded onto the platform: the three women are named in the pilot site as Evangelina, Ferdinanda and Tamaya (who are also mentioned in the linear documentary found on its home page). The manipulation, by editing, of these three testimonies is made apparent to the listener both via a blipping sound that is heard every time a cut occurs and via a drop in the horizontal line of the thread that visually symbolises each testimony. Both strategies are indicative of the curators' intention to declare to the audience the presence of the omniscient point of view (theirs): thus the flow of communication between the witness and the audience is reconfigured to become multi-directional. In addition, each of the three testimonies curated on the website presents a 'Share' option that allows the audience to share the link of the witness voice with a wider audience, thereby expanding the potential destination of the witness testimony. There is also an option for the listener to leave a message for the witness, which allows for a bi-directional flow between the witness and the audience. These devices are made possible by the features of the web platform, and are in stark contrast to the traditional linear narratives of the aforementioned documentaries.

The testimonies of the three witnesses are equally carriers of pain and anger, but also of a strong message of human rights awareness and willingness to speak. A recurrent theme in all testimonies is the reference to body pain, not only in relation to the procedure, but also to the brutal way in which it was carried out. Evangelina is particularly graphic in her recounting of pain, and talks about her body being cut when the anaesthesia was not yet effective. In her recording she says: 'They started cutting on me and it hurt' (*Quipu Project*). The cutting through the women's bellies and the reference to the 'tremendous pain' recurs several times in her statement, and this image epitomises, in her testimony, the physical and psychological violation these women suffered. Evangelina's testimony is the most extreme, as she was three months pregnant when she had the procedure done. She asked for her baby not to be removed, but as she (the baby) died during the operation she carried her dead baby in her belly until she had a haemorrhage and an abortion several months later. In Tamaya's testimony her need to vomit after the procedure becomes a mark of her disabled body. Ferdinanda constantly refers to her mutilated body, although more indirectly, when she talks about being an 'invalid' and leading a 'half-life'. She refers to the women who received the procedure as 'being on our knees' (*Quipu Project*).

Another theme the testimonies constantly refer to is resentment at having been deceived and coerced to go through the procedure. They all describe their experiences of 'being tricked' and 'forced' (*Quipu Project*). Evangelina and Tamaya, when describing their arrival at the medical centre where the procedure was carried out on their bodies, use the image of the prison, and Evangelina explains how the women were forced inside the clinic, after which the gates were closed. All talk about the women being forced to undertake the operation as 'crying', as they did not want to undergo the procedure (*Quipu Project*). Ferdinanda refers to the period in which the procedures were carried out as a 'time of violence' and to the women who received the procedure as being 'treated like animals', again as a metaphor of captivity and denial of human rights (*Quipu Project*). Evangelina and Tamaya talk about their embarrassment at being naked in front of the medical team and other male patients who had their tubes closed at the same time. Their modesty sounds almost out of place in a situation in which their very basic human rights are denied, but it is an indicator of their sense of dignity and perceived identity. This is in stark contrast to the medical team's understanding and appreciation of their social and personal value.

The testimonies by Ferdinanda, Tamaya and Evangelina provided on the pilot certainly portray them as victims in a similar fashion to the traditional linear documentaries that have been analysed above. However, all three testimonies end with an empowering message consciously given by the women themselves to their audience. In fact, the women who speak on the telephone are already involved in a collective project for reparation and for the production of shared histories. They meet regularly with the women from the *Quipu Project* and together they discuss the possibility of justice. The curators of the *Quipu Project*, via an interactive box on the website, explain that when they conceived of the project they had already heard of the grassroots activists of the Huancabamba region in the Northern Andes of Peru and had wanted to make their voices heard. The project was there-fore designed in collaboration with activists:

> Together we explored the experience of using the phoneline to record and listen to their stories. As they listened, they began to talk about how important it was to share their experiences and the possibilities the phone line opened up for their campaign.
>
> *(Quipu Project)*

The second stage of the project is under construction and at present con-sists of 20 unedited testimonies. These raw, unfinished statements are powerful evidence of the continuing trauma of that earlier experience: they are also evidence of the 'larger story' the project wants to tell (*Quipu Project*). Some of the women speak for less than a minute and are unable to articulate either their original experience or the subsequent, disabling effects. Their fragmented narratives, full of repetition and silence, reflect the on-going and unresolved trauma (Caruth, 1996; Nadal & Calvo, 2014). Other victims, in contrast, have clearly had other opportunities to speak and are actively involved in the project of political activism. They speak of meeting other women; they refer to the political context of their witnessing and they address directly the women involved in the *Quipu Project*. Santana, speaking very briefly, says: 'I also want to speak to find out about the other sterilised women to find out if they will help us. I feel bad, I want to find out about all of us who were sterilised' (*Quipu Project*). Though Santana's contribution is truncated and does not constitute a narrative or even a testimony as such, in her choice of language, and by saying 'I also want to speak', she positions herself as an agent in the project of reparation and in the campaign for justice.

Several of the witnesses use the word 'justice' and describe their words as 'testimony', signs that they are knowingly participating in a discourse of rights (*Quipu Project*). In the introduction to the linear documentary that frames these testimonies on the home page, the narrator explains that since '2000 there have been several attempts to bring those responsible to justice, without success' (*Quipu Project*). Some of the witnesses make reference to those attempts, and a note of cynicism and caution seeps into their testimony. An unnamed man, the eldest son of a woman who was sterilised says: 'They say there is going to be support and I see they're just tricking them − or maybe they're making a profit', a suspicion that he raises more than once. He also hints at what he considers to be the futility of meetings: '... they are losing their time going to meetings ... That's my testimony' (*Quipu Project*). At the same time, he makes more than one reference to 'hope'. The contribution of this eldest son highlights the way in which the 'routinisation of violence' in regimes such as Fujimori's was also accompanied by structures of 'deniability built into the very strategy of violent enactment' (Feldman, 2004, p. 172). It is a sign that 'political terror not only attacks the witness but also the cultural capacity and resources needed to bear witness' (Feldman, 2004, p. 172). This son's testimony is clear evidence of those strategies at work: women have not, and continue not to passively accept their victimisation. However, the repressive structures that encourage forgetting, in official records and in the public domain, have worked against their voices being heard.

Both the edited and unedited testimonies are delivered as part of a shared communal experience with each witness understanding that, however brief, their words count as evidence. They acknowledge that their presence at the meeting is a sign of political engagement, that they are agents of change and not simply women whose only identity is that they were forcibly sterilised. Another unnamed witness speaks graphically of her coercion, repeating 'I didn't want to, but my husband said it was okay' (*Quipu Project*). Like many other contributors, she says they 'threw us out' after the operation, despite the fact that they couldn't walk. She ends with a commitment to activism and a belief in collective action: 'sometimes one doesn't know and doesn't go, but I'll do what I can to go to the meeting to listen [...] There are many of us' (*Quipu Project*).

It is clear that each of the women and men attending the meetings are 'co-present' in the production of testimony: they participate both in the process of witnessing and in 're-living and re-experiencing the event' (Wake, 2013, p. 114). Unlike the more conventional examples of documentary analysed above, there seems in these archived contributions to be no interviewer, and therefore no-one in the formal role of 'secondary witness', listening to but separate from the 'primary witness' (Wake, 2013, p. 114). Although there clearly are women involved from outside the community, including the curators of the *Quipu Project*, rather than managing the production of testimony these other figures serve to facilitate the coming to voice of the primary witnesses. Rather than naturalising the production of testimony through conventional documentary, the project reminds us that 'the very condition of subalternity requires mediation by those with access to publishing and media venues' (Caminero-Santangelo, 2012, p. 452). In other words, the *Quipu Project* addresses, and in doing so forces the listener to address, the politics of its own production (Caminero-Santangelo, 2012; Szörényi, 2009).

Ferdinanda's edited recording concludes with: 'That is the testimony I give you now' (*Quipu Project*), addressing her audience directly and creating an instance in the narrative in which the storytelling mode gives way to a politically charged speech. Tamaya, like others in the unedited archives, concludes her testimony by thanking her audience for listening, and the *Quipu Project* team for giving her the opportunity to speak up: 'And thank you for all this, thank you very much. Very much' (*Quipu Project*). She is conscious of the power of the media to reach out beyond their marginalised community. The most powerful message comes from Evangelina who ends her testimony by announcing: 'But now we say these things that have damaged women in this area must not happen again. The women feel awful, and we won't allow young women to go through this again. This is why we are asking for women's rights. Thank you' (*Quipu Project*). It is clear that these testimonies do not function within the narrative merely as embodiment of pain but as an intervention into the political process.

These formal strategies underline a profound shift in the ideological stance of the project creators who see these women as the agents of a radical revolution with regards to campaigning for human rights. For the producers of the *Quipu Project* these women are not just the subjects of a media campaign aimed at raising awareness by mobilising audiences through compassion. Rather they are collaborators and negotiators of new meanings and understandings of their own stories through the means of technologies such as telephones and the online platform. As the voice over reiterates throughout the linear documentary found on the home page of the *Quipu Project*, the project invests in the potential of their oral testimonies to transform the women into globally networked subjects.

## DIGITAL TECHNOLOGIES AND INTERACTIVE STORYTELLING: RECONFIGURING THE WITNESS IN ONLINE TESTIMONY AND THE *QUIPU PROJECT*

The *Quipu Project* uses a specially developed telephone line devised to collate testimonies from the victims: the use of low-tech equipment, which is familiar to and approachable by the victims, allows a capillary outreach to a vast number of women. Their testimonies are then archived in a high-tech digital interface. This interplay between low-end and high-end technologies promotes the re-purposing and re-contextualisation of old tools into new media. It also involves the re-mapping and geographical reconfiguration of the victims' localised testimonies into the World Wide Web and its international audiences. By challenging the political, geographical and digital marginalisation of these women, described by the producers as 'collaborators', the creators of the *Quipu Project* aim to create a participatory mechanism for the women's testimonies. Ultimately, the ambition of the online platform is to keep building on data gathered in Peru and in other countries where women are facing similar problems. As a work-in-progress ad infinitum, it has the potential of reaching the most marginalised of global communities. As the curators of the site explain in one of the interactive boxes entitled 'Living Documentary':

> The Quipu Project is an experiment, a living documentary, a story that continues to evolve after its release. Its approach allows the story to emerge organically and people around the world to listen and to respond to each other. The people affected by sterilization without consent can connect with each other and the world, and so empower themselves to become active collaborators in the documentary-making process with their stories told with them, not about them.
>
> (*Quipu Project*)

The use of low-end technologies such as the phone lines to record the women's testimonies allows them to determine the form and content of their narrative. In fact, at the very core of the *Quipu Project* is the emphasis on the women's use of their own voices as evidence not only of their human rights violations but also of their journey from the margins to the centre of the story. One important feature of the project, that differentiates it from the aforementioned traditional media outputs, is its interactivity. This refers not only to the audience's ability to create an individual journey within the options offered by the non-linear audio narratives presented on the platform, but also to the relationship between the project curators, the women who provide the testimonies featured on the website and the visitors to the site. A simple technology allows listeners to post messages on the website either in the form of written posts or by leaving an audio message. As a result, rather than passive, illiterate victims, the women whose voices are recorded and curated on the site are offered an opportunity to revisit their testimony and to respond to others around the world, who have listened. The platform thus allows the construction of synergic and multifaceted narratives built by the women, the audience and the curators of the project and it positions the women's testimonies at the centre of this complex system.

The project reveals the conflicting nature of participatory ethnography: the subjects' empowerment and the self-representative authority allowed by the recording devices they are given and the pervasive presence of the expert, who provides in the background the contextual framework for the witnesses' testimonies (White, 2003). The crux of this tension is at the core of the conception of the web-curating role behind this project and of the producers' efforts to provide evidence, on the platform, of their interventions in the audio testimonies themselves. To this end, the *Quipu Project* aligns itself with other online content-sharing platforms that are the product of interesting synergies between user-generated content and curatorial involvements by the project leaders, as evidenced by the online project *Question Bridge* (http://questionbridge.com).

The fluidity of the digital aesthetic challenges the traditional medial delimitations and specificities, and provides the opportunity for medial configurations that blur traditional borders assigned to specific fields and practices. As Elleström (2010) explains, on the digital platform the properties of different media partly intersect. According to Ljungberg these hybrid forms 'generate something new and unique. These medial syntheses operate communication strategies which are both self-reflexive [...] and highly effective, as they give receivers access to different levels of meaning' (2010, p. 83). The *Quipu Project* website is an example of a multilayered and multimedia long-form content that relies on complex and sophisticated modes of web curation in which the negotiation of borders between traditional distinctive fields allows a cross-medial expansion of meaning. For online content delivery to be successful, a holistic cognitive experience is essential, one that promotes sensorial engagement (intermediality). Intermedial storytelling is a synthesis of different languages, such as writing, visual storytelling, the use of codes and design, and even social conversations. It is intended to produce meaning by its constant permutation through different senses and codes, such as the use of the quipu (thread) to visualise sound. In addition the project relies on specific immersive forms of audience engagement through the use of testimonies, case studies and short episodic storylines. Web engagement goes in waves rather than reaching an affective climax. As a result, the narrative structures that can be employed in digital storytelling engage lateral thinking as opposed to logical, step-by-step consequential, propositional exposition. On the *Quipu Project* website, sound is engaged both in propositional forms with the testimonies and as ambient sound in a non-directional form in-between digital spaces. These different acoustic systems are never integrated in an organic narrative structure and are left disembodied for the user to make sense of.

As we have seen, the women's accounts are presented without narration and description. This form of digital 'epic' storytelling has the effect of encouraging propositional thinking and critical understanding rather than climatic catharsis through immersion (Brecht, 1964). Through constant involvement in the interactive decision making process the listener is distanced, rather than completely immersed in the women's testimonies. In this way, the website aims to democratise the power dynamics of the production of information. Storytelling in this context can be seen as a form of sharing, an act of reciprocity and an example of more effective, participatory democracy (Lenart-Cheng & Walker, 2011). As a democratic, multivoiced and participatory medium, the website is not constrained by traditional linear storytelling strategies such as the use of vibrant examples that stir emotion – poignant stories that exemplify the problem analysed (as in the documentary videos analysed). The *Quipu Project* website goes beyond telling stories by immersion and thus challenges the user's ethical responses in ways that promote rational self-reflection. The technology, as we have argued, prompts an 'awareness of the mechanics of withholding' (Yaeger, 2006, p. 138) that in itself becomes productive of multiple levels of engagement. Such withholding demonstrates that 'proximity without intimacy can be an ethical stance' (p. 138).

## CONCLUSION

The object of the *Quipu Project*, as the voice over commentary of the linear documentary of the home page explains, is to enable 'a global dialogue which demands that justice is done' and to encourage listening. These women 'want you to listen' (*Quipu Project*). The experience we have of hypermediated witnessing (Wake, 2013), which is the effect of interactive, multimedia technology, mirrors the feelings of marginalisation and invisibility experienced by the women who testify. Their invisibility, on the other hand, frees them to speak without their voices being overly constrained either by the demands and structures of conventional documentary, or by the demands of legal and formal discourses. Although the form of the online project refuses easy familiarity and self-consciously works to undermine the work that compassion does to create points of empathy and identification, it does rely on viewer engagement and the willingness to listen. This is a challenge for the project's campaign as well as for viewers and academics. The effect of the form is to shift focus from the ontological to the ideological: from a concern with the ethics of witnessing, testimony and truth, to a concern about the function and ethics of the form itself (Wake, 2013). Certainly this complex form of engagement militates against voyeurism; indeed the audience is more accurately defined as listeners rather than viewers or spectators. The form of the project necessitates a reconsideration of the ethics of engagement, and an acknowledgement of the role played by conventional media narratives in the failure of existing systems of justice and reparation.

## NOTES

1. The website of the *Quipu Project* was at the time of writing this chapter under construction. However, the authors of the Quipu Project had made available a pilot site aimed at showcasing some of the work done to date. When writing the chapter, the authors accessed the pilot website (quipu.project-pilot.com) using the following login: User: Guest and Password: Quipu. In March 2016, a more developed site for Quipu Project went live at www.quipu-project.com. The new site retains all the principles that were discussed in this chapter regarding the pilot, but it is now fully developed with an improved interface and interactive features. Interactive digital projects and i-docs are a work in progress or, as Gaudenzi (2013) has called them, live documentaries, and as such always involve a degree of change. The making of the Quipu Project brings evidence of the continuous development that this type of project involves, both in terms of prototyping and final development stage, but also in terms of updating, maintenance and revision of the final web platform.

2. We changed the names of the women who gave their testimonies (which are provided on the pilot site) as the curators subsequently decided to maintain the women's anonymity in the final site.

## REFERENCES

Amnesty International. (2004). Truth and Reconciliation Commission, Final Report, Volume I, *The Faces and Profiles of the Violence*, cited in 'Peru: The Truth and Reconciliation Commission — A first step towards a country without injustice'.

Avci, A. K., & Spence, L. (2013). The talking witness documentary: Remembrance and the politics of truth. *Rethinking History*, *17*(3), 295–311.

Benavente, R. R. (2011). *Justicia Pendiente. Esterilizaciones forzadas Perú (Pending Justice. Forced Sterilization in Peru)*. Retrieved from https://www.youtube.com/watch?v=dabfwFkQAzM. Accessed on November 13, 2015.

Berlant, L. (2004). Introduction. In L. Berlant (Ed.), *Compassion: The culture and politics of an emotion* (pp. 1–14). London: Routledge.

Brecht, B. (1964). The modern theatre is the epic theatre: Notes to the opera *Aufstieg und Fall der Stadt Mahagonny*. In B. Brecht (Ed.), *Brecht on theatre: The development of an aesthetic* (pp. 33–42). London: Methuen.

Bruzzi, S. (2000). *New documentary: An introduction*. London: Routledge.

Burmiller, K. (2014). Feminist collaboration with the state in response to sexual violence: Lessons from the American experience. In A. M. Tripp, M. M. Fettee, & C. Ewig (Eds.), *Gender, violence and human security: Critical feminist perspectives* (pp. 191–213). New York, NY: New York University Press.

Caminero-Santangelo, M. (2012). Documenting the undocumented: Life narratives of undocumented immigrants. *Biography, 35*(3), 449–471.

Carrión, J. F. (2006). *The Fujimori legacy: The rise of electoral authoritarianism in Peru*. University Park, PA: Pennsylvania State University.

Caruth, C. (1996). *Unclaimed experience: Trauma, narrative and history*. Baltimore, MD: The Johns Hopkins University Press.

Elleström, L. (2010). Introduction. In L. Elleström (Ed.), *Media borders, multimodality and intermediality* (pp. 1–10). New York, NY: Palgrave.

Ewig, C. (2006). Hijacking global feminism: Feminists, the Catholic Church, and the family planning debacle in Peru. *Feminist Studies, 32*(3), 632–659.

Ewig, C. (2010). *Second-wave neoliberalism: Gender, race, and health sector reform in Peru*. University Park, PA: Pennsylvania State University.

Feldman, A. (2004). Memory theaters, virtual witnessing and the trauma aesthetic. *Biography, 27*(1), 163–202.

Gaudenzi, S. (2013). *The living documentary: From representing reality to co-creating reality in digital interactive documentary*. Doctoral Thesis. London: University of Goldsmiths. Centre for Cultural Studies (CCS). Retrieved from http://research.gold.ac.uk/7997/. Accessed on March 3, 2016.

Gorriti, G. (1999). *The shining path: A history of the millenarian war in Peru*. Chapel Hill, NC: University of North Carolina Press.

Henley, J. (2013). Firestorm. *The Guardian*. Retrieved from http://www.theguardian.com/world/interactive/2013/may/26/firestorm-bushfire-dunalley-holmes-family. Accessed on November 13, 2015.

Henriquez, N., & Ewig, C. (2014). Integrating gender into human security: Peru's truth and reconciliation commission. In A. M. Tripp, M. M. Fettee, & C. Ewig (Eds.), *Gender, violence and human security: Critical feminist perspectives* (pp. 260–282). New York, NY: New York University Press.

Kennedy, R., & Wilson, T. J. (2003). Constructing shared histories: Stolen generations testimony, narrative therapy and address. In J. Bennett & R. Kennedy (Eds.), *World memory: Personal trajectories in global time* (pp. 119–139). Basingstoke: Palgrave.

Lenart-Cheng, H., & Walker, T. J. (2011). Recent trends in using life stories for social and political activism. *Biography, 34*(1), 141–179.

Ljungberg, C. (2010). Intermedial strategies in multimedia art. In L. Elleström (Ed.), *Media borders, multimodality and intermediality* (pp. 81–97). New York, NY: Palgrave.

Nadal, M., & Calvo, M. (2014). Trauma and literary representation: An introduction. In M. Nadal & M. Calvo (Eds.), *Trauma in contemporary literature: Narrative and representation* (pp. 1–13). London: Routledge.

Nichols, B. (1981). *Ideology and the image: Social representation in the cinema and other media*. Bloomington, IN: Indiana University Press.

Nichols, B. (1991). *Representing reality: Issues and concepts in documentary*. Bloomington, IN: Indiana University Press.

Pieper-Mooney, J. (2010). Re-visiting histories of modernization, progress, and (unequal) citizenship rights: Coerced sterilization in Peru and in the United States. *History Compass*, *8*(9), 1036–1054.

Question Bridge. Retrieved from http://questionbridge.com. Accessed on November 13, 2015.

Quipu Project. Retrieved from http://pilot.quipu-project.com (User: Guest/Password: Quipu) (Accessed November 11, 2015). In March 2016 a more developed site for *Quipu Project* went live at www.quipu-project.com. Accessed on March 3, 2016.

Rabiger, M. (2004). *Directing the documentary*. London: Focal Press.

Rivas, R. (2006). *At highest risk*. Retrieved from https://www.youtube.com/watch?v = nRFzlTkQ6v4&list = PL816F26BD8B1B6536&index = 14. Accessed on November 13, 2015.

Secret Sterilization. (1999). Retrieved from https://www.youtube.com/watch?v = iv9GtGl4Odk&list = PL816F26BD8B1B6536&index = 9. Accessed on November 13, 2015.

Shepard, B. (2006). *Running the obstacle course to sexual reproductive health: Lessons from Latin America*. Westport, CT: Praegar.

Starn, O. (1995). Maoism in the Andes: The communist party of Peru – Shining path and the refusal of history. *Journal of Latin American Studies*, *27*(3), 399–421. Retrieved from http://www.latinamericanstudies.org/peru/shining-path.pdf. Accessed on January 12, 2016.

Szörényi, A. (2009). Till human voices awake us: Responding to refugee testimony. *Life Writing*, *6*(2), 173–191.

Tamayo, G., & Cardenas, C. (1999). *Nada Personal. Implementación de la Anticoncepción Quirúrgica en el Perú (Nothing Personal. Implementation of the Surgical Contraception in Peru)*. Retrieved from https://www.youtube.com/watch?v = QRcU_JZgatw&index = 8&list = PL816F26BD8B1B6536. Accessed on November 13, 2015.

Vasquez del Aguila, E. (2006). Invisible women: Forced sterilization, reproductive rights and structural inequalities in [the] Peru of Fujimori and Toledo. *Estudos e Pesquisas em Psicoogia*, *6*(1), 109–124.

Wake, C. (2013). 'Regarding the recording': The viewer of testimony, the complexity of copresence and the possibility of tertiary witnessing. *History and Memory*, *25*(1), 111–144.

White, S. (Ed.) (2003). *Participatory video: Images that transform and empower*. London: Sage.

Yaeger, P. (2006). Testimony without intimacy. *Poetics Today*, *17*(1), 339–423.

Zevallos, M. (2014). *Cicatrices del Engaño (Scars of Deception)*. Retrieved from https://www.youtube.com/watch?v = DCOSkhkO7Ww. Accessed on November 13, 2015.

# THE BODY CONTOURS OF CARNIVAL: MAS-PLAYING AND RACE IN TRINIDAD

Kavyta Raghunandan

## ABSTRACT

Purpose — *This chapter sets up the national event of Carnival in Trinidad as a contested space of liberation and tradition. It explores the intersections of gender and race for a group of young Indian Trinidadian women and highlights the ways in which agency, articulated as sexual liberation and 'free-up', is enabled and disabled in relation to mas[1] performance.*

Design/methodology/approach — *Based on ethnographic research conducted in Trinidad in 2011 (Raghunandan, K. (2014). The Dougla poetics of Indianness: Negotiating race and gender in Trinidad. Unpublished doctoral thesis, University of Leeds), this chapter draws on a selection of interviews conducted with a group of young Indian Trinidadian women between the ages of 18 and 25.*

Findings — *The binaristic positioning of modern, morally destructive masquerader vis-à-vis the traditional non-participant is an inadequate approach and this has, to a significant extent, dominated media*

Gender and Race Matter: Global Perspectives on Being a Woman
Advances in Gender Research, Volume 21, 193−212
ISSN: 1529-2126/doi:10.1108/S1529-212620160000021011

*representations of Indian women which draw on these monolithic stereo-types. There are many ways of 'doing' gender and race. Playing mas is only one of them.*

Research implications/limitations — *These findings are in no way representative of the entire Indian descent population, nor can the young women's talk be regarded as wholly representative of their lives. Rather, these are a snapshot of their discursively produced subjectivities within a particular time and space.*

Originality/value — *By problematising the mixed and multicultural image of Carnival, this chapter makes a contribution to Carnival scholarship in its analysis of Indian Trinidadian women's voices which do not typically feature in Carnival literature. In its drawing upon these voices as epistemological sources, it makes a contribution to wider discourses of race, gender and the nation in the Trinidadian context.*

**Keywords:** Carnival; bodies; Indian Trinidadian; mas; sexuality; Trinidad

# INTRODUCTION

The female body has always been a central force in the development of Carnival, as attested to in the media imagery of masqueraders in bikini, beads and feather costumes. Paradoxically, the participation of women in this national event has also led to wider debates on notions of sexuality, respectability and the morality of public performance. As such, the Carnival setting is revealed as one in which the centrality of gender and race gains prominence in discussions of national culture given how different women are positioned in the space. In considering how these young women negotiate sexualised Carnival culture, I have attempted to move away from the binary positioning of modern versus traditional by exploring the nuances of Carnival participation in talk.

Carnival, the annual festival of dance, music, food and culture, has come to be a major cultural force in the Caribbean post-colonial island-nation of Trinidad and Tobago. The centrality of this festival cannot be exaggerated and while this is indelibly linked to the nation's creole identity

(Nurse, 1999), it is also conceptualised as an event reflecting the diversity of the national body, with Black, Indian and European descent people taking part alongside others. Among the many aspects of Trinidadian culture that are expressed, reflected and constituted in Carnival celebrations, the treatment of the bodies of Trinidadian women is a fundamental part of the Carnival phenomenon of 'centering the periphery' (Nurse, 1999, p. 685).

That the experiences of Carnival are both gendered and raced is not a new revelation. The gendered and raced ideologies that shape Carnival experiences as both culture and community in Trinidad necessitate a continual and comprehensive exploration. As such, this chapter aims to address a gap in feminist scholarship on Carnival that supports or challenges the reality of Indian Trinidadian women's identities. The masks put on and played with in Carnival represent a paradoxical, challenging/challenge, but ultimately *real* and fundamental aspect of who these women (and other participants) are. Considering how women have partaken in Carnival throughout Trinidadian history will reveal more about this paradox.

Women's role in Carnival has transformed since the 1970s, the era when the first body of critical literature dedicated to Carnival emerged (Guilbault, 2007). The aesthetic of Carnival was markedly different in the 1970s when there was a greater emphasis on traditional mas characters which reflected the resistance to French, British and American colonial powers on the island. Analysed as a form of resistance against the social, economic and political elite, the impact of gender on Carnival as a cultural form in both pre-independence and contemporary Trinidad has garnered greater scholarly attention (Edmondson, 2009; Noel, 2010).

In recent decades, African descent women have begun to compose the majority of the masqueraders and become iconic in representations of Carnival. Referring to the 1970s, Noel (2010, p. 73) explained, 'Carnival was now more than ever associated with women', and this was attributed to their increasing economic power. Barnes (2006, p. 89) unpacks Carnival sexuality in terms of spectacle and stereotype:

> By re-enacting and embodying patriarchal stereotypes that depict women as sexually available, women consent to, rather than critique, their own subjugation [can] a resistive praxis emanate from the spectacle of women masqueraders gyrating in full view of television cameras? Is 'visibility' enough of a liberatory strategy to convert the subversive act into an emancipatory politics?

This type of analysis examines the double blind of increased sexual freedom and increased subjectification that has arisen for African Trinidadian women in recent years. While this is a necessary interpretation when looking at present day Carnival, it falls short of looking at the role of Indian descent women in this process, an underexplored area of inquiry. The politics of public performance for Indian descent women has long been, and continues to be, inflected by notions of respectability and control, whether it is through participation in the Trinidad Carnival, Bollywood representations of the female form in India or the marked racial disparities in American and British cultural industries. The history of Carnival may illustrate how women subvert the hegemonic order, but in its current guise we need to find out how Carnival speaks to the positionalities of women. Specifically, how it speaks to Indian descent women, who represent a different set of cultural expressions than African descent women in Trinidad.

## METHODS

In attempting to answer these questions the use of talk as a data method was employed, and this chapter draws on a selection of individual conversations and focus groups (of five participants per group) conducted with a group of 29 Indian descent Trinidadian young women. These methods drew on a black feminist ethnography (Hill-Collins, 2008) which propounds lived experience as a way of knowing, alongside talk as dialogue. This was identified as the most appropriate means through which to unpack the discursive repertoires. By engaging in an informal dialogue with the young women a range of themes emerged, one of the more pressing being notions of respectability in relation to playing mas at Carnival. In some of the young women's talk, there were a variety of attitudes towards this with some espousing conservative views and others talking about Carnival sexuality as a form of liberation albeit temporary. By embracing the changes that are bringing about a more permissive attitude to sexuality in Carnival, and simultaneously adhering to more traditional representations of female sexuality, patriarchal norms are being challenged but ultimately reproduced in different ways.

While this chapter is not a full representation of their narratives, I have attempted to convey some sense of tone by reproducing some of the quotes in their local dialect and noting where emphasis was given to particular expressions.

The participants mentioned in this chapter are identified as shown in Table 1.

***Table 1.***  Participants.

| Name | Religion | Age | Address | Occupation |
| --- | --- | --- | --- | --- |
| Esther | Presbyterian | 25 | Freeport | Psychologist |
| Hema | Hindu | 21 | Tunapuna | Student |
| Kelly | Hindu | 20 | San Fernando | Student |
| Lisa | Presbyterian | 25 | Woodbrook | Designer |
| Maariyah | Muslim | 24 | San Fernando | Human Resources Manager |
| Nafeesa | Muslim | 18 | Chaguanas | Student |
| Najma | Muslim | 22 | St Augustine | Trainee Engineer |
| Salma | Muslim | 19 | Chaguanas | Student |
| Samantha | Presbyterian | 24 | Williamsville | Teacher |
| Sattee | Hindu | 21 | Tunapuna | Student |
| Raadiyah | Muslim | 22 | San Fernando | Administrative Assistant |
| Riana | Presbyterian | 22 | Penal | Sales Assistant |
| Vaasha | Christian | 23 | Arima | Graduate Work Intern |

## PLAYING MAS

The complexities of gender involved in playing mas are frequently read as clashing with rules of propriety and dress inflected with ideas of respectability, as one of the respondents' anecdotes illustrated:

> I played last year and I would say around 3,000–4,000 people played. Many under 20s play because of the history of mas bands and it becomes a rite of passage when a young woman passes her CXC exams, she is allowed by her parents to play mas. So I was only allowed one time. My brother don't [sic] have this problem. He plays all the time! It was fun but my parents didn't stop me because of religious reasons. It was more 'cause of what goes on with the drinking and winin'[2] and that. So [...] as a parent I could see their reasons. (Samantha, 24, Teacher)

That Samantha was conditionally granted access to this public space, in contrast to her brother who could readily partake, evokes questions of equality. Women's participation may be evident at a surface level, but this does not signify equality nor is it a given. Playing mas has for a long time been a rite of passage for Indian Trinidadian women and men, but this is not accessible or acceptable for all. It could be said that to engage in a deeply national staging of public culture is only opening up to them in recent years. The question, then, of what meaning playing mas takes on for young women today becomes one which should be understood in the context of local understandings of gender and race.

Carnival is a paradoxical social phenomenon, as on the one hand it is celebrated as a national event that stages subversive social spaces and 'othered' identities. On the other hand these 'othered' identities are not sustainable outside of Carnival, despite its presence serving as a stabilising force in Trinidadian society (Isaac-Flavien, 2013). Individuals can demonstrate agency in their ability to alter the available discourses surrounding gender, whilst these alterations are always embedded within power structures. Playing mas exemplifies this tension between agency and structure. There are disparate strands of thought on the sexualisation of Carnival through the gendered, raced and sexualised practices of playing mas where normative/traditional ideologies of gender, race and class are represented, upheld and challenged. Most importantly, Carnival brings to the fore the fact that there are many different assertions about the appropriate breakdown of the categories of race, ethnicity, gender and class. Carnival demonstrates that there are multiple discourses of agentic female sexuality and not just the 'free up'[3] discourse that intersects with class, ethnicity and race producing particular limitations as to who can take these up. This chapter will go on to examine agentic female sexuality in terms of the Carnival dress and codes associated with the event.

Ethno-centrists have regarded Carnival as a strictly Creole or African event. A more recent example of their viewpoint is when the Carnival celebrations in 2012 coincided with the Hindu religious festival of Maha Shivratri.[4] The president of the National Council of Indian Culture (NCIC) was reported to have said in a local newspaper that he implored people to keep away from active indulgence in Carnival which can only degrade human values (Subero, 2012), and this was said with reference to women. From a gendered lens, the higher moral ground becomes underscored with notions of pollution and impurity, respectability and vulgarity. Puri (2004, p. 202) refers to this as a discourse about 'Carnivalesque degradation'. She argues that Carnival discourse represents the festival as something which epitomises Bakhtin's (1984, p. 20) 'double movement' which both 'bring(s) down to earth' and 'turn(s) (its) subjects to flesh.' This manifests in spheres of social interaction such as theatre and performance, all under the umbrella of Carnival. These 'performances' focus on the grotesqueness of bodily flesh and Puri (2004) argues that the grotesque represents the body of the 'people', which resists attempts by officials to be controlled and centralised.

Yet the common issue of what body best represents 'the people' surfaces again in the discussion of bodies in Carnival. The anxiety around the overlap of Indian women's sexuality with black women's sexuality interrupts the model of celebrated hybridity posited by the nation-state (Puri, 2004). The controversial reception of Drupatee's chutney-soca song, 'Lick down me nani',[5] as well as the disciplinary tone of the NCIC condemning women who play mas, are typical examples of how female involvement in Carnival usually draws the loudest condemnation from conservative Indian groups. The possibilities enabled by this agentic female sexuality become reduced to the homogenised portrayal of Indian descent people in the local media which represents different and competing, interests and therefore 'exists as the discursive fiefdom of the two major ethnic groups, African and East Indian' (Brunton, 2012, p. 1). Consequently, this tenuous representation of Carnival in the media puts forward a homogenised, normative ideal of beauty. Although mas was debatably a transgressive practice at other points in history (and to some extent still is) in its celebration of different female embodiments, through the mainstreaming of imagery of the Carnival queen, media representations reproduce normative beauty standards with a focus on slim, light(er) skinned, beautiful bodies with long, black or highlighted tresses dressed in the bikini and beads costume. The subversion is then tempered by who can participate in these practices and which groups tend to have the body-types that are presented as ideal, thereby creating or at least supporting a variety of social hierarchies. In addition to the 'body-types' and their accompanying variations, how one *dresses* for Carnival is an equally, if not more, important part of the performance.

## THE DRESS DILEMMA

In the post-war period and during the oil boom of the 1970s the aesthetics of the Carnival underwent a divisive change which was characterised as the ole' mas the pretty mas. 'Ole' mas refers to a ragged costume aesthetic prevalent during the early hours of J'ouvay[6] in addition to the depictions of the traditional Carnival characters. In contemporary Carnival, the pretty mas is referred to as the 'bikini, feather and beads' mas and is a major bone of contention in the debates about Carnival. This is encapsulated in Browne's (1994, p. 36) poem, 'Longtime was pretty copper, satin, silk and tin/Nowadays is bikini and bathing trunks dey playin in.' The preference for pretty mas over traditional mas was acutely observed and lamented on by some of the young women, for example:

> People have different points of view on this. But it is sexy! The old time costumes was for that time period. Some people do miss it. But the temperature gets so hot here. It's not practical to wear these long gowns with corsets on a road march in this blazing sun! So I prefer the pretty mas for this. (Hema, 21, University Student)

There were more elaborations on this but Green and Scher (2007, p. 216) also remark on the changing nature of Carnival:

> The masquerades, songs, music, and performative forms as well as the social organization of Carnival production during the colonial era mark a time of unambiguous resistance a period when the assertion of a pure national identity was untainted by crass commercialism, vaguely 'hybrid' cultures, or media manipulations. The Carnival of the present, on the other hand, is largely looked upon with a sense of loss and regret.

Far from being just cloth, feather and beads (mere objects), the sexual and cultural politics of the mas costume and how the body becomes the signifier for sexuality through it, was a concern for the young women. The dress and the body come together to make the woman embody the meanings of Carnival, the meanings of mas. Conventions of dress transform flesh into something recognisable and meaningful to a culture and are also the means by which bodies are made 'decent', appropriate and acceptable within specific contexts (Entwistle & Wilson, 2001, p. 33), and it could be argued that this is what mas clothing does. Bodies are sexualised in the appropriate way, or de-sexualised in the appropriate way, through both their taking on of traditional Carnival clothes (in the case of African Trinidadian women) and through refraining from Carnival clothing (in the case of Indian Trinidadian woman). The Caribbean cultural sphere of Carnival has frequently served as the site of questions about resistance or accommodation. In addition to this, women and women's bodies, as sites of difference and similarity, have come to dominate much of the scholarship on Carnival. However in terms of the 'pretty mas', the women's relationship to this, apart from the obvious stance of economic and sexual independence, has not been explored in detail. One insight into this comes from Riana who says:

> You know I think women wear these bikinis and thing because it's a time where anything goes. Pretty much. It is a time of liberation and you'll find some people judging it for xyz reason. But most people will tell you that what happens at Carnival, and what you wear, the clothes, you wouldn't wear this, like on a daily basis. That's why I think

we spend a fortune on Carnival. Coz for that time you can wear whatever the hell you want and do whatever. (Riana, 22, Sales Assistant)

The mas costume then plays a considerable part in constituting a parti-cular experience and selfhood despite a lot of the women's dismay at the homogenising effects of globalisation on the aesthetics of the mas costume. The bikini is also not part of Indian dress conventions so it does function as a form of taboo wear despite this being the most ubiquitous form of clothing during Carnival. This does not mean that the experience of wear-ing the mas is reduced to a single expressive form. Indeed, we see the differ-ent ways in which clothing and the mas costume, in the world of Carnival, play a key role in determining not only a classed position but also one's sense of selfhood and nationhood. Even though globalisation is often cited as having a long-standing influence on the nature of Carnival, how is the latter locally understood and consumed? Given the racial diversity of the nation, how specifically do Indian descent people consume Carnival? Reddock (1998, pp. 424–425) posited that ethnically-focused Indians, in their rejection of Carnival as a creole festival, held the following view:

Indian women who participated in Carnival until recently were seen as putting a stain on their sacred womanhood. The debauchery of this festival is seen as [an] example of the decadence and low moral standards of creole society and the African population in particular and have called for some Indians to refrain from participation. In this situa-tion, it is the Indian women in particular who have to be watched for it is they who have the responsibility of maintaining the image of their culture.

If the ethnocentric Indian Trinidadian view is that the 'wine and jam' Carnival is culturally destructive and morally suspect for women, then it is critical to note that this is not a singular view. Yet there are traces of race talk in categorisations of certain mas bands, for example, Harts[7] was termed 'the white man's band' and J'ouvay was categorised as the 'African party'.[8] One of the participants, Nafeesa, criticises the past and present political state marking out racial groups competing for cultural citizenship as highly problematic:

Indians and Africans went through the same thing. We are all one people. But we always [sic] fighting over an African party or an Indian party but what we don't realise is that it's the White man who set up the bacchanal that we see today. Politicians, man. The corruption you see with politicians don't help us. (Nafeesa, 18, Student)

Perhaps the key underlying issue here is the reinforcement of capitalist patriarchal structures through the consumption of Carnival. In other words, to truly participate in the nation, one has to perform the bikini, beads and feathers mas, which signals a middle-class position of being modern and agentic. This brought up another question, namely how mas is embedded within the Trinidadian social world for these young women. Of course there is no one single answer. There was certainly division about the meanings of mas, with some of the participants contending that it has sold out to consumerism and some positing that it is empowering, as exemplified by the following statements:

> Look it might not be feminist in the way that we learn this at school. But women work now, we earn our own money. So why can't we for a few days party up? (Maariyah, 24, HR Manager)

> It's just fun. I don't know why some people take this too serious. I mean girls take it seriously on a different level! With the workouts and culture around it. But I play once. It was pure fun. (Najma, 22, Trainee Engineer)

Salma counters this by saying:

> Yea true. But you know how much is to play? Them for rich people! I can't afford the costumes. Even if I want to play, the costumes are ONLY this bikini thing. And you see some girls wear knee high boots? With the bikini? You don't find that funny? It BOILING hot and they wearing these American fashions here. I feel like tellin' them it's not winter. This ain't New York. (Salma, 19, Student)

Moreover, while ideas of agency were articulated, these were wedded to notions of immorality and decadence. Bodies remain the site on which differences are constructed, and sexuality becomes signified through dress in this context. Clothing is used as the vocabulary through which notions of morality and sexuality are conveyed. The mas costume is invested with varying elements that pertain to these notions of morality and sexuality. Mas costumes speak to social and cultural capital as new identities are performatively brought into being through the costume itself. The fact that one has to pay a considerable sum of money highlights the issue of access to capital as determinants of who can wear what, and who can be what. This point is made more clearly below by Sattee, who points out that the costumes' vulgarity is problematic for respectable women:

> Yea I'd never play mas. You know it have people's band[9] where you can just wear whatever. I would probably play in people's band because I am not rich and cannot afford 4000TTD. It real expensive now and the thing about it is, it's basically underwear you're playing in. I would not go all out into this thing. It's too vulgar. Because you could just go in normal clothes and still enjoy yourself just as much with clothes on. (Sattee, 21, Student)

The point about the costumes' vulgarity can be likened to attitudes towards the swimsuit segment in Indian Trinidadian beauty pageants;

whereas Ragbir (2012, p. 14) comments that the pageant producers and participants are invested in:

> Protecting this staged space from swimsuits, westernized Bollywood and Afro-Creole culture the way that they do; it is the only site they can appear pure as Sita,[10] as devoted as Draupadi, as untouchable as Rapunzel and as much the star of their own fairytale as Cinderella, an ordinary girl who became queen — sexually desired, idealized, yet unique innocent, chaste, pious, untouchable — and in the end rewarded for their efforts.

In Ragbir's (2012) study, the critique of India for its use of swimwear as a way of inserting global ideas of beauty into the national arena and the concerns about putting women's bodies on display in a sexualised way, he echoes many of the ideas expressed in the young women's talk vis-à-vis both African and Indian women's bodies in Carnival. Vaasha's statement is the only one which made a distinction between perceived Indian and African norms and it could be theorised that this pertained to a colonial view of African 'untamed sexuality' (the discourse of hypersexuality that marked African descent women) and Indian 'restrained womanhood'. This is one view of the sexual politics of Carnival:

> I know a lot of Indian people who would say they would never play because of the costumes but for African people it's not a problem. Indian people like to party too but it's just that their parties are a bit different! (Vaasha, 21, Intern)

In investigating the sexual politics of Carnival, it is important to examine the extent to which these politics overlap with the sexual politics of the non-Carnival world. The ways in which sexuality as articulated in Carnival differs or adheres to the more everyday tropes of racialised womanhood will be explored in the following section.

## THE SEXUAL POLITICS OF CARNIVAL

The deployment of the body in a sexually suggestive manner as part of Carnival culture has been theorised as a safety valve for these women to vent frustrations over social inequities (Miller, 1991). I contend that two processes are occurring here. Mas takes on a dimension through which we see the reinforcement of patriarchal structures, but I take the view that mas-playing should also be explored as a series of moments of agency that respond to varying social tensions and inequities. Unmistakeably, the homogenisation of the mas bands in terms of their costumes does not afford the women a varied choice or afford varied alternatives in terms of the portrayal of characters and new identities they wish to convey. In this way, the body becomes the costume and the body vocabulary offered through wining and gyrating may symbolise economic and sexual freedom for women. On the other hand, the ways in which women masqueraders are conceived as not behaving properly indicates a racial hierarchy. In this sense, the woman who refuses to participate and pronounces a moral judgement about those who do is also enacting her classed racial position. It is important to analyse the refusal to perform mas as much as to examine those who do play it, in order to look at how Carnival entails the performance of one's race. Both inside and outside of Carnival, race is performed through these actions and discourses alongside tropes of patriarchal respectability and citizenship.

Following on from Butler's (1990) notion of performativity, the bodies of the masqueraders are enacted through these performances. They are 'worked out' from the physical body into a cultural form and 'worked back in' to the physical body. The physical practices of mas are reiterative and citational practices which evoke and reproduce images of femininity. The body becomes the materialisation of cultural norms but also materialises the masqueraders' interpretation of them. This was commented on by Kelly (20, student) who talked about 'winin' up on three men' as an undesirable way of performing mas, as compared to Lisa (25, designer) who said that 'you can tell from the way someone winin' where they from'. The borders of sexuality are drawn along classed lines in Lisa's statement in which she revealed the differences between wining for personal pleasure, indicating middle-class respectability, and wining for sexual arousal, which went against these norms. Kelly's account explicitly addresses this self-examination of respectability in Carnival:

> I think Carnival's just an excuse to get all naked and do all this revelry which is just not my domain. Because I guess it's this carnal instinct to run amok and just be primitive for two or three days. Everybody have this primitive instinct but I guess it just how it come out. Now there's a lot more Indian people going to the celebrations and partaking. They getting a lot more bold over time. Because normally very Indian people in the sense of 'traditional', they believe that Indians as a race, not Hindus specifically, are supposed to have a code of conduct. But nowadays people are rejecting this code of conduct. But even for normal stuff sometimes the way they behave [...] I feel ashamed when I see an Indian girl drunk, falling down, wining three to four men at one time. And it not like they're friends, it's a random man coming up behind and touching her up. I don't really support that. (Kelly, 20, Student)

Kelly's encounter with Carnival reveals how bodies are the markers of societal behaviour, moral codes and racial conduct, epitomising a Foucauldian disciplined body in which 'docile bodies' are mobilised in intimate ways (Foucault, 1977). The social control of sexuality, an indicator of power, is marked in Kelly's passage where the maintaining and establishing of docility takes place via a mode of observation of the bodies in question. In her positioning of respectable Indianness, in contrast to Trinidadian untamed sexuality, we see that sexuality is policed and maintained via codes of conduct. What are perhaps intended and coded as images of sexual desirability are not necessarily registered in a positive manner, leaving one to question whether there is room for multiple or alternative forms of sexuality. Desire and disgust map out the contours of sexuality in Carnival, where notions of morality and immorality are invoked. If there is talk about the possibilities of empowerment in Carnival it is accompanied by protests about what is perceived as aggressive sexuality performed in public. The body, in this sense, also becomes open to resignification through the way the women perform mas, but it could also be said that the masqueraders are not merely passive actors in terms of hetero-patriarchal power or docile bodies, but actively performing multiple femininities.

In the introductory paragraph to this chapter, Carnival is described as a space where capitalist, patriarchal and nationalist powers play a role in mediating the performance of mas. It is a space where stereotypes of a sexualised and racialised body are contested and where processes of resistance and domination, the seen and unseen, are merged. It could be posited that the young women negotiate with dominant powers in Carnival space to performatively produce new Indian Trinidadian femininities. For masqueraders there is an expectation to look fit, glamorous and beautiful and the 'body beautiful' look has to be attained through exercise, cosmetics and diets. The pursuit of the fit body is associated with experiences of freedom, fulfilment and feeling good. Through a Foucauldian lens, these masqueraders would be considered disciplined women who are not granted choice but follow regulations. Taking Butler's (1993) performativity concept as a useful tool here, I move past this Foucauldian assertion and argue that they are not passive recipients of a disciplined body but actively agentic through their performance, and their bringing into being of particular forms of identities. While in general terms the female masquerader's body at Carnival is sexualised and commodified, at the same time there are other forms of femininities being deployed, for example in fêtes, J'ouvay, at music events and so on. To a large extent the homogenised imagery of Carnival in tourist brochures, local press and other media outlets does not draw on this. It places a larger focus on the woman who plays mas, establishing her as the representative of Trinidadian racial and cultural hybridity. She also is a highly sexualised figure and is part of a long history of metaphors starting with the jamette[11] which also corresponds to Westernised stereotypes of Caribbean sensuality.

Carnival has a complicated relationship to race, gender and respectability, but these variables have almost always been approached through their significance for African Trinidadians (Barnes, 2006). The sexuality of Black women's bodies is often how the nation is read and imagined diasporically. The representations of Indian descent Caribbean women do not figure to any great extent in the exported versions of Carnival, and within the nation there are limiting discourses of Indian sexuality. In this construction of otherness it could be argued that Carnival is one of the ways through which sexuality produced tensions between African and Indian descent people. Mehta (2004, p. 70) extends this point by referring to the difficulties around forming alliances of solidarity even though Indians and Africans shared a common history of economic and political disenfranchisement. Colonial engineering played a huge role in this, and if the colonial policing of Black women's bodies marked hypervisibility, then for Indian women's bodies it emphasised invisibility (Ragbir, 2012). Bourgeois values were embodied in this notion of respectability, defined by Puri (2003, p. 23) as 'oriented towards bourgeois valuations of the centripetal, toward standard English, home, family, hierarchy, decorum, stability, honesty, economy, delayed returns, and transcendence.' The Indian woman was imagined as a character fitting into this set of bourgeois values through her invisibility, although this was never incorporated into the bourgeois class itself.

The young women, overall, stood at a highly charged crossroads between what they and others perceive to be 'traditional values', which are characterised by respectability, and 'modern' expectations, which involve more active selections about self-representation that incorporate sexuality more explicitly. They are exploring how the expectations of the statically constructed category of 'Indian Trinidadian woman' can be changed. In my view, if Carnival is seen as representing the social body, then this is also a gendered body with differences in the normative expectations of female and male bodies, as reflected in the mas costume. The social construction of the Carnival body is based on the nation's ideology of hybridity and modernity and the social pressure to discipline the body is reflected in the gym regimes that the young women speak of in their goal to achieve the 'body beautiful'. This, along with the pressure to participate, signals a stake in inclusion within the nation. The regulation of the Indian female body then takes on many guises as modernity is measured by which mas band one plays in, and simultaneously respectable Indianness is measured by silenced sexuality. Through the governmentality of these sociocultural discourses it could be said that some of the young women are 'bearers of their own surveillance' in the production of 'docile bodies' (Foucault, 1977, p. 136), as we see in the emphasis on being 'body beautiful'. The concept of the body panopticon operates in this sense as surveilling in order to fulfil the cultural imperative set forth by the business actors involved in Carnival. However, this is not to say the existence of the panopticon does not preclude the potential to resist this form of disciplining. These young women are very much aware of the ways in which they are being interpolated within the racial politics of their bodies.

Carnival as a national brand becomes an image that develops as much through the local contradictions of society as it is a part of an implicit debate about how people, particularly women, should be. This is an image with which some Indian people will identify while some will not or some only on certain occasions such as fêtes, the music monarchs and so on. It could also be said that the identity of being Trinidadian, which the young women placed a resolute emphasis on in the individual conversations, includes the presence of the African descent person as 'othered' in some ways. On one level they define themselves against and dis-identify with 'otherness', but at another level they incorporate it as part of their Trinidadianness. The dimension of ethnicity ascribed to Carnival is that some of the young women, in their attempt to resolve this contradiction of alterity, consume some forms of the Carnival, whether it is the act of playing mas, listening to the music or fêting, which provide identification with the 'othered'. Carnival femininities are not splintered solely by racial factors, as much of the earlier scholarship on Carnival claims, but also individual, class and ethnic factors, morality, respectability and body awareness. The discourse on mas-playing which I have explored in this chapter is just one example of the dynamic nature of gender and race. It would be a mistake to classify Indian female masqueraders as conformist to the 'Creole' nation, in the same way that it is reductionist to talk about non-participants as traditional or 'excluded from the nation' (Munasinghe, 2001, p. 214). The young women I spoke to, much like other women, react to and resist patriarchal discourses in varying ways, such that the question of how mas has the potential to disrupt 'tradition' should be expanded in classed and sexual-racial terms.

The varying viewpoints discussed herein indicate that it is unproductive to dichotomise Indians and Africans since within these groups there are further divergent views on playing mas. Within this sample, all the young women demonstrated extensive awareness of the mas costumes despite some of their apparent boycotting of the event. They also expressed their discomfort with the revealing mas costume and excluded themselves from the site which became an object of scorn and ridicule. One of the participants stated:

> I think when sex started to sell, that's when rum started to sell. We are a nation of rum drinkers whether it's social or everyday drinking. We're a nation that likes it and you know with our hypersexual moods, especially during Carnival both of them go hand in hand. So this is why the costumes have changed and become sexier. (Raadiyah, 24, Administrative Manager)

Behaviour that is usually associated with Carnival (e.g., drinking, wining and dancing provocatively) is looked down on by Raadiyah who views this as clashing with norms of respectability and civility. The act of wining, which she conceives of in negative terms, is theorised by Barnes (2006, p. 95) as a public display which could be transgressive in a 'extension of their new identities as modern, assertive feminist subjects' but also as working to reinforce the capitalist, male gaze. Indeed, Barnes (2006) talks about wining as part of the desire for visibility, but the association of wining with wild, untamed conduct is the discourse that is articulated in more detail by the young women. Another example arose when Esther spoke to me about the clash of 'jump up'[12] with norms of respectability:

> I have a four year old daughter. She was practising at school one day and come, she say 'Mummy, I jump up.' I was shocked. I know she don't know the real meaning of it 'cause she innocent right. She literally means jumpin. But you and I know that if she were older, it's no longer innocent. I'm not judging, but I think when it comes to your family you should know what is right and wrong and I don't want my daughter growing up, getting wrong ideas about that without knowing the consequences. I cannot have my daughter winin' in her childhood. I don't have a problem at all if she wants to play in the junior mas because other schools go and it's safer. Also, I find it more fun than the main mas. (Esther, 25, Psychologist)

Respectability is a significant issue in that it relates to Trinidadian, middle-class sensibility irrespective of race or colour. Also, we can see in this statement that the sexualisation of Carnival practices in which certain forms of perceived sexual expressions are the norm, such as 'jumpin up', 'wining' and dancing in the bikini mas, is a concern, as is safety, despite the discourse of freedom, free-up and change. Some women discussed this increased sexualisation as a serious break from respectability, and the emergence of a class of women and girls who would ultimately be at a loss because of their lack of respectability. This demonstrated a preoccupation with ensuring that Indian girls did not act 'Afro,' maintaining the historical understanding that Indian girls were respectable in their invisibility while African girls were dominant visually through their more vulgar behaviour. No side is right or wrong, and this debate will continue. However, women on both sides of the debate shared an emphasis on Carnival and performance as a site where the boundaries of respectability were established. While some wanted to open the existing boundaries, others wanted to police them more. Even those seeking more relaxed approaches to sexuality internalised a deep discipline about how to make their bodies more sexually attractive. Carnival emerges here as a site imbued with significance as both a set of limits and possibilities for the negotiation of the sexual identity of the gendered and raced Indian Trinidadian. In sum, the young women point to the objectification that takes place in Carnival as an effect of globalisation but in the same way have argued that this remains a localised image within a larger frame of gendered and raced identity. Carnival and playing mas then is not a universal experience and race is only one dimension where Carnival as myth deals with contradictions in value. Carnival, mas and even music carry temporal connotations. If Carnival retains a notion of modern subjectivity, fostered by its media representation and advertising, we have seen also that it has been a presence in Trinidad for many generations. It has become a site where nostalgia and tradition are wedded to modernity, liberalism and consumerism. The body acts as a signifier in this process, and playing mas, as a form of agentic female sexuality, also mirrors the contradictions between society and identity.

## CONCLUSION

In this chapter, the young women performatively produce the raced body in the hybridised space of Carnival through the practice of playing mas. Carnival, in its modern day incarnation, has come to stand for the fact that money is often translated into national belonging, so that playing mas within a particular band, is a signifier of a middle-class position and a modern, cosmopolitan subjectivity. So at once sexuality is discursively produced as agentic and as combating silenced sexuality but it is also contested as a limited act in which one has to exhibit a particular 'body beautiful' viewed as unrespectable, immoral and decadent. Thus, the possibilities of empowerment are revealed alongside protests about hypersexuality.

To take one position over the other is an oversimplification as we see a complex and more nuanced view of contemporary Indian femininities within the sexualisation of Trinidadian Carnival culture. I argue that the multiple ways of understanding femininities within the context of playing mas indicates the potential for them to be taken up subversively, and a potential for blurring gendered norms. However, historical and ethnocentric traces of sex in Trinidadian culture necessitate that any subversive act is likely to reinforce the patriarchal gaze, thus causing issues in the readability of mas performance.

In considering how these young women negotiate sexualised Carnival culture I have attempted to move away from the binary positioning which, in my view, is not an adequate approach to gendered and raced identities. This emphasis on the body is made simultaneously by those who want to uphold traditional social restrictions on bodily expressions and those who would like to adapt them. Both positions exemplify gendered experiences and the cultural production of Carnival through which we can observe how women use their bodies to challenge gender, race and class hierarchies. The body's expressions may be read through the traditional gaze that has emerged out of colonial history; however women's struggle to either uphold the traditional mode or to change it represents how they navigate between their own and others' expectations as raced and gendered beings.

## NOTES

1. Playing mas generally means to wear a costume during Carnival and perform a masquerade with one of the many mas bands which vary according to size: mini, small, medium or large.

2. To wine is a type of Caribbean dance with 'rotational hip movements (pronounced winin')' (Winer, 2009, p. 471).

3. To let go and behave in a relaxed and uninhibited manner.

4. The festival of Maha Shivratri is the most important festival for the millions of devotees of Lord Shiva. The festival has been accorded lot of significance in Hindu mythology. It is said that a devotee who performs sincere worship of Lord Shiva on the auspicious day of Shivratri is absolved of sins and attains moksha (see http://www.mahashivratri.org/significance-of-shivratri.html).

5. In the song, Ramgoonai employs two double entendres. 'Lick', a stock pun in typical calypso, contrasts with 'Nani', which is Trinidadian slang for vagina as well as the Hindi term for grandmother, that 'revered and idealised symbol of Indian womanhood' (Puri, 2004, p. 197).

6. J'ouvay is the official opening of Carnival at daybreak on the Monday preceding Ash Wednesday. The literal translation from French is 'day open' (Winer, 2009, p. 473).

7. Harts is an organisation that provides masqueraders with a package including costumes, goody bags, food and alcohol for the duration of Carnival.

8. In this case, this is to mean an event predominantly attended by African-Caribbean people.

9. D' People's Band entitled 'Mas for All' came about as a concept with the purpose of accommodating the ordinary man who cannot afford the exorbitant cost of Carnival mas bands (National Carnival Commission of Trinidad & Tobago, 2011).

10. Sita, in Hindu tradition is the wife of Lord Rama, and is esteemed as the exemplar for all Hindu women in discharging their wifely and womanly duties, for example, virtue, respectability and devotion (Ragbir, 2012, p. 14).

11. An African descent woman playing at Carnival typically considered obscene and vulgar (Winer, 2009, p. 46).

12. Jump up means to participate in Carnival masquerade.

# REFERENCES

Bakhtin, M. (1984). Rabelais and his world *(H. Iswolsky, Trans.)*. Bloomington, IN: Indiana University Press.

Barnes, N. (2006). *Cultural conundrums: Gender, race, nation, and the making of Caribbean cultural politics*. Ann Arbor, MI: University of Michigan Press.

Browne, M. (1994). *Trini talk: Dialect poetry and stories*. Trinidad: M. Browne.

Brunton, D. (2012). Ethnic minority media in Trinidad and Tobago. Retrieved from http://www.academia.edu/1970782/Ethnic_minority_media_in_Trinidad_and_Tobago. Accessed on September 7, 2015.

Butler, J. (1990). *Gender trouble*. London: Routledge.

Butler, J. (1993). *Bodies that matter: On the discursive limits of sex*. London: Routledge.

Edmondson, C. (2009). *Caribbean middlebrow: Leisure culture and the middle class*. New York, NY: Cornell University Press.

Entwistle, J., & Wilson, E. (2001). *Body dressing*. Oxford: Berg.

Foucault, M. (1977). Discipline and punish: The birth of the prison *(A. Sheridan, Trans.)*. New York, NY: Random House.

Green, G. L., & Scher, P. W. (2007). *Trinidad carnival: The cultural politics of a transnational festival*. Bloomington, IN: Indiana University Press.

Guilbault, J. (2007). *Governing sound: The cultural politics of Trinidad's carnival musics*. Chicago, IL: The University of Chicago Press.

Hill-Collins, P. (2008). *Black feminist thought: Knowledge, consciousness, and the politics of empowerment*. New York, NY: Routledge.

Isaac-Flavien, J. (2013). The translation of carnival in Trinidad and Tobago: The evolution of a festival. *Tusaaji: A Translation Review*, 2(2), 42–55.

Mehta, B. (2004). *Diasporic (dis)location: Indo-Caribbean women negotiate the Kala Pani*. Kingston: University of the West Indies.

Miller, D. (1991). Absolute freedom in Trinidad. *Man, 26*(2), 323–334.

Munasinghe, V. (2001). *Callaloo or tossed salad? East Indians and the cultural politics of identity in Trinidad*. New York, NY: Cornell University Press.

National Carnival Commission of Trinidad & Tobago. (2011). Retrieved from http://www.ncctt.org/home/index.php

Noel, S. A. (2010). De jamette in we: Redefining performance in contemporary Trinidad carnival. *Small Axe, 14*(131), 60–78.

Nurse, K. (1999). Globalization and Trinidad carnival: Diaspora, hybridity and identity in global culture. *Cultural Studies, 13*(4), 661–690.

Puri, S. (2003). Beyond resistance: Notes toward a new Caribbean cultural studies. *Small Axe, 7*(2), 23–38.

Puri, S. (2004). *The Caribbean postcolonial: Social equality, post-nationalism and cultural hybridity*. Basingstoke: Palgrave.

Ragbir, A. (2012). Fictions of the past: Staging Indianness, identity and sexuality among young women in Indo-Trinidadian beauty pageants. *Caribbean Review of Gender Studies, 6*, 1–21.

Reddock, R. (1998). Contestations over national culture in Trinidad and Tobago: Considerations of ethnicity, class and gender. In C. Barrow (Ed.), *Caribbean portraits: Essays on gender ideologies and identities*. Kingston: Ian Randle.

Subero, S. (2012). Chipping and chatting with Kamla. *Trinidad Express*. Retrieved from http://www.trinidadexpress.com/commentaries/Chipping_and_chatting_with_Kamla-140515733.html. Accessed on September 7, 2015.

Winer, L. (2009). *Dictionary of the English/Creole of Trinidad and Tobago: On historical principles*. Montreal: McGill-Queen's University Press.

# GENDER IN POST-LIBERALISATION INDIA: THE COMPLEX TRAJECTORIES OF GENDER AND (POSTCOLONIAL) NATIONALISM IN HINDI CINEMA

Priyasha Kaul

## ABSTRACT

Purpose — *The chapter explores how gender has been an integral part of the nation building project in post-liberalisation Hindi cinema, popularly, known as Bollywood.*

Design/methodology/approach — *This chapter is based on primary data gathered through interviews with prominent members of the Hindi film industry along with a detailed content analysis of commercially successful post-liberalisation mainstream Hindi films.*

Findings — *It highlights how the representation of gender has been a central axis around which the tension between tradition and modernity has been played out in Hindi Cinema. The construction of Indianness post-liberalisation has questioned gender politics but proposed easy*

Gender and Race Matter: Global Perspectives on Being a Woman
Advances in Gender Research, Volume 21, 213–229
ISSN: 1529-2126/doi:10.1108/S1529-212620160000021012

*resolutions which fit into the larger nationalist narrative. In doing so, it has used the diaspora as a category to produce a nationalist account which is simultaneously essentialised and transnational in the quest for projecting India's aspirations on the global platform.*

Originality/value — *The chapter provides important insights into the role of popular Hindi cinema, often brushed off as frivolous, in contributing to the mainstream discourse on nationalism post-liberalisation.*

**Keywords:** India; gender; nationalism; Bollywood; liberalisation; cinema

# INTRODUCTION

The year 1991 was an important year in Indian history as it was the year that the Government of India embarked upon the policy of economic liberalisation. It involved a series of economic reforms such as opening up the country to international trade and investment, deregulation and privatisation or disinvestment. In the decades since, these policy changes have had a significant impact not just on the economic development of the country, but also on the socio-cultural fabric of India as a nation. For instance, while until 1991 there was only one television channel, the state-owned '*Doordarshan*'[1] which broadcasted mainly Hindi language programmes for a limited number of hours each day, by 1998 there were more than 70 television channels in India (Thussu, 1999, p. 127). This included several international 24-hour television channels like 'Star Plus' broadcasting international programming including popular American soap operas such as *The Bold and the Beautiful*[2] and *Santa Barbara*[3] in India.

The mainstream cinema of this period, popularly known as Bollywood, provides a dynamic snapshot of these sociological changes in post-liberalisation India. In fact, the popularity of the term 'Bollywood' is itself a post-liberalisation phenomenon to market Hindi films globally through easy shorthand for conveying mainstream Hindi cinematic brand and sensibility. It is difficult to pinpoint the origin of the term but although it had been around for years, it was only after liberalisation that it gained mass usage. It was officially added to the Oxford English dictionary lexicon in 2001 (Govil, 2007, p. 77). It came into popular usage particularly as a tool for explaining mainstream Hindi cinema to those unfamiliar with the form, especially in the west. Thus, the usage of the term 'Bollywood' ties into various aspects of post-liberalisation Hindi films from its sense of conveying the banal mainstream *filmi*[4] melodrama to its marketing of the Indian brand particularly in the western context.

Hindi films, however, are almost a century-old with the first indigenous Indian film being released in 1913. It is the largest film industry in the world producing around 800 films a year and is watched by almost 14 million people every day within India (Chadha & Husband, 2006, p. 241). Mainstream commercial Bollywood films as a widely consumed cultural text provide a sociological insight for studying the changing dynamics of India as a nation. In spite of the massive cultural diversity in India, mainstream Hindi cinema has consistently been the most significant form of entertainment across the country. Bollywood films and film songs feature prominently in social life in India from political rallies using films songs for election banter to Bollywood trends marking religious festivals and marriage rituals. Mainstream Hindi cinema has been an extremely significant cultural force in Indian society. It is for these reasons that mainstream commercial Hindi cinema, often brushed off as frivolous and banal, is a crucial source of sociological enquiry with respect to changes in Indian society, not simply as a second-order reflection but indeed as an integral and visible part of the changing social dynamics in India.

This chapter explores the representation of gender in Hindi cinema post-liberalisation. Using primary data gathered through interviews with prominent filmmakers, it analyses the continuities and disjunctures in the representation of gender during this critical phase in the economic and socio-cultural journey of India as a nation. It demonstrates how gender has been employed as a trope for ironing out questions of nationalism and Indianness by locating it within the context of an idealised imagined diaspora. Post-liberalisation Hindi cinema has questioned gender politics but proposed easy resolutions which fit into the larger nationalist narrative. In the process, mainstream Bollywood cinema has thrown up contradictory representations of gender that both idealise and problematise gender issues in the nationalist context while also strategically positioning India's aspirations in the competition for acquiring soft power on the global platform.

*Women, Nation and Nationalism in Bollywood*

The issue of nationalism has historically played out in Bollywood cinema through the tension between the binary positions of tradition and modernity. Chatterjee (2008) notes that on one side of this debate have been proponents such as Dasgupta (1991) who argue that the Indian masses are deeply traditional and often do not distinguish between fact and myth, and thus Bollywood as popular cinema has developed itself accordingly over the decades by producing 'mythological and melodramatic rubbish' (Chatterjee, 2008, p. 1) which is eagerly popularly consumed by the masses. For Das Gupta, the godlike reverence for stars in India provides the biggest example of this hypothesis. While, for Chatterjee, the other end of this spectrum is represented by Nandy (1995, 1998) who argues that the non-modernity of Bollywood as a cultural form and sensibility depicts its refusal to accept western modernity. Thus, both the audience and filmmakers of popular cinema have subverted realism and mass culture by resisting western expectations of authenticity and realism and this can be viewed as a 'symptom of protest and resilience against an alien culture of modernisation' (Nandy in Virdi, 2003, p. 5).

The problem with these opposing viewpoints is that while the former is blatantly dismissive of non-canonical, non-western forms of modernity and cultural consumption, the latter carries the danger of falling into, what Virdi terms 'indigenous chauvinism' (Nandy in Virdi, 2003, p. 4) by privileging pure imaginaries of the self. In addition, this viewpoint reverberates with Charles Taylor's 'acultural theory of modernity which proposes that in order to achieve modernity, all societies no matter what their starting points will go through the same process of change in order to converge at a certain point' (see Gaonkar, 2001). Thus by corollary, it would seem that a society's digression from this predetermined pattern reflects its resistance to modernity. There is a need to move away from such simplistic accounts of non-western modernity which position these debates in terms of normative western modernity versus other alternatives. It is important to examine postcolonial modernity through the lens of the unique experiences of a particular nation, in this case India. Thus, it becomes crucial to steer clear of such zero-sum approaches in favour of a more nuanced understanding of the subject. Debates regarding issues of modernity have invariably taken the trope of the 'nation' in Hindi films. According to Prasad (1998), for instance,

> The binary modernity/tradition, whether it is employed to indicate conflict or complementarity, amounts to an explanation, 'a conceptual or belief system' which regulates thinking about modern Indian social formation. This binary also figures centrally, both thematically and as an organising device, in popular film narratives. (Prasad, 1998, p. 7)

Similarly, Virdi (2003, p. xiv) contends that Hindi cinema constitutes and is constituted by a shifting discourse that constantly reimagines the nation. In fact, the issue of the nation lies as the very foundation of the birth of Hindi cinema which later came to be known as 'Bollywood' particularly post-liberalisation. Rajadhyaksha (1993) points out that Dadasaheb Phalke who has been credited for being chiefly responsible for bringing filmmaking expertise to India, and who made the first indigenous film *Raja Harishchandra* [King Harishchandra] in 1913, was primarily fuelled by the desire to create a nationalist cinema capable of talking about India. This was quickly picked up by Indian filmmakers in the colonial period as a means to circulate political nationalist messages covertly. This role of Hindi cinema became even more significant and explicit with the ushering in of independence in 1947. Since independence Hindi cinema has been consumed with this project revolving around a 'fascination with the "new nation", its present, past and future' (Virdi, 2003, p. 1). It is indeed this unique ability of Hindi cinema to attract audiences across linguistic, regional and other cultural barriers in a massive country such as India that has earned it the badge of being a national cinema.

In fact, for Virdi, Hindi cinema has become a national cinema not just because of the number of audiences it involves across the country (in spite of the fact that the culture and language depicted in Bollywood films is only restricted to a certain section of North India, primarily the state of Punjab), nor because unlike other indigenous cinemas such as Latin American and British cinema, it is primarily produced, managed and consumed indigenously, but most importantly because it has been successful at.

> [...] inheriting and circulating notions of national identity, negotiating conflicts experienced by the imagined community, producing new representations of the nation, and constructing a collective consciousness of nationhood though special cultural referents. Hindi cinema is unique in using the family as the trope to negotiate caste, class, community and gender divisions, making for complex but decipherable hieroglyphics through which it configures the nation and constructs a nationalist imaginary. Deploying an affective mode of address, Hindi cinema is an emotional register and therefore a virtual teleprompter for reading the script called 'nation' [...] The concept of nation subtends imagination in Hindi films, and centers its moral universe. All ethical dilemmas revolve around the nation; good and bad, heroes and villains are divided by their patriotism and anti-patriotism. (Virdi, 2003, pp. 7–9)

In a similar vein, the *Daily Telegraph* and *Sunday Times* journalist Bose (2007), in his extensive book on the history of Bollywood, notes that, according to Faroukh Dhondhy[5], in the context of independence and the massive project of nation building, Hindi cinema became the 'discernable conscience of the nation' (Bose, 2007, p. 35). Hindi films came to define what being an 'Indian' should mean and to spell out how citizens should be in the newly independent nation. For Prasad (1998), the early years of Bollywood cinema of the 1950s to 1970s were the era of the 'socials'[6] or films that furthered the ideology of the state. This phase of Indian films has been known for its Nehruvian socialist optimism often focusing on issues of class, and the gulf between the rich and the poor through films by directors such as Guru Dutt, Raj Kapoor and Bimal Roy, dealing with the dream of a utopian modern India post-independence.

Chakravarti (1993), the first person to conduct a book-length study on the topic, argues that Indian national identity is central to Indian cinema. Drawing from the folk tradition of *nautanki* (performance), Chakravarti uses the metaphor of *imperso-nation* to show how Hindi cinema has constructed a sense of Indianness in accordance with notions of Hindu morality, thus, openly breaking class barriers while rarely attempting to cross religious or caste boundaries. For Mishra (2002), Bollywood films have used the device of 'excess and containment' for creating novel plots while refraining from producing any radical change, following the model of '*dharma* (virtue) − *adharma* (vice) − *dharma* (virtue)'[7]. This model allows minor transgressions to occur within the narrative but ultimately succeeds in restoring the ethical order or the *dharmik* (virtuous) form in Indian films. The Hindi film narrative follows this sequence of events to produce contained tension in the film. He notes that Bollywood therefore deals with social and political problems by converting them into a struggle between good and evil thus bringing about a co-existence of the modern within the realm of the pre-modern.

Bollywood does this most significantly by privileging collective identities over individualised ones, the 'family' as a metonym for the nation becomes the point of danger and the basis for forging the future (Virdi, 2003). The problems facing the nation come to be portrayed as ethical and/or moral dilemmas surrounding the family which the protagonist must overcome or defeat in order to vindicate himself/herself and in the process protect the family, and by implication, the nation. At the obvious level, it is played out by making the mother-son relationship especially laden in Hindi films, some classic examples being *Mother India* (1957), *Deewar* (1975) and *Karan Arjun* (1995). Hindi films up to the 1970s were explicitly involved in raising the question of class boundaries. The hero and heroine were inevitably from different class backgrounds and had to struggle against class boundaries in order to ultimately realise their romantic love. After the 1980s, however, Virdi notes that the issue of class receded into the background and class issues no longer held much significance. She conjectures that this could be for two reasons, firstly, the swelling of the middle class in the 1980s which meant that more opportunities for upward mobility were now becoming available to people, or secondly, due to the struggles of the women's movements, patriarchal authority replaced class as the enemy of romantic love. Interestingly, however, Virdi's explanation does not take into account that even in post-liberalisation Bollywood films, patriarchal authority was not flouted or disobeyed and instead romantic love was won only through gradual winning over of the patriarch through persuasion and devotion thus creating, what Patricia Uberoi calls the 'arranged love marriage' phenomenon (1999, p. 192), exemplified in commercially success-ful films like *Dilwale Dulhaniya Le Jayenge* [The romantic will take the bride] (1995) and *Hum Apke Hai Kaun* [Who am I to you?] (1994).

In fact, gender and patriarchy form an underlying theme that runs through all the continuing narratives on Indianness both pre- and post-liberalisation. Women's morality and bodies are the basis for reinforcing and transmitting Indian values inter-generationally. As Kishori Lal remarks in *Pardes* [Foreign Land] (1997), a film which dedicates itself to 60 years of Indian independence, good daughters personified by the character of Ganga[8] are essential for protecting Indianness and teaching it to way-ward young men, like his son Rajeev, through their love and affection, especially in the diaspora.

Since women have come to personify the cherished values of Indianness that need to be protected, one of the most important way to ensure the 'purity' of these Indian values is through the policing of women's sexuality (see Yuval-Davis, 1997). In what has come to be considered an iconic scene in Bollywood (Uberoi, 1999) from the film *Dilwale Dulhaniya Le Jayenge* (1995), Simran wakes up in the morning and is led to believe by Raj that they had had sex the night before, after she had to drink cognac to keep herself warm during a road trip in Switzerland, in spite of her insistence that 'girls don't drink alcohol'. Simran is so traumatised by the fact that she might not be a virgin anymore that she has a panic attack and Raj has to calm her down. He gives her a long speech explaining that even though she thinks he is not a nice person, he is an Indian and understands what an Indian girl's honour and virginity mean and he therefore can never imagine doing 'something like that' with her, even in a dream. Poignant as the scene is, Indianness here stands as shorthand for proving that he is a good guy at the end of the day, because even if he does not seem so from the outside, ultimately he will always have the good Indian spiritual core within him.

His being an Indian therefore proves that he will not do anything 'wrong'. Simran on the other hand is someone whose sexuality has to be protected by the Indian man since she is incapable of doing so herself. Interestingly, unlike Simran, Raj is depicted as a flamboyant character with an active romantic life which is never posed as a source of any moral dilemmas regarding his goodness and/or Indianness.

It is the women, therefore, who are the exclusive beneficiaries of the moral policing to protect their Indianness. This protection comes in the form of both direct and indirect patronage from the patriarchal set up. Chatterjee (1999) argues that the public-private dichotomy has been an important feature of the Indian nationalist discourse. During the struggle against colonial rule, this split was formulated as a devise used extensively by the nationalist leaders such as Mahatma Gandhi. The battle with the colonial establishment was negotiated by constructing the nationalist paradigm through the outer domain of the material, on the one hand, and the inner domain of moral spirituality on the other hand. This dichotomy corresponded with that of the *bahir/ghar*, or the world and the home. The outer, public material domain of the world was the masculine sphere while the inner, private domain of the home was the feminine sphere.

While the nationalist project allows women to participate in the outer sphere of the world, it does so on the condition that they display the signs of national tradition as evidence of an inner possession of Indianness thus making them essentially different from western women. For Loomba, the ideal woman constructed in this nationalist discourse 'fuses together old brahmanical notions of female self-sacrifice and devotion with the Victorian ideal of the enlightened mother, devoted exclusively to the domestic sphere' (1998, p. 183). Overt patriarchal symbols such as the *mangalsutra* and *sindoor*[9] are applauded as being the pride of an ideal Indian woman devoted to the upkeep of the patriarchal family set up. As Nandini's mother says to her recently married daughter in *Hum Dil De Chuke Sanam* [Straight from the heart] (1999), 'the day a woman understands that the black beads of the *mangalsutra* have the power of holding on to your husband, she will understand the value of her marriage'. These overt symbols stand as simple manifestations of the much larger patriarchal ideology of gender roles and expectations, and thereby the preservation of an essentialised Indianness. In *Taal* [Musical note] (1999), Manasi's father Tara Babu perhaps summarises this ideology, when he tells his daughter of how every father's dream is to hand over responsibility for his daughter to a good man so that he is free to die peacefully. It is this smooth anthropological exchange of women that seems to ensure the continuation of

Indianness. On a similar note, in *Yaadein* [Memories] (2001) we see the contrast between Isha as the good and Monishka as the bad NRI[10] woman. On the one hand, there is Isha, the dutiful daughter who willingly sacrifices her love and is ready to marry whoever her father selects. Her father feels that an Indian woman marries not just her husband but his entire family and thus it is important that the families should arrange the marriage. Monishka, on the other hand, is shown as the spoilt NRI woman who has forgotten her Indian values since she is too 'independent'. Her un-Indian values in the film are proven by the fact that she wants to live in a nuclear household with just her husband after marriage, continue to go to parties and have her own friends, and not have any children for at least the first five years after marriage since she wants to maintain her 'figure'. She is suitably punished for such behaviour when the male protagonist Ronit rejects her for Isha, the good NRI Indian woman who suffers in silence to win his family's heart and her own father's approval for the marriage.

Marriage, therefore, continues to be the most important factor defining the cinematic representation of a woman's life. In films such as *Aa Ab Laut Chale* [Come let us return] (1999) and *Judaai* [Separation] (1997), independent women like Pooja and Jhanavi become suitably demure and homely the moment they fall in love. From that point onwards they are shown as wearing only Indian clothes (salwar-kameez or sari) and cooking and taking care of the house to prove their worthiness of being the good Indian wife/mother who can pass on those values to the next generation. Gangoli (2005) has shown how women like Tina and Anjali in *Kuch Kuch Hot Hai* [Something Happens] (2005) establish their Indianness through sacrifice and devotion towards the patriarchal setup. Tina chooses to have a child even though she is medically advised against it just to honour her husband Rahul's desire for a child and dies shortly after childbirth, while Anjali leaves her education mid-way and has to become 'feminine' before Rahul eventually falls in love with her (Gangoli, 2005, p. 159). The female protagonists are all educated since they are shown going to colleges and universities, but that does not seem to translate into gainful employment, since this might indicate that the husband is not capable enough to 'provide' for the woman,[11] a deathly blow to the patriarchal system. In rare films such as *Chalet Chalet* (Along the Way) (2003), where the protagonist Rhea has a career before marriage, she soon gives it up after marriage to look after the husband/home. Men, on the other hand, are at least shown going out of the house to earn a living even though their occupational details also remain blurry.

Although the packaging of gender relations might have changed, the content continues to lag behind. Thus, in *Salaam Namaste* [Hello] (2005), when Ambar Malhotra, a very independent and financially self-sufficient woman in Melbourne, who is studying to be a doctor and works part-time as a radio jockey, finds herself pregnant and single after her live-in boyfriend, Nikhil, refuses to marry her, her 'predicament' makes Ambar think that she is being punished for disappointing her parents by not having lived a conventional life or agreeing to an arranged marriage as per their wishes. She repents her life decisions by concluding that the live-in relationship was 'wrong' but decides to carry the child since aborting it would be a sin. The situation is ultimately resolved only when Nikhil changes his mind and agrees to marry her. Thus, a woman's social and financial independence comes riddled with an overwhelming sense of guilt lying just below the surface for not following the ideal Indian values.

Interestingly, most respondents from the Hindi film industry agreed that these films in particular, and Hindi films in general, have been very patriarchal. They argue that this is what sells since this is what the cinema audiences in India want to see. Since no market research is done at the time of conceiving these films, however, there is no way of either confirming or refuting this claim, which is based purely on conjecture. These representations do however provide an ongoing image of the cinematic ideal Indian gender relations and roles that need to be upheld and glorified.

Some filmmakers also argued that the cinematic representation of gender should change, but worried about whether changing things too much might be risky both socially and economically. During my interviews with filmmakers there was an overwhelming agreement that Bollywood films have continued to be patriarchal when it comes to issues such as gender, sexuality and family. Director Tarun Mansukhani, for instance, suggested that directors do not want to introduce too much radical change into the narrative particularly in relation to sensitive issues such as gender and sexuality. Mansukahni's film *Dostana* [Friendship] (2008) was a romantic comedy narrating the story of three friends, two of whom pretend to be gay to find an apartment. He argues that the attempt is to introduce change slowly in small doses, in order to make it easily palatable. Citing his film as a landmark, he points out that it was the first time a mainstream Hindi film with a plot including homosexuality was a commercial success and did not result in any controversies. For him, introducing too much cultural change in the area of sexuality or gender relations and/or roles would only lead to a backlash and slow down the channels which could encourage dialogue and acceptance in Indian society. Others such as multiple national award winning veteran actor Anupam Kher, disagree with this. For Kher, mainstream films are about entertaining people and not intellectualising or analysing current or possible gender representations. Representation of gender particularly, therefore, is a topic that continues to be a vexed issue even among those involved in making these films. The preference is to remain within the conservative realm of gender representation, and even the films that do make an attempt to challenge certain stereotypes or preconceived roles do ultimately resolve the narrative through some sort of a *dharmik* compromise around the tradition-modernity dichotomy.

There is awareness that introducing too much radical or sudden change in relation to gender and patriarchy might close down existing channels of communication and change in society as these issues are seen to be too closely interconnected with core Indian identity. Any significant change in the internal sphere of the home, seen as the feminine domain, is a sensitive aspect of the nationalist project. While there is recognition of the need for change there is a simultaneous fear of letting too much external western influence into the domain of the home. Thus, when a film narrative attempts to challenge conventional patriarchal gender roles and relations, this is quickly resolved by adopting solutions favouring conventional expectations, as for instance in films such as *Pardes* [Foreign Land] (1997), *Yaadein* [Memories] (2001) and *Dilwale Dulhaniya Le Jayenge* [The Romantic will Take the Bride] (1995), where the female protagonist wants to marry the person she loves but is willing to sacrifice for her family and patiently wait for the patriarch's approval. The marriage happens only when the father gives her the permission to marry, this avoiding the disobeying of patriarchal norms and authority, leading to the arranged love marriage phenomenon in post-liberalisation Hindi films.

# THE POST-LIBERALISATION INDIAN NATIONALIST PROJECT

This representation of gender issues can be seen within the larger narrative of the Indian (post)colonial project's construction of the masculine external domain of the world and the feminine inner domain of the home. While the nationalist project is eager to establish itself as on a par with the west in terms of material achievements and skills externally, it is resistant to change that might be seen as 'western' in the inner domain of the home. For Partha Chatterjee this does not, however, mean that the spiritual domain is left untouched or unchanged but that this change has to be brought about from within the private domain. Women and the family are believed to be an integral part of the spiritual domain since they are believed to play a crucial role in the physical as well as the cultural and ideological reproduction of the nation. Thus, for instance, while women's education was recognised as being important by the nationalists in the colonial phase of the Indian nationalist project, women were constantly reminded not to become too westernised as a *memsahib* [European woman] and forget that their foremost devotion in this nationalist narrative should always be towards the home and family (1989, p. 240). Women are singled to carry the burden of imparting spiritual and cultural values that define the nation to subsequent generations in this nationalist project.

Post-liberalisation Bollywood films' treatment of gender issues therefore follows this larger nationalist trajectory by allowing space for superficial change in areas such as dress and appearance but resists any significant deeper changes in gender roles and identity which might be seen as compromising women's ability to transmit the nation in moulding further generations. Women therefore continue to be seen as repositories of the nation by being the embodiment of the inner feminine domain of the home as the core of the Indian identity. Thus, in keeping with the larger trend in the Indian nationalist project, the inner domain of the home continues to be configured as patriarchal and brahmanical in its portrayal of gender and religion.

What is significant about the post-liberalisation Indian nationalist project is that it has successfully combined this essentialised Indian core identity with overwhelming overt materialism and transnationalism without any mutual conflict. This construction of the post-liberalisation Indian identity is tied to the rising influence of the right-wing hindutva forces on the one hand and rising global ambitions following the sudden and rapid economic boom and increasing aspirations of the upwardly mobile Indian middle classes on the other hand. The post-liberalisation Indian nationalist discourse has been successful in forging a delicate balance between these two opposing trends by glossing over the contradictions in its account and making the external material and inner spiritual domain fully compatible. Thus, this new nationalist reformulation allows post-liberalisation Indianness to celebrate its new found material accomplishments and consumerism in this phase, alongside glorifying a highly essentialised notion of patriarchal, brahmanical Hindu identity as the ideal form of Indianness.

The post-liberalisation construction of the seamless fluid ideal Indianness, however, is not just a nationalist project but a postcolonial nationalist project. The public-private interplay represented by the easy marriage of worldly success and patriarchal morality is made more potent by cinematically representing it through an imagined diaspora, strategically located in these films almost exclusively in Britain and the United States of America, to highlight the significance of this nationalist construction. Even though the Indian diaspora is spread throughout the globe, the diasporic location in the west is seen to carry special significance in conveying a sense of accomplishment and material success that success in other parts of the world is seen to lack. Thus, an overwhelming majority of these ideal Indian characters in post-liberalisation Bollywood are shown to be a part of the Indian diaspora in the west since it establishes the potency of the Indian nationalist project in a postcolonial world. Britain and the United States as former colonial and neo-imperial nations, respectively, therefore form the focus of these diaspora-based nationalist film narratives. It is, in fact, the material success of this strategically located imagined diaspora in the heart of the capitalist first world west that makes its possession of an essentialised Indian core even more central in its significance for the postcolonial Indian nationalist discourse. Post-liberalisation nationalism co-opts this imagined diaspora in the west to highlight the co-existence of the material and spiritual domains irrespective of geographical boundaries. Thus, this gendered Indian spiritual core is presented as disconnected from territorial compulsions and becomes capable of travelling transnationally as per the requirements of achieving material success. This combination becomes most poignant when placed in the west as the conventional epicentre of modernity.

Post-liberalisation Bollywood cinema with its entrenched popularity in the south Asian region also enables in highlighting the new Indian nationalist project as a benign power for the welfare of the South Asian region. It is significant for instance that this discourse is often presented in terms of '*desis*[12] versus foreigners', to include not just Indians but other diasporic nationals from the Indian subcontinent as well. This marketing of oneself as a *desi* has, in fact, been an important aspect of the strategic deployment of Bollywood cinema internationally in the post-liberalisation era. Hindi cinema has, for instance, been extremely influential in establishing Indian cultural influence across the Indian subcontinent. In spite of the longstanding diplomatic tension between India and Pakistan, Hindi films have consistently been extremely popular in Pakistan. Even though Hindi films were officially banned by the Pakistani government following the 1965 war with India, pirated DVDs of most Bollywood films become available in Pakistan within days of the film's release. After decades of the ban on Hindi films, often cited as the reason for the decline of local Pakistani cultural industries[13], in 2008 the Pakistani government revoked this ban due to the economic benefits (such as entertainment tax) accrued from screening immensely popular Bollywood films in Pakistani cinema theatres (Press Trust of India, 2008). Similarly, Bollywood films have been extremely popular in neighbouring countries such as Bangladesh, Nepal, Afghanistan, Bhutan and Sri Lanka.

Diasporic populations from these countries, therefore, have increasingly been drawn under the 'desi' umbrella to highlight the growing cultural influence of the Indian brand in the South Asian subcontinent. In recent years, films such as *Namastey London* [Hello London] (2007), *Jhoom Barabar Jhoom* [Swirl Around] (2007) and *Dhan Dhana Dhan Goal* [Come On Goal] (2007) have had a token Pakistani diasporic character (often as a friend) who is reminded of the importance of remembering cultural values by the Indian hero. In *Namastey London*, for instance, the supporting character, British Pakistani Imran Khan agrees to give up his religion and any association with his parents or culture and convert to Christianity by getting baptised as Immanuel, as a condition laid down by the parents of Susanne, his white British girlfriend, to allow their marriage. It is the good Indian hero Arjun who convinces Imran otherwise by reminding him of the importance of his cultural values and traditions and persuades Imran's parents to forgive him. Thus, the Indianness of the hero emerges not only as the protector of the woman's morality but also as a shining example to men from the neighbouring countries by having successfully negotiated the tension between tradition and modernity without losing his core Indian identity.

Politically, there has been a growing effort to expand this marketing of the Indian brand using Bollywood films as a tool. Internationally promoting the image of the new Indian modernity based on a privileged and essentialised notion of Indianness enables the strategic positioning of India as a soft power in contemporary globalised world politics. This representation of Indianness, thriving in former colonial countries like Britain or neo-imperialist countries such as the United States, through the diasporic Indian characters, portrays the image of Indian modernity as an enduring power capable of successfully establishing itself under any circumstances. The projection of this Indianness enables post-liberalisation Bollywood cinema to attract middle-class audiences within India by showing their aspirations of affluence and emigration to the west as being achievable while reassuring them of their innate ability to establish their Indianness, as a portable entity that is easily compatible with the material demands of the host society, in any location. Thus, post-liberalisation Indianness has negotiated the changes in Indian society by reworking its capability to what Chatterjee (1989) calls selectively appropriate western modernity by successfully adapting to the demands of western capitalism in the public sphere while retaining an essentialised gendered identity within the private realm of the home. The postcolonial nationalist project reconfigures itself strategically by using this conception of Indianness to promote India's rising ambitions of being a more prominent player in global world politics.

The postcolonial Indian nationalist project has constructed this imagined diaspora located in the west to position itself vis-à-vis the west. The nationalist project post-liberalisation uses this figure of the imagined diaspora to showcase its new confidence in being able to establish itself by gaining material influence in the heart of the first world west without compromising its essentialised spiritual core. It highlights a self-assured nationalist discourse which presents itself as being eager to take on a more mainstream role globally while holding on to an abstraction of its identity as an innate enduring core. In the process, a seemingly paradoxical account is presented that simultaneously challenges Eurocentric notions of western modernity while enabling an essentialised gendered cultural core to project India's rising self-confidence and global ambitions post-liberalisation.

# NOTES

1. The name 'Doordarshan' literally means seeing a vision from far away.
2. *Bold and the Beautiful*, first aired in 1987, is a long running popular American soap opera aired on the CBS network in the United States.
3. Santa Barbara is an American soap opera that was from 1984 to 1993 on the NBC network in the United States.
4. The term '*filmi*' is a colloquial euphemism in Hindi meaning a melodramatic candyfloss manner characteristic of films.
5. Faroukh Dhondhy is an Indian-born British activist and playwright, who has written several short stories and plays including the Channel four sitcom '*Tandoori Nights*' (1985–1987) featuring the story of rivalry between two Indian restaurants in London. He uses the term 'Bollywood' generically for Hindi cinema at all times.
6. Prasad (1998) uses the term 'socials' to refer to feudal family romance genre in Hindi cinema between the 1950s and 70s.
7. Drawing on the Hindu religious idea of '*dharma*' meaning virtue/duty.
8. The word 'Ganga' also refers to the river Ganges, considered the holiest of rivers in Hindu religion. It is believed that bathing in the Ganges absolves one of all past sins and ultimately leads to salvation.

9. The *Sindoor* [vermillion] and *Mangalsutra* [a particular necklace of black beads] are symbols of marriage, usually worn by 'upper caste' Hindu women after marriage.

10. NRI or Non-resident Indian is term used by the Government of India to refer to Indians living abroad.

11. This representation of the ideal Indian woman not having a career is quite a paradox since a large percentage of women are employed in contemporary Indian society. Traditionally however there does continue to be a caste dimension to this, since the notion of prestige associated with women of the family not working outside of the home is strongly related to the perception of a higher status in the caste hierarchy.

12. 'Desi' is an umbrella term used to describe someone from the Indian subcontinent. It derives from the Hindi word 'des' that refers to one's own country.

13. As well as other national cinemas in neighbouring countries like Bangladesh and Nepal.

# REFERENCES

Bose, M. (2007). *Bollywood: A history*. New Delhi: Roli Books.

Chadha, R., & Husband, C. (2006). *The cult of the luxury brand: Inside Asia's love affair with luxury*. London: Nicholas Brealey.

Chakravarti, S. (1993). *National identity in Indian popular cinema, 1947—87*. Austin, TX: University of Texas Press.

Chatterjee, P. (1989). The nationalist resolution of the women's question. In K. Sangari & S. Vaid (Eds.), *Recasting women: Essays in Indian colonial history* (pp. 233—253). New Brunswick, NJ: Rutgers University Press.

Chatterjee, P. (1999). *The Partha Chatterjee omnibus*. New Delhi: Oxford University Press.

Chatterjee, P. (2008). Critique of popular culture. *Public Culture, 20*(2), 321—344.

Dasgupta, C. (1991). *The painted face: Studies in India's popular cinema*. New Delhi: Roli Books.

Gangoli, G. (2005). Sexuality, sensuality and belonging: Representations of the 'Anglo-Indian' and the 'Western' woman in Hindi cinema. In R. Kaur & A. K. Sinha (Eds.), *Bollyworld: Popular Indian cinema through a transnational lens* (pp. 143—162). New Delhi: Sage.

Gaonkar, D. P. (2001). On alternative modernities. In D. P. Gaonkar (Ed.), *Alternative modernities* (pp. 1—23). Durham, NC: Duke University Press.

Govil, N. (2007). Bollywood and the frictions of global mobility. In D. K. Thussu (Ed.), *Media on the move: Global flow and contra-flow* (pp. 76—88). London: Routledge.

Loomba, A. (1998). *Colonialism postcolonialism*. Abingdon: Routledge.

Mishra, V. (2002). *Bollywood cinema: Temples of desire*. New York, NY: Routledge.

Nandy, A. (1995). *The Savage Freud and other essays on possible and retrievable selves*. New Delhi: Oxford University Press.

Nandy, A. (1998). Introduction: Indian popular cinema as a slum's eye view of politics. In A. Nandy (Ed.), *The secret politics of our desires: Innocence, culpability and Indian popular cinema* (pp. 1—18). New Delhi: Oxford University Press.

Prasad, M. (1998). *Ideology of the Hindi film: A historical construction.* Oxford: Oxford University Press.
Press Trust of India. (2008). *Pak senate panel wants ban on bollywood films lifted.* Retrieved from Times of India website http://articles.timesofindia.indiatimes.com/2008-01-29/pakistan/27749080_1_indian-films-number-of-pakistani-movies-indian-movies
Rajadhyaksha, A. (1993). The Phalke era: Conflict of traditional form and modern technology. In T. Niranjana, P. Sudhir, & V. Dhareshwar (Eds.), *Interrogating modernity: Culture and colonialism in India* (pp. 47–82). Calcutta: Seagull.
Thussu, D. K. (1999). Privatizing the airwaves: The impact of globalization on broadcasting in India. *Media, Culture and Society, 21,* 125–131.
Uberoi, P. (1999). The diaspora comes home: Disciplining desire in DDLJ. In V. Das, D. Gupta, & P. Uberoi (Eds.), *Tradition, pluralism and identity: In honour of T. N. Madan* (pp. 163–194). New Delhi: Sage.
Virdi, J. (2003). *The cinematic imagiNation: Indian popular films as social history.* New Brunswick, NJ: Rutgers University Press.
Yuval-Davis, N. (1997). *Gender and nation.* London: Sage.

# FILMOGRAPHY

*Aa Ab Laut Chale* [Come let us return] (1999), Dir Rishi Kapoor, India.
*Chalet Chalet* [Along the Way] (2003), Dir Aziz Mirza, India.
*Deewar* (1975), Dir Yash Chopra, India.
*Dhan Dhana Dhan Goal* [Come On Goal] (2007), Dir Vivek Agnihotri, India.
*Dilwale Dulhaniya Le Jayenge* [The romantic will take the bride] (1995), Dir Aditya Chopra, India.
*Dostana* [Friendship] (2008), Dir Tarun Mansukhani, India.
*Hum Dil De Chuke Sanam* [Straight from the heart] (1999), Dir Sanjay Leela Bhansali, India.
*Jhoom Barabar Jhoom* [Swirl Around] (2007), Dir Shaad Ali, India.
*Judaai* [Separation] (1997), Dir Raj Kanwar, India.
*Karan Arjun* (1995), Dir Rakesh Roshan, India.
*Kuch Kuch Hot Hai* [Something Happens] (2005), Dir Karan Johar, India.
*Mother India* (1957), Dir Mehboob Khan, India.
*Namastey London* [Hello London] (2007), Dir Vipul Shah, India.
*Pardes* [Foreign Land] (1997), Dir Subhash Ghai, India.
*Raja Harishchandra* [King Harishchandra] (1913), Dir Dadasaheb Phalke, India.
*Salaam Namaste* [Hello] (2005), Dir Siddharth Anand, India.
*Taal* [Musical note] (1999), Dir Subhash Ghai, India.
*Yaadein* [Memories] (2001), Dir Subhash Ghai, India.

# PART IV
# HAVING A VOICE: LITERATURE AND POETRY

# MIGRATION, AFRICAN WRITING AND THE POST-COLONIAL/ DIASPORIC CHIMAMANDA ADICHIE MOMENT

Carole Boyce Davies

## ABSTRACT

Purpose — *This chapter examines the current incarnation of African literature as written by a younger generation, less concerned with writing back to the colonial empire, and more with examining issues of migration and the consequences of living in diaspora. It contrasts the concerns and experiences of the older generation of African writers such as Chinua Achebe and Ngugi wa Thiongo with the current generation, especially Chimamanda Ngozi Adichie and Mukoma wa Ngugi.*

Design/methodology/approach — *It engages in literary and cultural analyses of selected texts, revealing how a range of current issues, such as women's rights, are discussed therein.*

Findings — *A new generation of African writers, many having already been through the migratory experience before writing, are engaging a range of issues that are no longer identical to those concerning writers of*

Gender and Race Matter: Global Perspectives on Being a Woman
Advances in Gender Research, Volume 21, 233–248
Copyright © 2016 by Emerald Group Publishing Limited
ISSN: 1529-2126/doi:10.1108/S1529-212620160000021001

*the immediate colonial experience. Issues of sexuality, migration and post-independence challenges become prominently articulated.*

Originality/value — *Women's rights were raised by an earlier generation of African women writers and are seen now not so much as radical positions but as assessments of how men and women are socialised. The ways in which people are encouraged or discouraged from articulating full equality as part of the larger critique of post-independence African states is a focus.*

**Keywords:** African literature; decolonial; diaspora; feminism; migration

# INTRODUCTION

When Chimamanda Ngozi Adichie presented a London talk in which she claimed boldly, 'We Should All Be Feminists' (April 12, 2013) we witnessed, within the same time frame as Chinua Achebe's passing (March 21, 2013), another major transition: a fitting representative of a second generation of African writers[1] made a major political intervention, such as that which had taken place at an earlier historical juncture via writers of the Achebe generation. As a young African woman writer, Adichie was advancing some of the intellectual and creative positions that women writers of that same earlier generation as Achebe, had advanced without the major international recognition that she is now afforded.[2] Writers such as Ama Ata Aidoo, Buchi Emecheta, Nawal el Saadawi, Flora Nwapa and Bessie Head had consistently articulated positions on women's experience in African contexts and were often critical of African traditions which disadvantaged women, but also of looming problems in the rising post-independence states.

The fact is that much as we celebrate the contributions of Achebe, with the kind of world renown that he received, he was also locked into some specific representations of the political issues of decolonisation, in which African women were represented in a less than favourable light and, for sure, in which African masculinity was posed as the only response to European colonial dominance. However, an entire body of writing by African women created a more nuanced examination of African realities, which included critique of some of the limitations of the post-colonial state, and therefore of male leadership. Thereby, the presentation of the other side of the story, the one in which women lived complex lives of 'joys' (*The Joys of Motherhood* by Emecheta, 1979) and 'pains' (*Woman at Point Zero* by El Saadawi, 1975) was made significant.

In this period, actually half a century of literary production defined as modern African literature, we witnessed a writing back to colonial empires and their constructions, coupled with revision or correction of the ways in which Africa had appeared in the Western imagination. Achebe ended up at the forefront of this discourse with his early and representative *Things Fall Apart* (1958) which rapidly came to be defined as the 'archetypal African novel'.

## THE CHIMAMANDA ADICHIE MOMENT

The Chimamanda Adichie moment represents a totally different articulation of African literature outside of those frames set by the earlier writers in the waning days of colonialism, who dealt with tradition in the immediate and post-independence realities. Much of the writing in that modern African literature period, nationalist in orientation, did not include women in its thinking about the construction of new nations. And even in the documentation of that literature, a standard text such as *A History of Twentieth-Century African Literatures* (1993) had to be pushed by its editors to include women writers, resulting in one chapter accounting for the place of women in African literary history (Boyce Davies & Fido, 1993). Today, migration is suggesting a whole different reading of African literatures and presenting a variety of other narratives. These include recognition of the contributions of African women writers to the larger field of African writing *and* the rise of a new generation of young writers who are living the experience of migration. It is this new generation which is pursuing a variety of different angles, often ushered in by a series of diasporic realities. This presents the need for a complete rethinking of the contours, nature, themes and concerns of African literature today, in which women writers are central and no longer marginal. As such, a writer such as Chimamanda Adichie, in my reading, brings together, and therefore best represents, the convergence of these new realities.

Among the members of this generation of African writers some, like Tope Folarin (2013) who won — the 2013 Caine prize for his short story *Miracle*,[3] describe themselves as born in the United States of Nigerian parents, with more global concerns, many of these generated from their experiences of migration. Folarin's representative story *Miracle*, for example, is centred in a Nigerian community living in the Midwest United States and deals with a blind prophet in a small church community of Nigerian migrants who is unable to produce the unlikely miracle of giving sight to a young boy who actually needs his glasses. Folarin indicates that he had never travelled to Nigeria, largely because his working class family could not afford to purchase tickets for such a journey.[4]

Several members of this new generation of African writers have lived in Europe, with writers such as NoViolet Bulawayo having studied in the United States and gained an MFA at Cornell University. Hailing from Zimbabwe, she wrote about these two experiences in her book *We Need New Names* (2013). Hers is a stark portrayal of the world from the point of view of a young girl who is wise beyond her years, due to having to confront all the ills of the post-colonial state and also manage life in the United States and all that this entails as a black immigrant. Many of the writers of this generation have travelled outside of Africa before becoming recognised, unlike the Achebe or Ngugi generation, who were often writing at home before gaining outside acclaim, although their publications written in Western languages (English and French mostly) were for foreign audiences. The second generation, diasporically literate, navigate home and abroad conceptually if not personally. Writers writing in the home space, such as Binyavanga Wainaina, still gain in international recognition and have developed continental readerships. Wainaina publicly announced his sexuality in an article in *The Guardian*[5] in response to repressive anti-homosexual laws in some African countries.

For the international audience though, Chimamanda Adichie comes across as at the forefront of this group and indicates that she lives both experiences. The recent story of her father being kidnapped in Nigeria poignantly captures this experience of being a writer with international acclaim who has to navigate difficult experiences at home (Adichie, 2015a, 2015b). It will be interesting to see if her novel *Americanah* (2014) becomes the 'archetypal novel' of its generation. In an earlier essay on Ama Ata Aidoo, I made the claim that in the field of African women writers Aidoo[6] should be identified as setting some of the early themes and arguments for a more gender-balanced modern African literature (Adams, 2012). Writers of Adichie's generation are able now to articulate these, and other related issues raised by Aidoo, because writers in that cohort had already done 'daily battle', for example in Fatima Mernissi's Doing Daily Battle and thereby claimed a place for African women's writing. Chimamanda is very clear about this history and of Achebe's placement in the hierarchy and African women's location in all of this. During a visit to India, she was quoted as saying:

> Being a sub-Saharan African writer, you're supposed to be like Chinua Achebe, who is called the father of modern African literature. But you're probably compared to him because people don't know any other writers from Africa […] Then I always want to know who the mother of African literature is. And also, why does African literature need a father and a mother at all? (Umachandran, 2011)

She claims literally to have been raised in the house of Achebe at The University of Nigeria (Nsukka) on the Eastern Nigeria campus, and identifies herself as coming out of the house of Achebe, for reasons of literary history, but also ethnicity, and a certain descent as an African writer. Despite this patriarchal inheritance in African writing, there is clearly a gap between the two writers in terms of age, influence, concerns, gender and time. Chimamanda Adichie's 'The Headstrong Historian' in *The Thing Around Your Neck* is clearly a rewriting of the Okonkowo narrative in *Things Fall Apart*, even with the word play on 'Thing' in the book's title. Things have already fallen apart we assume from her narrative. In 'The Headstrong Historian' the person affected by colonialism is a woman, the grandmother, who develops as a resisting subject, but who importantly is able to take the fight forward via the female line. It is the granddaughter who becomes a thinker and a scholar of African history who re-captures her grandmother's innate resistance and unfulfilled quest for justice. Interestingly, Adichie mentions the presence of such a dynamic and resisting grandmother in her own life.

I read Adichie's 'The Headstrong Historian' as writing back to Achebe by reworking some of the same turf that he had covered: time frame, names, traditional cultural practices that maintained inequality, colonial incursion and the arrival of the white man, Christianity and its effects, and colonial schooling. She even re-writes Achebe's imagined colonial text which ends *Things Fall Apart*, entitled *The Pacification of the Primitive Tribes of the Lower Niger*, with the title *Pacifying With Bullets: A Reclaimed History of Southern Nigeria*.

In the context of this discussion, what is significant about 'The Headstrong Historian' is that Adichie focuses on women — a grandmother who was wronged by both family (tradition) and coloniality. She presents a granddaughter who re-writes her grandmother's power of creativity and political sensibility. In this story, she makes the person affected by colonialism (the grandmother) a resisting subject from childhood, bypassing the colonised son for a granddaughter, Grace, who takes back her African name, resists colonial educational tendencies in the academy and writes books that reclaim African history.

Chimamanda Adichie's TED Talk 'We Should All Be Feminists' is loaded with anecdotes about gender inequality in contemporary Africa that span class, age and circumstance and that range from her childhood experience of being denied adult privileges like walking into a hotel unaccompanied, because she would be assumed to be a sex worker, or being rendered invisible when in the company of men. Claiming her own feminism and asserting that her grandmother was also a feminist in practice, she highlights the ridiculous conclusions of men and women in her community (some of them educated) that attempt to return her to a place of acceptance of gender inequality. From Adichie's point of view we have evolved but our ideas about women have not.

There is an additional critique of the valorising of tradition in Achebe's *Things Fall Apart* in Adichie's reference to the practice of destroying twins which appears in the Achebe novel. She uses her beautiful twin nieces who would have been victims of that tradition had they been born during those times to exemplify her opposition to this practice. Her conclusion is, of course, that people make culture and therefore we can change those things that remain inappropriate. Thus she provides for her audience a simple definition of feminism, advanced a bit beyond the definition she acquired via a dictionary in her childhood search, as that of a man or a woman who says 'yes there is a problem with gender and we must fix it'. For scholars it is a much more complicated set of definitions with a body of scholarship to match. Adichie is clearly aware of the variety of feminist positions, for in the same TED talk she indicates that she is very familiar with the 'systems of oppression' approach which is one of the hallmarks of black feminism. Relatedly, the most advanced articulation of African feminist positions carries the class/race/gender articulation of African women's rights. The *Journal of African Marxists* in an editorial to a special issue on women, entitled 'Women on the March' in 1986 quoted the following which proposed an economic/class based feminist approach to the democratisation of African women's rights:

> Our vision of feminism, born of our experience as activists and analysts, has at its very core a process of economic and social development geared to human needs through wider access to economic and political power. Equality, peace and development by and for the poor and oppressed are inextricably interlinked with equality, peace and development by and for women. (Sen & Grown, 1986, p. 18)

One immediately sees in this formation a 'systems of domination' approach, linked to the development of a full humanity in which political and economic power is shared. Adichie is also well aware of this logic of the critique of inequality as she cites Wangari Maathai's claim that women appear infrequently in leadership in Africa. She engages a range of feminist issues anecdotally and descriptively by asserting that equal pay for equal work is a fundamental right and that rape reveals the depravity of men and not women's lack of inhibition. Adichie pays significant attention to the issue of sexuality in this talk and challenges the assumption that women are raised to marry while men have choices. She describes a woman she knows who pretended domesticity in order to get married and critiques the idea that women must silence themselves and not express their sexuality. In a 2010 interview, around the time of the publication of her book of stories, *That Thing Around Your Neck* (2010), Adichie described among her current preoccupations the idea that marriage is not set up for the benefit of women and indeed can be dangerous because women are conditioned to behave 'as though marriage is a prize'. But Ama Ata Aidoo, as already indicated, made similar arguments, which are well developed in her novel *Changes: A Love Story* (1993).

Adichie's novel *Americanah* deals with the international migration of Africans to the United States and the United Kingdom and the related issues of living in the center of these global powers as a black immigrant. Yet it also offers an unabashed engagement with all salient aspects of sexuality, in and out of Africa, for her generation. The lead character, a young Igbo woman, reveals a range of tentative sexual escapades as a teenager in Nigeria, her migration to Lagos then to the United States as a student, where she experiences a level of poverty that leads to an encounter in which her dignity is compromised. She ends up living in long-term relationships with white and black American men before returning to Nigeria where things have indeed fallen apart, way beyond even Achebe's version. *Americanah* is about sexuality as much as it is about transnational migration, and about the full realisation of the African woman as literary subject, but it is also a critique of life in the post-colonial state.

As indicated above, Achebe, as the representative voice of his generation, documented the period of the British colonial incursion into Africa and the im/possibility of a concerted and organised response. In contrast, Adichie is aware of the colossal importance of the United States as a world hegemon. The titling of the book, while a play on the way Nigerians referred to those who had gone abroad to the United States and returned with affectations, is also about the Americanisation of the world, which renders Africans and others around the world at times totally dispossessed both at home and abroad and having to make their way in this world of American dominance which impacts upon everywhere. For this reason, the experience of her Nigerian boyfriend in England is less than appealing, as he is reduced to toilet cleaning and this period of his life in England ends in humiliating deportation. Ironically he is able to achieve a measure of financial support through well-known Nigerian patronage systems in which economic structures are negotiated via a series of connections and the acquisition of lucrative government contracts with help behind the scenes from corrupt officials and the like. So he was able to use a friend made during his difficult days in London as a representative English man, which makes colonial England not really significant in the Adichie scheme of things, as it should not be for the contemporary African writer. Our protagonist returns home to Nigeria but it is not an idyllic return and rather one fraught with myriad cultural adjustments along the lines of the critique of independence genre of novels. Nonetheless it is home.

Taking the recognition of Adichie to another level, popular singing icon Beyoncé sampled Adichie's TED talk, 'We Should all be Feminists' for her recent album.[7] In my view, it fulfils perhaps a more elaborate marketing and recognition model than has been seen before. Achebe's *Things Fall Apart* became a bestseller because of its iconic significance in documenting the pre-colonial. Furthermore, it documents colonial incursion into Africa and associated decolonial politics across the world, thereby becoming necessary reading for all those interested in learning about a representative African culture at the period of colonial arrival. It was used in classes from anthropology to political science, and of course in literature, a staple on everyone's reading list.

By contrast, the new generation of African writers, who Ali Mazrui[8] recently described as American Africans (as opposed to African-Africans), are becoming adept at giving us a more advanced or nuanced understanding of some of the intricacies of the results of the secondary African Diaspora's experiences. For example, Mukoma Wa Ngugi's *Nairobi Heat* (2011) is a detective story set both in the United States and in Africa which follows the experiences of an African American detective from Wisconsin who travels to Nairobi and meets up with a like-minded African detective to unravel a murder that had taken place in the United States. The experiences they have occur in and through the seamy underbelly of a postcolonial state with all the sordid experiences and thrills that accompany such journeys. Indeed Mukoma, by these means, has extended the range of African literature for this post-colonial period and indicates that the detective genre he works in may be more relevant to this contemporary period. With the existence of groups like Boko Haram in Northern Nigeria and the Somalian group al Shabaab able to bring mayhem to a mall in Kenya, we are presented with a different set of foci which still relate to, but are larger than, the earlier address to the ill-effects of colonial experiences.

What I am calling 'the Post-Colonial/Diasporic Chimamanda Adichie Moment' then is a totally different articulation of African literature outside of those frames set by the earlier writers who dealt with coloniality, tradition, and the immediate and post-independence realities. Just as the formal recognition of women has advanced the field and it is now assumed that any discussion of African literature must include women writers, experiences of migration and diaspora are suggesting a whole different set of themes and presenting a variety of other narratives.

## GLOBAL CITIZENSHIP

This new global citizenship for African writers is summarized by writer Uche Umez, who indicates that for his generation:

> Their focus is not as overtly political as the pioneer generation of writers [...] Maybe because Achebe's generation inherited the insidious burden of colonialism, nationalism and independence, whereas the only burden we have so far inherited was military rule and the overwhelming ineptitude of civil rule [...] we have all become global citizens, exploring new identities, subjectivities, sexual orientation and experiences at home and abroad. (2012)[9]

In a conversation with Sokari Ekine, a Nigerian social justice activist and blogger living in Spain, who writes an award winning blog, 'Black Looks', which deals with a range of topics such as LGBTI rights in Africa, gender issues, human rights, the Niger Delta and Land Rights.

Still, what becomes clear immediately in this analysis is that the issues which contemporary writers (male and female) foreground, such as issues of global citizenship, new identities and subjectivities, sexual orientation and experiences at home and abroad, were and still are clearly part of the framework of earlier women writers. My argument remains that the work of African feminist writers of the earlier generation must be taken into account in examining contemporary writers. In all of Aidoo's works one can identify a conscious women's rights positioning, in her early affirmative critique of issues which were of concern to African women in key areas such as marriage policy, divorce, 'herstory', rape and sexual harassment.

Indeed, these political issues raised by women writers, some from their own experience, provide an operational context for what followed and have become useful information for those embarking on some form of women's rights analysis. This is Ama Ata Aidoo's summary, from over 20 years ago:

> [...] marriage has proved singularly effective as an instrument of suppression. It has put half (or often more than half) of humanity through mutations that are thoroughly humiliating and at best ridiculous. (p. 263)[10]

By the time we get to Chimamanda Adiche we see an assumption that these are normal issues relating to living in the contemporary world. Thus, in a CNN 'African Voices'[11] presentation, besides the critique of heterosexual marriage and its effects on women, often the subordinated partner, she added the hypocrisy concerning the denial that same sex relationships existed/exist in Africa. Aidoo (1992), in her generation, like other continental African feminists, saw the emancipation of women as political and the last possible hope for ourselves and for everyone else on the continent. Chimamanda Adichie sees these as assumptions of equality in the treatment of men and women as human beings.

This brings us to the African Union's Protocol on the Rights of Women in Africa (2005) (ratified by 23 countries as of this date) which has enshrined many of the advances that African feminists have been battling for over the years, claiming women's rights as human rights. Article 6 of the Protocol for example deals with marriage, with 10 items pertaining to women's rights in marriage, from rights to property to fair treatment and relations to children. Article 5 discusses the elimination of harmful practices, defining these as 'all behaviour, attitudes and/or practices which negatively affect the fundamental rights of women and girls, such as their right to life, health, dignity, education and physical integrity'.[12] Article 7 deals with separation, divorce and annulments of marriage, Article 12 the right to education and the removal of barriers which discriminate against women in educational settings. In the definitions category, violence against women is defined as follows:

> 'Violence against women' means all acts perpetrated against women which cause or could cause them physical, sexual, psychological, and economic harm, including the threat to take such acts; or to undertake the imposition of arbitrary restrictions on or deprivation of fundamental freedoms in private or public life in peace time and during situations of armed conflicts or of war. (African Union's Protocol on the Rights of Women in Africa, 2005)

These rights, now fundamentally enshrined in an international law instrument, were issues that a writer/activist like Ama Ata Aidoo, as we have shown, had already challenged as limiting the full possibilities of African women. Thus a work such as *Anowa*, as I have argued in *Migrations of the Subject*,[13] can be read as one of the most important theorisings of diaspora and middle passage textualities with reference to the struggles of African women. Ama Ata Aidoo, then, remains one of a small group of African writers to actually engage some of the historical, personal and ideological issues on the African side which ushered in the forced migration that helped shape the African Diaspora. But within that framework she skillfully embeds the talented, creative and ambitious woman as not at all complicit, as her character Anowa navigates outside of traditional inequities and is on the road to independence and full partnership. However, along the way she is stymied by male dominance which is also read as male impotence.

Another work by Aidoo, *Our Sister Killjoy or Reflections from a Black Eyed Squint*, had also dealt with the African woman's appearance in the West as sexualised and racialised. As Adichie confronts this same theme in the contemporary world in her novel *Americanah*, we can also reconfigure Aidoo's earlier and tentative attempt to deal with the issues of same sex sexuality, which appear as a kind of minor subtext at the level of the desire of a German woman for the African woman's sensuality. The larger narrative structure, experimental in form, engages the African student abroad and signifies what we begin to see as the development of the second level African diaspora (see Zeleza, 2009).[14] The diaspora being described now is different from the previous version which was identified as the absence of a commitment to return. The character Sissie does return, having navigated Europe, with a surprised recognition of the inherent limitations of those who had colonised others.

Interestingly, like Sissie in Ama Ata Aidoo in *Our Sister Killjoy*,[15] Adichie has written several stories wherein a variety of characters encounter the contemporary experience of living abroad, this time in the United States, and then return home to Africa or, as in the American Embassy story, decide not even to bother accepting the humiliation. The colonial role that the United States plays, not in the acquisition of territory, as in the older colonial model, but in the acquisition and control of military power and markets, explains why it is a destination of choice for migrants of all sorts.

Thus Adichie's *Americanah* centres migration, sex and sexuality, class, education and race as the African experiences them in the United States. They are all launched in a hair braiding salon, indicating the bifurcated nature of migration to the United States and the United Kingdom, which

Caribbean writers have been adept at articulating. With reference to form, there is a movement between blogging and writing, with Adichie using blogging for her main character Ifemelu to express her thinking on race and identity. The novel's narrative explores the experiences of Ifemelu in diaspora. Therefore, what we see in the work of writers of the 'Post-Colonial/Diasporic Chimamanda Adichie Moment' is a line of thinking and writing that demonstrates a decolonial assumption across Africa and the African Diaspora. This is a full and prominent Pan-Africanist/feminist sensibility, expressed in essays as in creative writing (poetry and prose), but also an engagement with the problematics of exile, of migration in multiple directions and the implications of engaging a larger world with eyes wide open to the limitations of 'Miracles'.

Still, in the essay 'Beauty, Mourning and Melancholy' in *Africa 39*, a review essay, Mukoma Wa Ngugi, the son of Ngugi wa Thiong'o, identifies the meaning of the second generation, migrated and at home, as having already lost any connections with 'traditional practices'. While the older generation of his father could write about the loss happening in their child-hoods, the loss has already happened by the time of the post-colonial generation, sometimes violently through destruction by the colonial state. So it is no longer about mourning that which has been taken away by colonialism but about not even being aware that it had been taken, while somehow feeling the melancholy of separation and absence in diaspora. He describes Tope Folarin's father as 'mourning things he has lost — country, wife, culture and so on'. The son, meanwhile, raised in Utah of Nigerian parents, with little knowledge of Africa, not even a visit, writes about their experiences in diaspora.

Taiye Selasi's *Ghana Must* go begins with the death of the father, lit-erally, who was one of that generation who qualified as a medical doctor in the United States, returns home after a humiliating professional experi-ence and leaves his family in the United States to fend for themselves. His death is the catalytic event in the novel which triggers his family's return to Ghana and their engagement with all the missing history and related diffi-cult experiences of his children in the African diaspora as on the African continent.

As indicated earlier, a section of Adichie's TED talk was sampled on Beyoncé's popular self-titled album's 11th track, 'Flawless'. According to reports 'At 5 p.m. on December 12, 2013 (the day before Beyonce's album came out) Amazon ranked *Americanah* #861 of all hardcover books. Five days later, the book was ranked #632. Today, the book is ranked #179. It's a staggering rise up the rankings'.[16]

Incorporating social media directly into the novel *Americanah* in the form of a blogging lead character, Adichie uses a form familiar to her generation. A series of blogs are placed directly into the text, indicated by a different font, and are actually used to advance the narrative, as proverbs or stories would have been used by Achebe. New challenges, new media, different forms and different audiences than earlier generations were available to present a different approach to textualities as to political realities. If groups such as Boko Haram and their kidnapping of over 200 young Nigerian girls from school generated the Bring Back Our Girls Movement, we are witnessing a different engagement with some of the failures of the post-colonial African state in which the lives and conditions of women cannot remain marginal issues.

# CONCLUSION

A new generation of African writers, many having already been through the migratory experience before writing, are engaging a range of issues that are no longer identical to those concerning writers of the immediate colonial experience. Whereas writers such as Chinua Achebe, in classics like *Things Fall Apart* (1958), deliberately wrote to challenge colonial enterprises, a second generation is obviously less concerned with establishing Africa's humanity in the eyes of the world. Instead, issues of sexuality, migration and post-independence challenges become prominently articulated. The post-colonial/diasporic moment is marked by an assessment of the meanings of enduring coloniality and the still pervasive need to confront additional and enduring challenges. The position of women in society remains fundamental in each of these scenarios, as raised by an earlier generation of women writers whose works paralleled that of the men of their generation. Still currently relevant, a new generation confronts at times more insidious forms of fundamentalisms and the incomplete tasks of decolonisation.

# NOTES

1. A panel discussion on Africa's Literary Identity was dedicated to this question of identifying the new generation of writers, Moderated by Uzodinma Iweala, award-winning author of *Beasts of No Nation*, it featured this writer, TMS Ruge,

Hannah Pool and Tope Folarin and was held at Pace University on 27 September 2013. Podcast available: http://bit.ly/16CWGBN

2. See, for example, Ogundipe (1984). 'Women on the march' in the *Journal of African Marxists* which proposed an economic/class-based feminist approach to the democratisation of African women's rights in the following terms:

> ... Our vision of feminism has at its very core a process of economic and social development geared to human needs through wider access to economic and political power. Equality, peace and development by and for the poor and oppressed are inextricably interlinked with equality, peace and development by and for women. (Ogundipe, 1984, p. 3)

3. www.caineprize.com/pdf/2013_Folarin.pdf

4. At the panel discussion organised by Africare at Pace University on Africa's Literary Identity, 27 September, 2013, New York City, mentioned in note 1 above, Tope Folarin indicated that his father sold ice cream and cleaned buildings, and his mother worked as a nursing assistant in the Midwest U.S. where he was one of only a few black children in the school he attended.

5. Kenyan writer Wainaina (2014) declares: 'I am homosexual'. http://www.theguardian.com/world/2014/jan/21/kenyan-writer-binyavanga-wainaipina-declares-homosexuality. Accessed on June 23, 2015.

6. Chimamanda Adiche, in an interview on CNN 'African Voices' (2010), described the themes that preoccupied her in her then most recent collection of short stories, *The Thing Around Your Neck*.

7. 'Flawless' (stylized as '***Flawless') is a single from the album 'Beyoncé', released on 12 August 2014 (Parkwood − Columbia).

8. See introductory essay by Isidore Okpewho in Okpewho and Nzegwu (2009) which discusses this idea.

9. http://nigerianstalk.org/2012/11/05/interview-with-uche-umez-sokari-ekine/. Accessed on June 23, 2015.

10. Aidoo (1984).

11. CNN International (2009).

12. http:www.african-union.org/root/au/documents/treaties/documents/test/protocol. Accessed on February 14, 2011.

13. *Black Women Writing and Identity: Migrations of the Subject* (1994).

14. See for example Paul Zeleza's essay in (2009).

15. Longmans edition, 1997. Published initially by NOK Publishers International with the subtitle. *Reflections from a Black-Eyed Squint* (1997 [1979]).

16. *The Atlantic* (2013).

# ACKNOWLEDGEMENTS

A version of this chapter was presented at PKU − Peking University, Beijing, China in October 2015. Thank you to my assistant Han Xiu for her consistent work during my stay at BFSU and to the students excited about African literature, who asked wonderful questions after my presentation.

# REFERENCES

Achebe, C. (1958). *Things fall apart*. London: William Heinemann.
Adams, A. (Ed.). (2012). *Essays in honour of Ama Ata Aidoo at 70: A reader in African cultural studies*. Banbury: Ayebia.
Adichie, C. N. (2010). *The thing around your neck*. New York, NY: Anchor Books.
Adichie, C. N. (2013). We should all be feminists. *TEDx Euston*, April 12.
Adichie, C. N. (2014). *Americanah*. New York, NY: Anchor Books.
Adichie, C. N. (2015a). My father's kidnapping. *The New York Times*, May 30. Retrieved from http://www.nytimes.com/2015/05/31/opinion/sunday/chimamanda-ngozi-adichie-my-fathers-kidnapping.html. Accessed on June 22, 2015.
Adichie, C. N. (2015b). *We should all be feminists*. New York, NY: Anchor Books.
African Union's Protocol on the Rights of Women in Africa. (2005).
Aidoo, A. A. (1984). Ghana: To be a woman. In R. Morgan (Ed.), *Sisterhood is global. The international women's movement anthology* (pp. 258−263). New York, NY: The Feminist Press, CUNY.
Aidoo, A. A. (1992). The African woman today (Keynote address). Women in Africa and the African Diaspora Conference, Nigeria.
Aidoo, A. A. (1993). *Changes: A love story*. New York, NY: Feminist Press.
Aidoo, A. A. (1997 [1979]). *Our sister Killjoy. Reflections from a black-eyed squint*. London: Longmans.
Beyoncé. (2013/2014). 'Flawless'. Retrieved from http://www.latimes.com/books/jacketcopy/la-et-jc-beyonce-flawless-chimamanda-ngozi-adichie-20131213,0,3338347.story#ixzz2pe TdpJeV
Boyce Davies, C. (1994). *Black women writing and identity: Migrations of the subject*. London: Routledge.
Boyce Davies, C., & Fido, E. (1993). African women writers: Towards a literary history. In O. Owomoyela (Ed.), *A history of African literature in the twentieth century* (pp. 311−346). Lincoln, NE: University of Nebraska Press.
Bulawayo, V. (2013). *We need new names*. London: Chatto and Windus.
CNN International. (2009). African Voices. Broadcast date 7.11.2009.
Ekine, S. (2012). Interview with Uche Umez − Sokari Ekine. *Nigerians Talk*, November 5. Retrieved from http://nigerianstalk.org/2012/11/05/interview-with-uche-umez-sokari-ekine/. Accessed on June 23, 2015.
El Saadawi, N. (1975). *Woman at point zero*. London: Zed Books.
Emecheta, B. (1979). *The joys of motherhood*. New York, NY: George Braziller.
Folarin, T. (2013). Miracle. In *The Caine prize for African writing: A memory this size and other stories* (pp. 10−21). Oxford: New Internationalist Publications Ltd.
Mernissi, F. (1995). *Dreams of trespass: Tales of a harem girlhood*.
Mernissi, F. (1998). *Doing Daily Battle*. London: The Women's Press.
Ngugi, M. (2011). *Nairobi heat*. New York, NY: Melville House Publishing.

Ngugi, M. W. (2014). Beauty, mourning and melancholy. *Africa 39*, November 9. Retrieved
    from https://lareviewofbooks.org/review/beauty-mourning-melancholy-africa39.
Ogundipe, M. (1984). African women, culture and another development. *The Journal of
    African Marxists*, *5*(77), 92.
Okpewho, I., & Nzegwu, N. (Eds.). (2009). *The new African diaspora*. Bloomington, IN:
    Indiana University Press.
Selasi, T. (2013). *Ghana must go*. New York, NY: Penguin.
Sen, G., & Grown, C. (1986). Development crisis and alternative visions: Third world women's
    perspectives development alternatives for women with a new era. *Canadian Woman
    Studies/Les Cahiers De La Femme*, *1*(3), 16−18.
*The Atlantic*. (2013, December 23).
Wainaina, B. (2014). Kenyan writer Binyavanga Wainaina declares: 'I am homosexual'. *The
    Guardian*, January 20. Retrieved from http://www.theguardian.com/world/2014/jan/21/
    kenyan-writer-binyavanga-wainaina-declares-homosexuality. Accessed on June 23, 2015.
Zeleza, P. (2009). Diaspora dialogues: Engagements between Africa and its diasporas. In
    I. Okpewho & N. Nzegwu (Eds.), *The new African diaspora* (pp. 31−58). Bloomington,
    IN: Indiana University Press.

# SUHA

## Jocelyn Watson

## INTRODUCTION

As I read the papers and listened to the news, I appreciated that there was little written about how the present crisis in Syria affects women and this prompted me to investigate further. I began to read what I could online, in newspaper articles from Britain and across the world, reports written by charities and NGOs, the UNHCR, and the UN as well as British Government. I then wanted to use my skills as a writer to give voice to what I had read. I felt compelled to write something that I thought might provide an insight into the trauma and suffering that women are enduring. I wanted to write a story that could provide some insight into the risks for female-headed households and the realities of gender-based violence that many women have to endure. Dry newspaper articles, detailed reports, erudite academic journals may sometimes fail to engage people in a way that touches their humanity, whereas I believe, literature sometimes can. Literature, in this case the short story can take people away from the familiar, bringing people of different backgrounds, cultures, experiences and ways of life together. People are better able to relate through a piece of literature as it makes us understand we are not alone, and that people, in this case refugees, are enduring horrendous suffering and persecution. My hope is that Suha's plight will open readers' minds to the inhumanity and the scale of human suffering that displaced peoples and refugees, who may include abandoned children, disabled people, families, isolated single

Gender and Race Matter: Global Perspectives on Being a Woman
Advances in Gender Research, Volume 21, 249–260
Copyright © 2016 by Emerald Group Publishing Limited
ISSN: 1529-2126/doi:10.1108/S1529-212620160000021013

people and the elderly, who have had to endure the brutality of war and devastation in order to survive. As the reader learns about other cultures and experiences I hope it assists in self-reflection about the kind of world we live in.

I have attempted to bring the reader into the mind of a young woman who finds herself alone and having to take on responsibilities that she never anticipated. Even if Suha's surroundings and experiences are completely different from what the average reader has lived through, her story is a way to engage, to understand, to learn, to sympathise and empathise and in the final analysis, to better understand what humanity, compassion and integrity really mean. For me as a writer, literature not only represents our world to us but it also shows us ways in which we can change the world we live in or adapt to changes which have already taken place that we had little or no understanding of. I believe that literature's powerful force is that it helps us with current as well as future challenges by helping us to think about ourselves, our worlds, our societies and those who are impoverished, excluded, marginalised and discriminated against across the globe.

This is Suha's story, punctuated by happiness, naivety, fear, tragedy and hope...

## SUHA

Let me tell you what happened and then you can judge for yourselves. In those early days, dreams used to fuel my imagination, lift me and sweep me off to different spaces and places. Whenever and wherever there was an opportunity I planted a dream and I was thrilled by all the excitement that lay ahead. And then ... and then, I realised how foolish I was. How could I have known, how could any of us have known ...

I look out of the window of this room that has nothing of me. There is a dusty blue sky. It looks as though a child has taken a piece of chalk and drawn bubbles and lines, circles and oval shapes, as though there is no story. But like everything, there is a story. The white parallel streaks are the trails left behind by planes criss-crossing through the London skyline. A journey I had thought Wassim and I would make together one day.

*** 

Wassim and I were close playmates from childhood and so it was expected. It had become part of everyone's dream. I was only sixteen in 2009 when it was discussed. I hadn't imagined it would happen so soon. Though I knew Wassim wasn't like Moonif or Nizar, he always still felt like my brother. But after Mama and Papa spoke to me, I started to look at him with different eyes. It wasn't difficult. Soon it was like eating *maamoul bi ajwa*, I could taste the sweetness of the dates in my mouth. In the beginning, Wassim was like me, a little shocked, but as we talked and laughed about it, we no longer found it strange. Wassim's parents spoke to Mama and Papa. They agreed *the mehr*, the bride money, and Wassim and I agreed that I would continue to study because there were so many things I wanted to learn.

Everyone was invited and everyone came. There was a huge tent erected near where we live on the outskirts. The arada bandleader organised the music. It was loud, and noisy and full of life. We walked three times around the saint's tomb asking for his blessing and walked backwards still facing the saint. Wassim nearly forgot to put his right foot first, but I quickly reminded him so there was no disrespect.

My thick wavy long black hair was curled into ringlets. I was dressed in white, Wassim in a smart black suit with a white tie and the singers in bright orange and red embroidered vests, white cotton shirts, loose dark trousers. They had Damascene swords, which they drew up in the air as they sung and danced. Everyone clapped and cheered. All the elders smiled to see that Wassim and I had not forgotten; we still valued the old wedding customs. When Wassim arrived and gave me the gold and silver jewellery, I gave them to Mama to look after. I went with him in the car decorated with the white and yellow fragrant jasmine flowers. The others followed behind, going round and round the square, honking their horns. There was music, the songs of Sabah Fakhri and Farid Al-Atrash and my favourite singer, Asala Nasri, and dancing. The tables all had dishes of apricots, peaches, pears, juicy ripe maroon fruit from the trees of joy and ice cream and cups of juice and coffee. During the day, women had gathered to bake dusty brown tannour and kebbeh and there was a feast of *halabi* with spicy tomato sauce and Aleppo pepper, *mahshi* stuffed with beef and rice and nuts, tabbouleh, minced beef and *fatteh*. It was a day where everyone was eating and smiling and though the food looked so good, I could not eat a thing. There was plenty of food for everyone, too much when I think about it now. We had too much food. What a waste. When the women's party ended, Wassim came with his father and Papa and Moonif. My cousin helped Nizar so even he was able to come.

Wassim and I left to go to the room that Mama had prepared for us in the back of our house. It was a special day, one I shall never forget. The only noise I remember was the sound of everyone singing; singing to Wassim and me.

For the next year, I continued to study and Wassim worked at his father's business. Though there was so much happening, our lives were full of joy. Fruit trees lined our old property that lies in the south-east. We had an abundance of food and ate meat every day.

Our first sadness came when I lost the baby. I cried and cried but Mama told me these things happen. Wassim told me it was not my fault and we had plenty of time and that I was not to worry, but it was hard. In January 2011, I returned to my studies. I worked hard trying to learn English and Wassim promised that one day we would go to London so I could use the English I had learnt.

It happened or seemed to happen quickly after that. It was a cloudy, rainy day, I came home from Al-Baath University and heard shouting in the house. Wassim was never one to raise his voice. If he was in a bad mood, angry about something, or upset for some reason, he would walk out of our room. I would hear doors bang as he left the house, but he would come home calm.

I leant against the wall and listened.

'She has to go,' Wassim was saying.

'Will you go too?' I heard Mama ask.

'I can't. I have to help my father.'

'How can she go alone?'

'It is too dangerous here.'

'But on her own. What is the matter with you? That's dangerous too, no?' Papa shouted.

'But if she stays who knows what will happen?'

'It's all becoming more uncertain. There is no protection for anyone,' Moonif added as though he was supporting Wassim.

'What about Nizar?' Papa asked.

'What about Nizar?'

'He can't look after himself.'

'It will make it more difficult for her.'

Papa's voice was harsher than I had ever heard him speak, 'I will not let her go unless she takes her brother. His condition means that if anything more happens here, and we are not by his side to help him, there is no one. I will not let her go unless she goes with Nizar.'

There was silence and that was when I walked into the room.

'Why are you all shouting?'

Mother looked across at me and sighed. I stared at her and then across at Wassim; his tall slim body shaking, his eyes staring down at his slippers. His face was drooping and he didn't look up at me.

Only Papa spoke, 'I have told Wassim I will not let you go unless you take Nizar with you.'

'You will not let me go where? What are you all talking about?'

They all began to talk at the same time, 'The Alawite government forces,' Papa said raising, his hands to the air.

'The militias,'

'The Shia groups, the Sunni groups, everybody is fighting now.'

As they kept calling out names, I realised how little I knew or understood. I felt so stupid.

'The Jabhat al-Nusra.' Moonif said, thumping his hand against the wall.

'Al-Dawla Al-Islamiya fi al-Sham,' Papa said, looking across at me, but I didn't know what to say.

'This unrest is out of control. No government has come to help us. We are alone. These are terrible times. That is what we are talking about. It is no longer safe.' Wassim was almost shouting.

'If it's not safe we must all go,' I said, unable to grasp why I was being singled out.

'We can't all go. Your grandparents, aunties, uncles, cousins, who will take care of them? Our businesses and our homes, who will look after everything if we are not here? If we all go, we will lose everything. Everything that we have worked so hard for.' Papa lifted his hands to his head as though I was talking rubbish.

'I want your father to allow me to arrange safe passage for you. There are others who are fleeing, and you can go with them. But he insists you must take Nizar. I don't think you can manage.'

In this same way, we talked, argued, cried and shouted for months. Though they have seen me cry many times, it was the first time I had seen Papa weep. Before I had tried to ignore the background sounds, pretending they weren't there, but soon the shelling, and the gunfire grew louder and more frightening than ever before. By March of 2012, the fighting and shelling had become too real and distressing. With further pressure from Mama and Moonif, and still more tears, Wassim and I finally agreed that I would leave and take Nizar.

Nizar was only eight years old but he has had problems from the time he was born. He always found talking and learning hard. If he had to find the answer to a problem, he got upset. The doctors told Mama and Papa that he had a problem in the brain. It took him a long time to sit up, crawl and walk. If we were ever in a hurry, Moonif would carry him on his shoulders. He didn't speak very much and understood little but because Mama has always been by his side, he was never alone. She has taken care of him since he was a baby, cleaning him, washing him, feeding him. Mama had no children after Nizar was born so there is only Moonif, Nizar and me.

I promised Mama and Papa, Wassim and Moonif that I would take care of Nizar, and myself, and be very, very careful. Mama gave me a soft red purse that contained all my wedding gold and silver. It was left to Wassim to organise how I would go. He talked to many people and came home one day and told me that his friends had recommended people who we could trust.

'They are good people. They will look after you and Nizar. We won't be apart for long. I won't change. I won't forget you. We will all be together soon. But it is too dangerous now for you and Nizar to stay here. I have taken care of everything and you will both be safe,' he told me. The night before we left, family and friends came to our house. There were no words to be said but Papa began, and everyone joined in, and the room was suddenly filled with hope and pride, as we sang, Homs: The Land of Peace.

So my journey began.

Wassim delivered us into the hands of some people who had been recommended to him by friends whose families had fled. He paid these smugglers and they promised him they would take us safely to Europe. Wassim gave me money that he hid in pockets that he stitched into my clothes and into the one leather bag I carried, strapped to my breast. He told me to hide my rings and bangles on my body where no one could see, and to make sure no one could hear them jingling. When he held my hand before he left, I felt his tears. Nazir didn't understand anything about what was happening. Whatever these men promised Wassim, they were liars and thugs. When I spoke to Wassim over the phone, I never told him or Mama and Papa what was happening.

They took us to the Jordanian border and left us there. We were alone and there was no one to help us. At that point, life, as I knew it, changed forever. Overnight I became a breadwinner with no bread, a caretaker with no real knowledge of what I should do, the Decision-Maker who was afraid.

A Syrian woman, who was herself a refugee, led us to an abandoned factory site where we stayed for several months before an older Palestinian woman approached me.

'You and the child can come and live with me and my six children. If you can give us a little money that would be good.'

I agreed and so Nizar and I found space in the dusty desert Za'atari camp in Jordan. Nizar and I lived in a tent with this woman and her six children. It was in a terrible state and Nizar didn't like the children who teased and made fun of him, so I decided to move. I found a rundown shelter where a lot of families lived. It too was dirty and dusty, and smelled of sickness and filth. There was nowhere for people to clean themselves. It was overcrowded and we had nothing. I had to take Nizar once a week to wash him. There was no room to stand up, nowhere for him to play and hardly any space to cook. Sometimes I only had enough to cook one meal a day for us. I felt so bad and so alone.

If any of the women from the camp told me about work like cleaning, washing, or selling vegetables I would eagerly take it, but it was hard because I had no one to look after Nizar so I had to take him with me. He didn't like the places I took him to. I kept telling him to sit quietly and touch nothing, but he never listened and so I quickly I lost these jobs. One woman told me that perhaps I could go to a Jordanian university close to the Za'atari refugee camp through a scholarship from the UNHCR's DAFI programme, but I knew that was impossible, as there was no one to look after Nizar.

My role, as a wife, sister, daughter, switched. Suddenly I became a mother. I was Nizar's Mama and Papa. There was no Wassim to support me. I had to take on responsibilities that I was totally unprepared for. I didn't know how to cope. I was exposed to risks I never knew even existed. I struggled to find food, to take care of Nizar, to just make it through the day. It was always harsh and lonely.

My most difficult night came when Nizar was crying with hunger. We hadn't eaten properly for two days. He stopped saying even the few words that he used to say in Homs. I didn't know what to do. That night, after I had put him to bed, I crept out of the tent and told myself I would do any work so long as I could get money for food. A man came to me and told me he would help me. I was so happy when he said, 'I'm going to take you to a place where everyone will give you money.' He then handed me a veil.

It was dark when we arrived at a busy area full of men. I panicked. I was afraid. The man left me there and walked away. I didn't recognise where I was. I had never been to that area before. It was far from the shelter. I began trying to walk back. Not knowing where I was going, I began to cry. I was lost and terrified. As I walked, I fell over onto the ground three times. Two men grabbed me and I screamed. Another came and he helped me. He walked me back to the shelter and gave me some money to feed Nizar and warned me not to go out at night again. He told me I had been in 'a dirty place'.

I was haunted by the constant struggle for money. There was no one to talk to. No one to share my worries, my fears, no one to comfort me when I cried, which I did, every night. There was no Wassim by my side to protect me. When I went out, to get food the men would stare at me, calling me a whore. These men knew how desperate we women alone were. They would approach, not just me, but any woman on her own, knowing how we all needed money. They would tell us they could give us what we needed. I couldn't bear it. One afternoon, a woman in the camp saw the men leering at me and pulled me aside, 'I have an abaya which I could sell you if you like.' I nodded and gave her the little money I had, and took the black cloak and threw it over myself and felt a bit more protected.

Nizar became more and more difficult to take care of. He didn't speak anymore but would scream and shout. He wanted Mama and the safety of her arms around him. When I tried to hold him, he pushed me aside.

I heard some Syrians talking about how they were getting out and going to Europe where they said the conditions for refugees were better. Although my experience of the smugglers in Syria had been awful, I was confused and lost. I gave them my two gold bangles for a place for Nizar and I. Why did I listen to people I didn't know? I shouldn't have believed there was a better future ahead.

People were saying Egypt was cheap. They didn't mention the living conditions. Nizar and I were forced to sit on a bus for six hours. Nizar's screams were ear-piercing and the others on the bus yelled at him, telling him to shut up. I put his head in my lap to try to calm him, whispering in his ear to stay quiet, as I knew that they would leave us behind if he continued. When we arrived, we were all taken to a shabby, overcrowded flat where the smuggler demanded more money. I gave him a silver ring.

The next night he picked us up and took us to the harbour. There were all kinds of boats but the one he showed us to was small. He shouted at us to hurry up and get on board even though there were far too many of us. It was dark and terrifying as I clutched hold of Nizar. I couldn't see the others properly but I could hear them just as they could hear Nizar. Dozens of us were crammed onto this wooden dinghy. If any of us tried to shift position, we were kicked by the smugglers. We didn't even know where the boat was going, just that it was bobbing up and down in the darkness, lurching between the waves with all of us screaming. Neither Nizar nor I knew how to swim so I wouldn't let Nizar move and held onto him with all my strength. As the boat lurched and advanced further and further into the darkness, the waves grew. We were all tossed about, shuddering and swaying as the boat struggled over one wave and then another.

The swells grew higher and higher. Each time it lurched to one side, every-one rushed to the opposite end. The waves just kept on coming and coming until a huge wave covered us all, and the boat overturned.

'Nizar, Nizar, Nizar,' I called out Nizar's name, again and again, as I struggled to keep afloat in the water. I heard others shout and scream but I couldn't hear Nizar. In the blackness, the water swallowed me and I began sinking. As the current pulled me deeper and deeper into the sea, I tried to fight back. When there was no more fight left in me, I closed my eyes, accepting that I was going to drown. I had failed to look after Nizar when he needed me. I couldn't forgive myself. I was ready to die and to beg his forgiveness in heaven.

As I was sinking, someone grabbed hold of the black cloak. It tore and I slipped back under the water. They stretched out and tugged again and eventually pulled me out, shocked, and shivering, into a small boat. I was in a state of shock, choking and vomiting. People were screaming in Arabic and other languages that I didn't know. There were men and women and children but there was no sign of Nizar. Someone was sick all over me but I didn't care. I just kept looking out onto the fearsome darkness ahead thinking I would see Nizar. The people in charge were foreigners. I didn't understand what they were saying. I started to plead with them to look for Nizar. I was on my knees crying, begging them, pointing to the darkness, to the sea, in fear and despair, screaming his name, but they did nothing, and refused to listen to me. The boat ferried us to a larger boat. I watched as they spent hours rescuing people from the sea but there was no sign of Nizar. When the captain decided they had done all they could, despite my cries and screams, he fired up the engines, and the big boat moved forward, more secure than the smaller boats in battling against the stormy waves.

For many, they felt salvation had come at last. For me, it was death. I had failed Nizar. He was my brother, my flesh and blood, my link to Homs, to my family and home. I no longer wanted to live. I lay in despair for the two-day journey to Sicily, neither eating nor talking. Life no longer held any meaning for me. After I don't know how long, I was shaken awake, and told the Italians had arrived. Four huge red inflatable boats were circling the ship. People were clapping and chanting but I looked out at the crystal blue sea and cried. I was the last one to leave. At the port, a woman, another refugee who I later learnt was from Somalia, saw me bleeding and crying as I squatted in the street, and took me to the doctor. The doctor examined me, bandaging my cuts and bruises. She gave me medicine to take and then told me to go. The Somali woman gave me some bread but I couldn't eat. After a few hours, many buses turned up and we were all piled inside. None of us knew where we were going. Night fell but the bus driver kept on driving. Hours later we reached a northern Italian city I had never heard of called Milan. It was surrounded by statues and gardens and buildings that once upon a time I would have thought were beautiful, but as I got off the bus, I didn't care.

I had nothing to say to anyone. No one knew what I had been through. As they all excitedly talked about the next stage, I said nothing. A young Syrian woman called Shireen could see the desperate state I was in. She forced me to eat and kept shaking me. 'You are my sister. I saw you on the boat with that little boy.'

I began to cry. I howled. She put her arms around me.

'Nizar, Nizar,' I called out.

Shireen stroked my hair, 'who is Nizar?' she asked.

I told her and she held me tight as sorrow took over my mind and body.

'I will take care of you as you tried to take care of your brother.'

She did.

'Do you have any money?' she asked.

I shook my head, as I had nothing. All that remained was my red pouch, which I had pushed into my bra. I reached in, pulled it out and gave her the last of my wedding jewellery. She took me to a place where there were five young Syrian women lying on the floor. When we walked into the room, she told them all what had happened to me and about Nizar. They lowered their heads. They had little but what little bread and water they had, they shared with me. They took care of me because I couldn't look after myself. They saw me pulling my hair as I cried out in despair and decided it was best if my hair was cut. I didn't care. By then my hair was thin and ragged and itchy.

For two days, Shireen left them to look after me while she went in search of an escape route for us all. Late one night she came back and told us what she had arranged.

'We are to be smuggled in a lorry to England.'

All of us stared back at her, saying nothing. We were five young women, all desperate, all alone, frightened, scared and sick. We did as we were told, and the next day we climbed into the container in the lorry.

The driver looked at us with a cold stare. He put a finger over his lips.

'Not a word. He is telling us we are not to say a word until he lets us out of the container,' Shireen explained. Each time I or any of the girls was about to cry or speak, Shireen put her finger to her lips to silence us. We stayed quiet. We ate nothing. We spread water over our dry lips, but didn't dare to drink. Each of us wet ourselves — what could we do? Shireen was sick and the foul smell and sight of urine, diarrhoea and vomit filled the container. As the lorry moved on, we became sicker and sicker. We covered our mouths and noses to try to stop ourselves from making the mess even worse but it was pointless. When the lorry eventually stopped after what seemed a lifetime, we thought we had arrived in England. We didn't move and stayed still and remained quiet. When the container lid was opened, though they were repelled by the stench, but they pulled us out, and it was only then that we realised that they were the police. Shireen held onto me, as I was faint and unsteady. The police put us in a van. We had no idea where they were taking us. They drove and drove. We sat silent. Numbed by the knowledge that we didn't know what they would do to us. When the van stopped, we were told to get out. Instead of a hospital or a place of safety, they had brought us to a prison. We stayed there for many months not knowing what was to become of us. Though Shireen tried to encourage me, saying that at least we were away from the bombs and shelling, I didn't care what happened.

One morning, an elderly English woman who we had never seen before, came to the prison. It was then, that I had to use the little English I knew, to help Shireen and the others. The woman said she was a lawyer and told us that because we were young and alone we might be given legal protection and medical care, and that she was going to apply on our behalf for asylum. She was impressed that I could speak English and told me that I might be able to apply to study English. She explained that the situation back in Syria was very bad. I begged her to find out about Wassim and the family.

Each time she came, I asked her. One day in August 2014, she arrived with her briefcase and her eyes lit up in a way we had never seen before. It was clear she had good news to tell and for the first time I too smiled at her. She told us about where we might live, and that it seemed likely that we would be allowed to remain in England. All the girls were so pleased but I looked at her, waiting for her to tell me what I wanted to hear.

'Suha, I am so sorry. Your husband, your father and your brother have all been killed and I can't find out where your Mother is. I am so sorry.'

***

I have been here a year now. All the time I try to call home, but I never get an answer.

Nothing makes any sense. Why am I alive and not Mama, Papa, Wassim, Moonif, Nizar, my cousins, aunties, uncles, grandparents, the rest of my family and friends?

The Refugee Group people have helped me to stand up again. They have introduced me to a choir — a choir of refugees. The music we sing isn't loud and noisy and full of life but we are learning to sing together. It is not that music is a blanket that I wrap around myself to shut out all the horrors of my life, but the melody, the sounds, the chords say what I can't. They are like gestures of friendship, a warm hug that throws light into the darkness of my heart. I am slowly learning the English words which Mama, Papa, Wassim, Moonif, Nizar would not have understood. Perhaps when I am stronger, no longer a broken-winged bird that cannot fly, when I can dream again, I will teach them to sing — Homs: The Land of Peace.

# WOMAN WITH GOLDEN APPLE (NO ORDINARY FRUIT)

After Lotte Kramer's 'Boy with Orange (Out of Kosovo)'

## Dorothea Smartt

A woman holding a golden apple in her palms
has crossed the boundary, uncertain yet hopeful.

She waits there, glances back at stony ground — scenes
when her desire was too held in check, diminishing.

Now, with this globe she's grasping, something beckons;
its small oval assurance, a piquant promise of juiciness

no one shall deny. She dares a smile at signs of surrender
within her. Packed precariously about a soft-spiky seed.

Soon she will uncover the arousing body, touch tangy lips,
kiss a loving woman; traverse any stings of this asylum.

## ACKNOWLEDGEMENT

'Woman with Golden Apple (No Ordinary Fruit)' from *Reader, I married him & other queer goings-on*. Leeds: Peepal Tree Press, 2014.
    We are grateful to the publisher and author for permission to reprint this copyrighted material.

**Gender and Race Matter: Global Perspectives on Being a Woman**
**Advances in Gender Research, Volume 21, 261**
© **Dorothea Smartt**
**ISSN: 1529-2126/doi:10.1108/S1529-212620160000021015**

# ABOUT THE AUTHORS

**Carole Boyce Davies** is an African Diaspora Studies scholar, she is Professor of Africana Studies and English at Cornell University. She is author of *Left of Karl Marx: The Political Life of Black Communist Claudia Jones* (Duke University Press, 2008) and *Black Women, Writing and Identity: Migrations of the Subject* (Routledge, 1994) which is considered a theoretical base for many studies in the field of black feminist literary theory and the writing of migration. In addition to over a hundred scholarly articles, Carole Boyce Davies has also published the following critical editions: *Ngambika. Studies of Women in African Literature* (Africa World Press, 1986); *Out of the Kumbla. Caribbean Women and Literature* (Africa World Press, 1990); a two-volume collection of critical and creative writing entitled *Moving Beyond Boundaries*, Volume 1: *International Dimensions of Black Women's Writing* and Volume 2: *Black Women's Diasporas*. She is co-editor with Ali Mazrui and Isidore Okpewho of *The African Diaspora: African Origins and New World Identities* (Indiana University Press, 1999) and *Decolonizing the Academy: African Diaspora Studies* (Africa World Press, 2003). She is general editor of the three-volume *The Encyclopedia of the African Diaspora* (Oxford: ABC-CLIO, 2008). She recently published a collection of the writings of Claudia Jones titled *Beyond Containment: Claudia Jones: Autobiographical Reflections and Essays* (Banbury: Ayebia, 2011). *Caribbean Spaces: Escape Routes from Twilight Zones* (University of Illinois Press) was published October, 2013. From Trinidad and Tobago, Carole Boyce Davies studied African Literature, earning a PhD from the University of Ibadan, Nigeria. She has travelled extensively in Africa and has been a visiting professor in South Africa, Trinidad and Tobago and Brazil. Her next project is on women and political leadership in the African Diaspora.

**Maria Martin de Almagro** is a post-doctoral researcher at the Université libre de Bruxelles and Adjunct Professor at Vesalius College (Belgium). Her research focuses on gender politics, international relations and critical security studies. More precisely, she has conducted research on peace and security governance and on the United Nations Women, Peace and

Security Agenda. She currently investigates post-structural accounts of gender and transitional justice mechanisms.

**Adrija Dey** has completed her PhD from the University of Hull in Media, Culture and Society, focusing mainly on gender violence and digital gender activism in India post December 16, 2012. Currently she is working as a Research Associate in the "Equally Safe in Higher Education" Project in the University of Strathclyde. This project is funded by the Scottish Government to implement "Equally Safe" the Scottish Government's strategy for preventing and eradicating violence against women and girls and to maintain a safe campus environment for all staff and students.

**Jaya Gajparia** – currently teaches a range of undergraduate and postgraduate courses at London South Bank University and at Ithaca College, London Center. She completed her doctoral research titled "Gender, Poverty and Development in Mumbai: A Study of Policy, Perceptions and Practice" funded by the Institute of Social Science Research (ISSR) in 2015. Her research interests are on gender, ethnicity, poverty, sustainability, social justice, education, postcolonial and third world feminism. She also has several years of experience in voluntary and community sector organisations working on disability, age, gender discrimination and human rights.

**Hala Kamal** is Associate Professor of Gender Studies at the Department of English, Faculty of Arts, Cairo University; and co-founder of the Women and Memory Forum – an Egyptian NGO concerned with the study of women in cultural history. She teaches undergraduate and postgraduate courses in Women's Writing, Autobiography, and Translation Studies. Her research interests and publications in both Arabic and English are in the areas of feminist literary criticism, autobiography theory, women and gender studies and the history of the Egyptian feminist movement. She has also translated several books on gender and feminism into Arabic. (https://cairo.academia.edu/HalaKamal)

**Priyasha Kaul** is Assistant Professor of Sociology at FLAME University in India. Before joining FLAME, Priyasha worked as Assistant Professor of Sociology at Miranda House, University of Delhi. In the past, she was employed as a researcher at Bristol University where she worked on several EU funded international research projects in collaboration with City University, Queen Mary, University London and the Equal Opportunities Commission, United Kingdom. She has taught undergraduate and postgraduate courses at several universities, including Bristol University, Delhi

University and the Indira Gandhi National Open University. Prior to this, she has also worked as an independent researcher with the Centre for the Study of Developing Societies (CSDS Delhi) and the Developing Countries Research Centre at Delhi University. Priyasha has a doctorate in sociology and a masters in management from Bristol University in the United Kingdom. She also has a masters and a bachelor's degree in sociology from Delhi University in India. She has published and presented her research at various international conferences and academic fora. Her wider research interests include gender, media, organizations, culture, diaspora and migration, globalization and contemporary social change.

**Donatella Maraschin** is a Senior Lecturer in Journalism and Film at London South Bank University. She has published on the intersections between mainstream cinema and the practice and concerns of Visual Anthropology. Her publications include articles on the work of Italian film director Pier Paolo Pasolini published in the journals *The Italianist* (24:2) and *South Asian Cinema* (5:6), and her recent book *Pasolini: Cinema e Antropologia* [*Pasolini: Cinema and Anthropology*], published by Peter Lang in 2014, which engages with the most recent theorisations of the 'Anthropology of the Senses'. Her recent work focuses on the development of storytelling on the digital platform and on the latest innovations in online journalistic content delivery.

**Bev Orton** is Fellow in Criminology and Criminal Justice at the University of Hull. Her doctoral thesis was on women and political activism in South Africa. She teaches on the Criminology programmes at undergraduate and postgraduate level. Bev also supervises PhD and MA students. Bev's research interests are women and political activism in apartheid South Africa, restorative justice and mothers, women and disability in prison and feminist issues in apartheid South Africa. She is working on projects that include film making with women from refuges, prison and various women's organisations. Her doctoral thesis was on women and political activism in South Africa, specifically the acknowledgement of South African women's contribution to the struggle against apartheid. The representation of women in the apartheid era is analysed through play texts.

**Tara Povey** is Senior Teaching Fellow in the Comparative Politics of the Middle East at SOAS. Her research focuses on social movements, neo-liberalism, gender and political movements in the Middle East. She is the author of Social Movements in Egypt and Iran (Palgrave Macmillan, 2015) and she is the co-editor of Women, Power and Politics in 21st Century Iran

(Ashgate, 2012). She has published articles and book chapters on women's activism and Islamophobia and social movements and political change in Egypt and Iran.

**Kavyta Raghunandan** is currently an Associate Fellow at the Institute of Commonwealth Studies in London, has an interdisciplinary background ranging from the arts and humanities to sociology and cultural studies. Her doctoral research, which was conducted at the University of Leeds in the School of Sociology and Social Policy, explored the production and performativity of Indian identities in the postcolonial Caribbean island nation of Trinidad and Tobago. Influenced by a black feminist ethnographic approach, Kavyta is largely interested in the dynamics of intersectionalities across the global South and North and to this end, continues to critically engage with gender, race and sexuality as concepts in nuanced and non-binaristic ways from academic, cultural and digital platforms.

**Elaheh Rostami-Povey** is an academic, researcher and writer. Her research and writings focus on Iran, Afghanistan and the role of Iran in the Middle East. She is the co-editor, with Tara Povey, of the book *Women, Power and Politics in 21st Century Iran* (2012 Ashgate). She is also the author of three books published by Zed Books: *Iran's Influence: A Religio-Political State and Society in its Region* (2010); *Afghan Women: Identity and Invasion* (2007) *and Women, Work and Islamism: Ideology and Resistance in Iran* (1999; 2nd edition 2010). She has also written on feminisms in Iran, women and civil society organisations in Iran, women, war, conflict and diaspora in Afghanistan in the *Feminist Review Collective, The Journal of Development Studies, The Journal of Iranian Studies* and *the Journal of Development in Practice*. She has contributed chapters on similar topics to books published by I.B. Tauris, Macmillan, Routledge, Lynne Rienner and Oxfam. Her books and articles have been translated into Farsi, Arabic, Portuguese and Korean languages.

**Suzanne Scafe** is a Reader in Caribbean and Postcolonial Literatures at London South Bank University. She has published several essays on Black British writing and culture and Caribbean women's fiction. She is the co-editor of a collection of essays, *I Am Black/White/Yellow: The Black Body in Europe* (2007), which includes her chapter on the drama of Roy Williams; other chapters on Black British drama are published in *Hidden Gems* (Oberon: 2007) and *Modern and Contemporary Black British Theatre* (Palgrave Macmillan: 2014). She has written several articles and book chapters on the Caribbean short story and on contemporary Caribbean and Black British women writers such as Diana Evans, Merle Collins, Erna Brodber, Brenda Flanagan, Donna Hemans, Zee Edgell and on the Caribbean−diasporic poets Dorothea Smart, Jean Binta Breeze and Amryl Johnson. She is currently co-editing a Special Issue on Caribbean Women's short fiction for the journal *Short Fiction in Theory and Practice* and a collection of essays on Caribbean co-presence for Rutgers University Press. Her recent work includes essays on Black British women's autobiographical writing, published in the journals *Changing English* (17:2), *Women: A Cultural Review* (20:4) *Life Writing* (10:2) and for a forthcoming volume for Cambridge University Press.

**Dorothea Smartt** is a literary activist, live artist and established and respected poet with an international reputation. Born and raised in London she is described as a 'Brit-born Bajan international'. With two full collections, Connecting Medium and Ship Shape (Peepal Tree Press) her years of experience include engagements with the British Council in Bahrain, South Africa, United States, Egypt, and Hungary. In 2013 she was keynote speaker at Barbados' Frank Collymore Literary Endowment Award. She is an honorary member and advisor to Cambridge University's Caribbean Poetry Project; Co-Director of Inscribe: national writer development programme; Associate Poetry Editor of "Sable Litmag", and guest co-editor of their LGBTQI issues. Her recent chapbook *Reader, I Married Him & Other Queer Goings-On*, is a sampler to her forthcoming collection where she continues to rework standard narratives, this time examining sexuality as a factor contributing to 'West Indians' going to work on the Panama Canal.

**Shaminder Takhar** is Associate Professor in Sociology at London South Bank University, teaching across a range of undergraduate and postgraduate courses. Her research interests and publications are centred around race, ethnicity, gender, education, social justice and sexualities. She recently competed research funded by the British Academy on the under-representation of South Asian women in local politics published in 2013. A sole authored book, Gender, Ethnicity and Politcal Agency: South Asian women organizing was published in 2013 (Routledge) and she has also co-edited a special issue on Diversity, Inclusion and Social Justice for the *Race Equality Teaching* journal (2010).

**Jocelyn Watson** − The Asian Women's Writers Collective was Jocelyn Watson's first writing home. In 2015 and 2011, she won a Jane Austen Short Story Award for her short stories and in 2013, she was the winner of the UK Asian Writer Short Story Competition for *The Gardener*. Her play, *Cornelia Calling* was part of the Kali Talkback 2013 at Tristan Bates Theatre. In 2012, she won the Freedom From Torture Short Story Competition for *London Plane* and was one of the winners of the SAMPAD '*Inspired by Tagore*'. Her story, *X* was published by Dahlia Publishing in an anthology of New Writing by British Asian women in 2014 entitled *Beyond the Border*. In 2015, her autobiographical piece, *Words* was part of the Tangled Roots Anthology and her short story, *Nana's Navartan Set* was published by Momaya Press in their Treasure anthology. She is active in feminist, BME and socialist politics.